**THE KLUWER INTERNATIONAL SERIES
IN ENGINEERING AND COMPUTER SCIENCE**

**PARALLEL PROCESSING AND
FIFTH GENERATION COMPUTING**

Consulting Editor

Doug DeGroot

Other books in the series:

PARALLEL EXECUTION OF LOGIC PROGRAMS,
John S. Conery ISBN 0-89838-194-0

PARALLEL COMPUTATION AND COMPUTERS FOR
ARTIFICIAL INTELLIGENCE
Janusz S. Kowalik ISBN 0-89838-227-0

MEMORY STORAGE PATTERNS IN PARALLEL PROCESSING
Mary E. Mace ISBN 0-89838-239-4

SUPERCOMPUTER ARCHITECTURE
Paul B. Schneck ISBN 0-89838-234-4

ASSIGNMENT PROBLEMS IN
PARALLEL AND DISTRIBUTED COMPUTING
Shahid H. Bokhari ISBN 0-89838-240-8

MEMORY PERFORMANCE OF PROLOG ARCHITECTURES
Evan Tick ISBN 0-89838-254-8

DATABASE MACHINES AND KNOWLEDGE BASE MACHINES
Masaru Kitsuregawa ISBN 0-89838-257-2

PARALLEL PROGRAMMING AND COMPILERS

by

CONSTANTINE D. POLYCHRONOPOULOS
Center for Supercomputing Research and Development
and The University of Illinois at Urbana-Champaign

KLUWER ACADEMIC PUBLISHERS
Boston/Dordrecht/London

Distributors for North America:
Kluwer Academic Publishers
101 Philip Drive
Assinippi Park
Norwell, Massachusetts 02061, USA

Distributors for the UK and Ireland:
Kluwer Academic Publishers
Falcon House, Queen Square
Lancaster LA1 1RN, UNITED KINGDOM

Distributors for all other countries:
Kluwer Academic Publishers Group
Distribution Centre
Post Office Box 322
3300 AH Dordrecht, THE NETHERLANDS

Library of Congress Cataloging-in-Publication

Polychronopoulos, C. D. (Constantine D.)
  Parallel programming and compilers/by Constantine D.
Polychronopoulos.
  p. cm.—(Kluwer international series in engineering and
computer science ; 59)
  Bibliography: p.
  Includes index.
  ISBN 0-89838-288-2
  1. Parallel programming (Computer science) 2. Compilers (Computer
programs) I. Title. II. Series: Kluwer international series in
engineering and computer science ; SECS 59.
QA76.6.P653 1988   88-21632
004'.35—dc19   CIP

To Gerasimoula, Katerina, and Dimitri,
my Precious Trio

CONTENTS

PREFACE

The second half of the 1970s was marked with impressive advances in array/vector architectures and vectorization techniques and compilers. This progress continued with a particular focus on vector machines until the middle of the 1980s. The majority of supercomputers during this period were register–to–register (Cray 1) or memory–to–memory (CDC Cyber 205) vector (pipelined) machines. However, the increasing demand for higher computational rates lead naturally to parallel computers and software. Through the replication of autonomous processors in a coordinated system, one can skip over performance barriers due technology limitations. In principle, parallelism offers unlimited performance potential. Nevertheless, it is very difficult to realize this performance potential in practice. So far, we have seen only the tip of the iceberg called "parallel machines and parallel programming". Parallel programming in particular is a rapidly evolving art and, at present, highly empirical. In this book we discuss several aspects of parallel programming and parallelizing compilers. Instead of trying to develop parallel programming methodologies and paradigms, we often focus on more advanced topics assuming that the reader has an adequate background in parallel processing. The book is organized in three main parts. In the first part (Chapters 1 and 2) we set the stage and focus on program transformations and parallelizing compilers. The second part of this book (Chapters 3 and 4) discusses scheduling for parallel machines from the practical point of view (i.e., macro and microtasking and supporting environments). Finally, the last part (Chapters 5, 6, 7, and 8) considers program partitioning and task scheduling from a more theoretical point of view.

ACKNOWLEDGEMENTS

I would like to thank all those who contributed directly or indirectly to the writing of this book. Foremost, I want to thank my wife and my children for their constant love and support. Many thanks are also due to my friends and colleagues Perry Emrath, Stratis Gallopoulos, David Kuck, Duncan Lawrie, Dave Padua, Alex Veidenbaum, and Harry Wijshoff for many fruitful and enlightening discussions. A good part of this book has its origins to my dissertation work which was completed under Dave Kuck's direction. I am grateful to Dave for introducing me to this exiting research area and teaching me the art of research. Finally, I want to thank all my relatives and friends whose love and encouragement keeps me going.

This work was supported in part by the National Science Foundation under Grants NSF DCR84–10110 and NSF DCR84–06916, the U.S. Department of Energy under Grant DOE DE–FG02–85ER25001, the IBM Donation, IBM Parafrase Contract 632613, the AT&T Affiliates Program, and the Control Data Corporation.

PARALLEL PROGRAMMING AND COMPILERS

CHAPTER 1

PARALLEL ARCHITECTURES AND COMPILERS

1.1. INTRODUCTION

The ever increasing demand for computational power in many areas of science and engineering is an undeniable fact. In the first few generations of computer systems, increased computational speed was primarily obtained through advances in technology that allowed higher degree of integration and faster circuits. As technology approaches certain physical limitations, parallelism seems to be the most promising alternative for satisfying the ever–increasing demand for computational speed. Through the replication of computational elements that are interconnected in some regular structure, programs can execute on multiple processors and access multiple memory banks. In other words computations (and memory transfers) can be performed in parallel. Parallelism is an old concept and was applied to a limited degree in some of the early computer systems. First in the form of I/O channels that allowed overlapped computation and I/O, and later in the form of multiple functional units that could operate in parallel. Technology constraints and software limitations however did not make it feasible to design and build parallel machines until later in the 70's.

It is indisputable that the shared memory parallel processor model is and will continue to be one of the dominant architectures for the near future supercomputers. The flexibility, scalability, and high potential performance offered by parallel processor machines are simply necessary "ingredients" for any high performance system. The flexibility of these machines is indeed greater than that of single array processor computers and they can execute more efficiently a larger spectrum of programs.

But there are divided opinions when the question comes to the number of processors needed for an efficient and cost–effective, yet very fast polyprocessor system. A number of pessimistic and optimistic reports have come out on this topic. One side uses Amdahl's law and intuition to argue against large systems [Mins70], [Amda67]. The other side cites simulations and real examples to support the belief that highly parallel systems with large numbers of processors are practical, and could be efficiently utilized to give substantial speedups [PoBa86], [Cytr84], [Krus84], [Kuck84], [Bane81], [FlHe80]. However, we have little experience in efficiently using a large number of processors. This inexperience in turn is reflected in the small number of processors used in modern commercially available supercomputers.

Truly parallel languages, parallel algorithms, and ways of defining and exploiting program parallelism are still in their infancy. Only recently the appropriate attention has been focused on research for parallel algorithms, languages, and software. Several factors should be considered when designing high performance supercomputers [Kuck84]. Parallel algorithms, carefully designed parallel architectures and powerful programming environments including sophisticated restructuring compilers, all play equally important roles on program performance. In addition several crucial problems in scheduling, synchronization, and communication must be adequately solved in order to take full advantage of the inherent flexibility of parallel processor systems. The investment in traditional (serial) software however is so enormous, that it will be many years before parallel software dominates. It is then natural to ask: " How can we efficiently run existing software on parallel processor systems?" The answer to this question is well–known: by using powerful restructuring compilers.

The primary challenge with parallel processor systems is to speed up the execution of a single program at a time, or maximize program speedup (as opposed to maximizing throughput). One of the most critical issues in parallel processing is the design of processor allocation and scheduling schemes that minimize execution time and interprocessor communication for a given program. A significant amount of theoretical work has been done on the subject of scheduling, but because of the complexity of these problems, only a few simple cases have been solved optimally in polynomial time. Moreover, almost none of these cases is of practical use. Another important issue is program partitioning. Given a parallel program, we need to partition it into a set of independent or communicating processes or tasks. Each process can then be allocated (scheduled on) one or more processors. Program partitioning affects and can be affected by several factors. It is a complex optimization problem where the variables to be optimized are not compatible.

1.2. BOOK OVERVIEW

This book discusses and proposes solutions to some important problems in parallel programming and processing. In particular we consider problems on program restructuring and parallelism detection, scheduling of program modules on many processors, overhead and performance analysis. Based on past experience and future trends, we propose a new framework for a sophisticated tool that performs not only automatic restructuring, but it also provides a comprehensive environment for automatic scheduling and overhead analysis at all levels of granularity. The present chapter gives an introduction of the tools and concepts used throughout the book.

As mentioned earlier, a vast amount of existing software has been coded either in a serial language (e.g. Fortran, Pascal, Lisp, C), or for a serial machine. The need to run serial software on vector or parallel machines without reprogramming gave rise to program restructuring. During program restructuring, a compiler or preprocessor identifies the parts of a program that can take advantage of the architectural characteristics of a machine. Two equally important reasons for program restructuring are ease of programming and complexity. Coding a particular problem to take full advantage of the machine characteristics is a complex and tedious task. For non–trivial programs and on the average, a compiler can perform better than a skillful programmer. As is the case with traditional code optimization, restructuring can be automated. A very significant amount of work has been performed on program restructuring primarily in the case of Fortran [KLPL81], [Kuck80], [Kenn80]. However more remains to be done in this area. Chapter 2 defines data dependences and associated concepts briefly and gives an overview of the most useful transformations for automatic restructuring. Most of the transformations which have been developed so far were targeting mainly vector machines. Transformations targeting hierarchical parallel computers are the current focus of research in this area. Chapter 2 presents four transformations which are particularly suited for parallel machines. Hybrid transformations are used when information about a program is not adequate for the compiler to make the correct decision. Chapter 2 discusses the usefulness of such transformations and gives specific examples.

Given that a program has been written or transformed into a parallel form, the next issue of parallel programming is to find ways to exploit that parallelism on a given machine. This is our well known scheduling problem. In this book we discuss both, static and dynamic scheduling strategies. Static scheduling can be accomplished by the user or the compiler. Dynamic schemes are enforced through the operating system or the hardware and are more commonly employed in real machines. A number of dynamic scheduling schemes have been proposed in the past few years [KrWe85], [Mann84], [Bain78]. Most of these schemes are based on specialized scheduling hardware or operating system functions. In the case of hardware schemes the drawbacks are cost and generality. The majority of these schemes are designed for special purpose machines [Bain78], or for scheduling special types of tasks, e.g. atomic operations. On the other hand, the disadvantage of dynamic scheduling by the operating system is the high overhead involved. Especially when the granularity of tasks is small, the overhead involved with the invocation of the operating system is likely to outweigh the benefit of parallelism. It is more appropriate to implement dynamic scheduling without involving the operating system, by using low level primitives inside the program. This is the focus of Chapter 3 which gives an overview of the design of a hypothetical supercompiler for this purpose.

In Chapter 3 we propose a general framework for compiling, scheduling and executing parallel programs on parallel computers. We discuss important aspects of program partitioning, scheduling and execution, and consider possible realistic alternatives for each issue. Subsequently we propose a possible implementation of an auto–scheduling compiler and give simple examples to illustrate the principles. Our approach to the entire problem is to utilize program information available to the compiler while, at the same time, allowing for run–time "corrections" and flexibility.

Auto–scheduling compilers offer a new environment for executing parallel programs in a dedicated mode without the involvement of the operating system. This allows for spreading tasks across processors during run–time in an efficient and semi–controlled manner which involves little overhead. Furthermore, the small overhead of spawning new tasks makes possible the parallel execution of medium to fine granularity tasks, which is not possible under existing methods. We also consider the many flavors of program partitioning and scheduling in detail and argue that a combination of compile and run–time schemes offer, in general, the most efficient and viable solution.

Our work on scheduling differs from the previous work in several aspects. Instead of considering simplified abstract models [CoGJ78] [Coff76] [KaNa84], we focus on the aspects of scheduling of real programs. Particular emphasis is given to parallel loop scheduling. Since parallel loops account for the greatest percentage of parallelism in numerical programs, the efficient scheduling of such loops is vital to program and system performance. Little work has been reported on this topic so far [Cytr84], [PoKP86], [TaYe86], [PoKu87] although it becomes an area of great theoretical and practical interest. This book discusses optimal static and dynamic solutions for the general problem in Chapter 4. Most of the loop scheduling efforts consider the simple case of singly nested parallel loops. No significant work has been reported for the case of multiply nested loops until recently [PoKP86] [TaYe86]. Most of the modern parallel computers are able to exploit parallelism in singly nested loops only. This is partially justified by the small number of processors used in these machines; one level of parallelism would be adequate to utilize all processors. However it is often the case where several nested parallel loops can be executed at once, assuming an unlimited number of processors. Also, with such nested parallel loops, parallelism can be better utilized if a limited number of processors are allocated to more than one loop.

The first part of Chapter 4 discusses dynamic loop scheduling approaches and suggests an efficient dynamic scheme (GSS) to solve the loop scheduling problem. Two important objectives are automatically satisfied by this method: low overhead and load balancing. By guiding the amount of work given to each processor, very good (and often optimal) load balancing is achieved. The assignment of large iteration blocks, on the other hand, reduces the number of accesses to loop indices and thus the run–time overhead.

Next, we consider optimal static processor allocations for complex parallel loops. Even though static processor allocation may not be as useful as GSS in general, there may be cases where loop characteristics are known in advance and static allocation may be a viable alternative.

During the execution of a program on a parallel machine run–time overhead incurs from activities such as scheduling, interprocessor communication and synchronization. This overhead is added to the execution time in the form of processor latencies and busy waits. As overhead increases, the amount of parallelism that can be exploited decreases. In Chapter 5 we consider two models of run–time overhead. In the first model overhead increases linearly with the number of processors assigned to a parallel task. In the second case, overhead is logarithmic on the number of processors. We discuss ways of computing optimal or close to optimal number of processors for each case, as well as critical task size.

Extensive work has been done on the problem of static scheduling of independent tasks on parallel processors [Sahn84], [Liu81], [CoGJ78], [Grah72], [CoGr72]. Most of the instances of this problem have been proved to be NP–Complete. Optimal algorithms have been developed for special cases of the problem that restrict the tasks to be of unit–execution time and/or the number of processors to be two. These theoretical results however are of little help to practical cases. Heuristic algorithms for approximate solutions [CoGJ78], [CoGr72], also use simplifying assumptions that make them difficult to use in practice. In Chapters 6 and 7 of this book we consider the general partitioning and static scheduling problem. By considering the nature of tasks that occur in real programs one is able to design optimal algorithms and approximation heuristics that can be used efficiently in practice. Of course, before scheduling one must partition a given program into a set of identifiable tasks. Partitioning can be done statically or dynamically and it is discussed in Chapter 3. A more theoretical (but less general) approach to partitioning is also discussed in Chapter 6.

Chapter 8 presents three models of program execution and analyzes their corresponding speedup bounds. A generalization of the doacross model is also discussed in Chapter 8. It is clear that parallel programming is a rapidly growing area of research and interest. As such it is an evolving art, even though certain future aspects of parallel programming are predictable at present.

1.3. VECTOR AND PARALLEL MACHINES

Several attempts have been made to characterize computer systems based on their instruction sets, control, processor organization, and so on. So far there is no universally acceptable taxonomy. Some of the most commonly used terms to characterize the functionality of computer systems are pipelined, vector, array, and multiprocessor systems. However there is no clear distinction from the instruction set point of view for example, between pipelined or array organizations.

One could say that "vector" refers to computers with vector instructions in their instruction repertoire. Pipelined and array machines fall into this category. Pipelined systems usually have pipelined functional units, as the term implies. Examples include the Cray 1, the CDC Cyber 205, the Fujitsu VP–100/200, the Hitachi S–810, and the Convex–1 computers [MiUc84], [NIOK84]. Pipelining though can also be used at a higher level. One common activity that is pipelined in most modern computers is the instruction execution cycle. The three different phases (instruction fetch, decode, and execute) can be pipelined by having different instructions going through different phases of execution simultaneously. Array computers usually come with a number of identical ALUs interconnected in some symmetric structure (e.g., linear array, mesh, ring). Some existing array machines include the Goodyear MPP, ICL DAP, Illiac IV, and the Connection machine. Pipelined and array systems are also characterized by their single control unit. According to Flynn's taxonomy these are single–instruction–multiple–data or SIMD architectures. They are synchronous systems in the sense that the control unit and all computational elements are driven by a common clock.

A different organization are the multiprocessor or parallel processor systems. These computer systems are composed of a set of independent and autonomous processors that are fully or partially interconnected in some way. Multiprocessors can be synchronous or asynchronous where each processor is driven by its own clock. In Flynn's taxonomy these are multiple–instruction–multiple–data or MIMD systems. In MIMD computers the control is distributed, with each processor having its own control unit. Global control units may be used to coordinate the entire system or allow for the design of hierarchical MIMD systems.

Two major subfamilies of parallel processor machines are the shared memory and message passing. In the former organization all processors share the same memory address space, and are connected to a shared physical memory through a high bandwidth bus or a multistage interconnection network. Communication between processors is accomplished through the shared memory. Examples of shared memory systems include the Cray X–MP, Cray 2, ETA–10, Alliant FX/8, and IBM 3090 [Alli85], [Chen83].

In the message passing organization each processor has its own private memory and there is no physical shared memory. Processors communicate asynchronously using message passing mechanisms. Most of message passing systems require a host or some sort of global control unit (which can be one of the processors) that is used to initialize the system and keep global status information. The Intel hypercube, the Caltech cosmic cube, and the N–cube/10 are examples of message passing multiprocessors.

Kuck's taxonomy [Kuck78] was a more recent attempt to categorize computer organizations based on their instruction sets. It is more detailed than Flynn's taxonomy, and it will be used through the rest of this book. According to this taxonomy, the previous systems can be characterized as SEA, MES, or MEA. SEA stands for single–execution–array and includes pipelined and array machines. MES stands for multiple–execution–scalar and is identical to MIMD. Note that MES refers to multiprocessors with scalar processors. A more interesting category is the MEA or multiple–execution–array machines that are multiprocessors with SEA processors. These are generaly more powerful than all previous categories since they provide two levels of parallelism and larger instruction sets. Examples of MEA systems are the Cray X–MP, the Cedar, and the Alliant FX/8. We will return to this taxonomy in Section 1.4.

1.4. PARALLELISM IN PROGRAMS

In a parallel computer all processors must be used at all times to keep utilization at maximum level. There are two ways one can use to achieve this goal. Either by making the machine available to many users, or by exploiting program parallelism. In the former (extreme) case, different processors would be executing different user jobs (probably in a timeshared mode). The throughput of the machine may be high, but the individual turnaround time would most likely be worse than that on an equivalent serial machine. In the latter (extreme) case all processors are put to work on a single user program, in which case program execution time is minimized. This can only be done with parallel programs.

One could argue that the primary purpose of designing and building parallel computers is to minimize program execution time (especially for critical applications) as opposed to maximizing throughput [PoKu87]. It is well–known that many important questions in science and engineering cannot be answered adequately, simply because their computational needs far exceed the capacity of the most powerful computer systems of today's. It is thus very important to exploit parallelism in such applications. On the other hand, needs for increased throughput may be satisfied by having several different machines, each taking part of the workload. Clearly throughput needs can be satisfied without the use of parallel computers.

1.4.1. Sources and Types of Parallelism

Parallelism can be structured or unstructured. Structured parallelism (e.g., a set of independent identical tasks that operate on different data sets) is more easy to deal with than unstructured parallelism (i.e., different instruction and/or data streams).

At the algorithm design level the user can choose the most appropriate algorithm to carry out a particular computation. This is the first and the most important step in the parallelism specification process. After selecting the most appropriate (parallel) algorithm, the user must select appropriate data structures. For example, in Pascal or in C a set of data items can be stored in a linked list or in a vector. In terms of parallel access, a vector is clearly a more suitable structure since we can address each of its elements independently.

The next step is to code an algorithm using the "most appropriate language". If the language provides parallel constructs (unfortunately very few do) the user may explicitly specify all or some of the parallelism in a program using these language constructs. Alternatively the user may write a program in a serial language and leave the responsibility of parallelism detection to the compiler. A restructuring compiler can also be used to discover more parallelism in a program that has already been coded in a parallel language.

During coding, parts of the computation may be organized into subroutines or coroutines. In particular, independent modules of computation can be implemented as independent subroutines. During execution of the program these subroutines can execute in parallel. Parallelism at the subroutine level is *coarse grain.*

At the loop level, parallelism can be specified again by the user or it can be discovered by the compiler through dependence analysis. Parallel loops is one of the most well studied topics in program restructuring. Several different types of parallel loops exist depending on the kind of dependence graph of the loop, and we will define and use most of them in the following sections. Because most Fortran programs spend most of their time inside loops [Kuck84], parallelizing loops is one of the most crucial activities during program restructuring and it may result in dramatic speedups [Kuck84], [PoBa87]. We can classify loop parallelism as *medium grain.*

Parallelism at the basic block level can be medium or *fine grain* depending on the size of the block. Basic blocks can execute concurrently if no interblock dependences exist. In some cases basic blocks with interdependences can also execute in parallel [PoBa87]. Fine grain parallelism at the statement or operation level is also important even though the average resulting speedup (at least for numerical programs) is far smaller than at the loop level. Due to the overhead involved, fine grain parallelism is usually exploited inside each processor by utilizing different or multiple functional units, or by using pipelining.

1.4.2. Expressing Parallelism in Programs

If we have a powerful parallel language at our disposal, then parallelism at all levels can be explicitly specified by the programmer [ANSI86], [MeRo85]. The higher the level the easier it is to do this. As we go though deeper into each program module, it becomes increasingly cumbersome to specify parallelism even if the language provides all necessary constructs. This is true partly due to the unstructured nature of parallelism at low levels.

An unpleasant fact of life, so far, is that there are no languages available that can be characterized as truly parallel. Even if such languages emerge in the near future (which is inevitable) they will probably be unusually complex for the "casual" programmer. Another problem is the fate of "dusty–decks". In the numerical world the amount of Fortran 66 and Fortran 77 code that is currently in use, translates

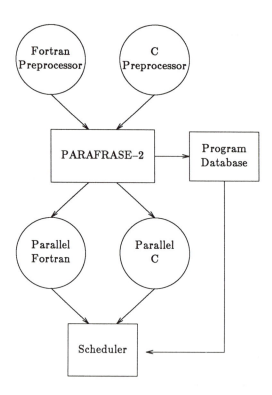

Figure 1.1. The structure of Parafrase–2.

into billions of dollars investment in human and machine resources. Rewriting these codes is a parallel language would take several years and serious financial commitments.

Restructuring compilers offer a very attractive solution to both of the above problems. If the techniques used to discover parallelism are language independent (which is approximately true) changing a restructuring compiler to generate code for different versions of a programming language (e.g., Fortran) requires little effort. The task of parallelism detection and specification is very complex even for skillful programmers. A restructuring compiler can do a better job than the average programmer, especially with large size programs.

1.4.3. Utilization of Parallelism

Assuming that parallelism has been specified by the user or has been discovered by the compiler, the next step is to find ways of utilizing this parallelism. That is, find the best mapping of parallel program constructs onto a given parallel architecture. Finding the optimal mapping is a crucial and very complex problem [PoKu87].

There are several components in the mapping problem: processor allocation and scheduling, communication, and synchronization. An optimal solution that takes all these components into consideration would result in optimal execution times. However, in general an optimal solution to one of the subproblems implies a suboptimal (and maybe inefficient) solution to the other subproblems. For example, interprocessor communication alone is minimized (in the absolute sense) if the program executes on a single processor. The same is true for synchronization.

A few approaches have been proposed recently that solve some important instances of the mapping problem very efficiently and are discussed in this book [PoBa87], [PoKu87]. The complexity of the mapping problem calls for automated solutions through the use of more sophisticated software tools. It is simply not practical to assume that the responsibility lies entirely with the programmer.

1.4.4. The Role of the Compiler

The complexity of parallel programming increases as the organizations of parallel computers become more and more complex. This complexity makes the need of sophisticated software tools more clear. As it is "natural" for traditional compilers to carry out register allocation and other standard optimizations, it is also more appropriate for serial–to–parallel program restructuring to be the compiler's responsibility. Even though restructuring compilers emerged several years ago, there is still a long way to go before we can consider the problem as adequately solved.

Most current supercomputer vendors supply such compilers for their machines [Alli85], [Cray85], [MiUc84], [NIOK84]. Several commercial and experimental restructuring compilers are in use including the Vast, the KAP, the PFC, and the Parafrase restructurer which was developed at the University of Illinois [AlKe82], [AlKe87], [Kenn80], [KKLW80], [KKPL81], [Kuck84]. All of these compilers focus on program restructuring alone and they ignore other important problems such as scheduling, synchronization, and communication [PoKu87]. We believe that these activities can be carried out (at least in part) by the compiler.

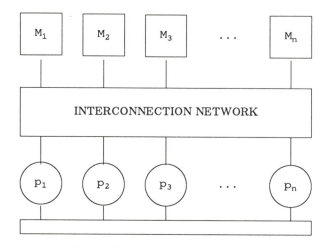

PROCESSOR INTERCONNECTION

Figure 1.2. A shared memory parallel processor model.

Parafrase–2, an undergoing project (at the Center for Supercomputing R & D of the University of Illinois), aims towards the development of a powerful parallelizing compiler that it will not only restructure serial programs into a parallel form, but it will also perform communication and synchronization overhead analysis, memory management, and it will help the scheduling of the resulting program for execution on parallel machines. Another goal of this project is to develop a restructurer that will be able to parallelize several different languages. The structure of Parafrase–2 is shown in Figure 1.1. Parafrase–2 is currently being developed to restructure Fortran 77 and C programs for shared memory parallel machines. Long term goals include memory management and automatic analysis of the expected overhead incurred during parallel execution of a given program. Experience with parallel machines, so far, has indicated that only a small fraction of the available parallelism in programs can be exploited on such machines. This is due to several types of overheads that severely restrict performance. Typical overhead activities during parallel execution include synchronization, communication, and scheduling activities, as well as extra random delays due to memory and network conflicts. These sources of overhead can be reduced significantly by compiler optimizations and architectural enhancements. The restructurer will also perform the first phase of scheduling called pre–scheduling. Parafrase–2 will encompass most of the existing technology in this area, as well as new methods that have been developed recently. The compiler is designed to allow easy integration of new technology with minimal effort.

The next section introduces the basic assumptions, notation, and definitions that are used throughout this book. Notation and definitions that are relevant only to a particular chapter are given at the beginning of that chapter. A brief overview of the Parafrase compiler which was used for experiments is also given.

1.5. BASIC CONCEPTS AND DEFINITIONS

The architecture model used throughout this book is a shared memory parallel processor system as shown in Figure 1.2. The machine consists of p processors (numbered $1, 2, \ldots, p$) that are connected to a shared memory M through a multistage interconnection network. The memory can be interleaved and each processor can access any memory module, or can communicate with any other processor through the memory. Each processor has its own private memory that can be organized as a cache, register file or RAM. Each processor is a stand–alone unit. It has its own control unit and can operate independently and asynchronously from the other processors. Our machine model therefore is multiple–instruction, multiple–data or MIMD. We also assume that each of the processors is a vector or array processor and thus it can operate in single–instruction, multiple–data or SIMD mode. It is apparent that this taxonomy cannot uniquely characterize our machine model. According to Kuck's taxonomy, the model of Figure 1.2 is an MEA system.

In this book we consider parallel programs which have been written using language extensions or programs that have been restructured by an optimizing compiler. For our purposes we use output generated by the Parafrase restructurer [Kuck80], [Wolf82]. Parafrase is a restructuring compiler which receives as input Fortran programs and applies to them a series of machine independent and machine dependent transformations. The structure of Parafrase is shown in Figure 1.3. The first part of the compiler consists of a set of machine independent transformations (passes). The second part consists of a series of machine dependent optimizations that can be applied on a given program. Depending on the architecture of the machine we intend to use, we choose the appropriate set of passes to perform transformations targeted to the underlying architecture. Currently Parafrase can be used to transform programs for execution on four types of machines: *Single Execution Scalar* or SES (uniprocessor), *Single Execution Array* or SEA (array/pipeline), *Multiple Execution Scalar* or MES (multiprocessor), and *Multiple Execution Array* or MEA (multiprocessor with vector processors) architectures [Kuck78]. SES is a uniprocessor machine and optimizations for serial architectures include the traditional code optimizations used in most compilers [AhUl77]. SEA architectures include all single instruction multiple data models such as vector or pipeline and array machines. The MES model includes parallel processor systems with serial processors, or more commonly referred to as MIMD. In other words MES systems are composed of a set of independent SES machines (that may operate out of a shared memory). In case of a parallel processor system where each processor has an SEA or SIMD organization, the corresponding machine is called MEA. The machine models used in this book are MES and MEA.

The most important aspect of the restructurer is its ability to perform sophisticated dependence analysis and build the data dependence graph (DDG) of a program [Bane79], [Wolf82]. The DDG is an internal representation of the program that is used by most subsequent passes to carry out a variety of transformations and

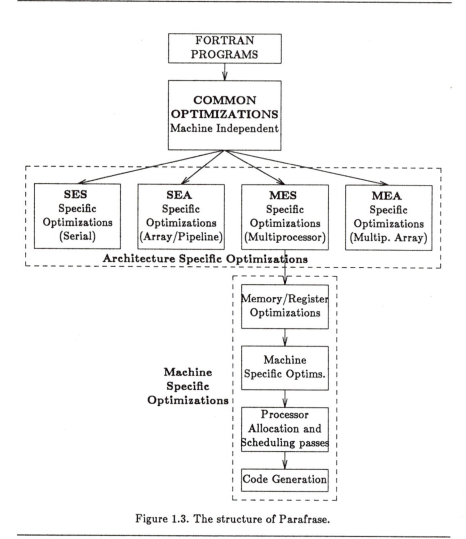

Figure 1.3. The structure of Parafrase.

optimizations without violating the semantics of the source program. The DDG is a directed graph, where nodes correspond to program statements and arcs represent dependences. Dependences in turn enforce a partial order of execution on the program statements. For most of our work we make an implicit assumption that Parafrase can supply us with any *compact data dependence graph* or CDDG. A CDDG is a directed graph that can be derived from the DDG by condensing several nodes into a single *composite node*. A set of consecutive program statements for example can define a composite node. The arcs in DDGs represent collections of dependences. Clearly several different CDDGs can be constructed from the same DDG. Data dependences are defined in Chapter 2.

Through a series of transformations, Parafrase is able to restructure Fortran loops into a parallel form. There are three major types of loops in a typical restructured program. *Doserial* (or DOSERIAL) are loops that must execute serially on any machine due to dependence cycles. An important transformation in the restructurer is the *do-to-doall* pass that recognizes and marks *Doall* (or DOALL) loops [Davi81], [Padu79]. In a DOALL loop cross–iteration dependences do not exist and thus all iterations can execute in parallel and in any order. A restricted case of a DOALL is the *Forall* loop. In a FORALL loop cross–iteration, forward–pointing dependences of constant distance may exist, but synchronization can be used to execute such loops as DOALLs. Another pass in Parafrase is the *do-to-doacross* that recognizes and marks *Doacross* (or DOACR) loops [Cytr84], [PoBa87]. A DOACR is a loop that contains a dependence cycle in its loop body. If the cycle involves all statements in the loop, a DOACR is then equivalent to a DOSERIAL loop. Otherwise partial overlapping of successive iterations may be possible during execution. A DOALL loop can also be thought of as an extreme case of a DOACR.

In addition to restructuring Fortran programs Parafrase supplies the user with program statistics that include speedup of execution for different numbers of processors, parallel and serial execution times, and efficiency and utilization measures. For a given program, T_1 denotes its serial execution time. T_p denotes the parallel execution time of a program on a p–processor machine. For a given p, the *program speedup* S_p is then defined as

$$S_p = \frac{T_1}{T_p}.$$

The *efficiency* E_p for a given program and a given p is defined as the ratio

$$E_p = \frac{S_p}{p}$$

and $0 \le E_p \le 1$. Often in this book the terms *parallel execution time* and *schedule length* are used interchangeably.

The overlapped execution of disjoint modules of a parallel program is referred to as *spreading*. If spreading is performed for fine grain parallelism it is called *low–level spreading*. If high level or coarse grain parallelism (e.g. disjoint loops) is used it is called *high–level spreading* [Veid85]. A *block of assignment statements* (or BAS) is a program module consisting exclusively of consecutive assignment statements. A BAS is also referred to as a *basic block* [AhUl76]. Basic blocks have a single entry and a single exit statement which are the first and last statements in the BAS. A *program task graph* is any compact DDG. Nodes in a program task graph correspond to program modules and are called *tasks*. Arcs represent dependences and are labeled with *weights* reflecting the amount of data that need to be transmitted between tasks. The arcs of a CDDG define a partial order on its nodes. The *predecessors* of a task are the nodes pointing to that task. The tasks pointed to by the arcs originating from a given node are *successors* of that node. Tasks may be *serial* or *parallel* depending on whether they can execute on one or more processors. A parallel task may *fork* or *spawn* several *processes* with each process executing on a different processor. Serial tasks are composed of a single process. A task is said to be *active* if it can spawn more processes, or if some of its processes have not completed execution. A task is *ready* when it does not have predecessor tasks, and it is *complete* when all of its processes have completed execution.

A *processor allocation* is the assignment of a number of processors to each task of the program task graph. A *schedule* is the assignment of tasks to processors under time constraints. Note that processor allocation specifies the number of processors assigned to each task but not the actual binding of tasks to physical processors. Scheduling on the other hand binds a specific task to one or more physical processors at a specific time interval. Processor allocation takes into account the timing constraints implicitly. A schedule may be *static* or *dynamic*. A static schedule specifies the assignment of tasks to processors deterministically before execution. Dynamic scheduling performs the binding dynamically at run–time in a nondeterministic approach. A variation of dynamic scheduling is *self–scheduling* [Smit81]. During self–scheduling idle processors fetch their next process from a shared pool of ready tasks. A *schedule–length* is the time it takes to execute a given program (graph) under a specific scheduling scheme. The execution time is determined by the moment the last processor working on that program finishes. For the same program graph different scheduling schemes have (in general) different schedule lengths. *Finish time* and *completion time* are synonyms to schedule length.

CHAPTER 2

PROGRAM RESTRUCTURING
FOR PARALLEL EXECUTION

2.1. DATA DEPENDENCES

The effectiveness of automatic program restructuring depends on how accurately we can compute data dependences. In general, data dependences give us information about how data are computed in a program and how they are used. This information is then used to parallelize the program automatically. The resulting parallel program should be such that during its parallel execution it computes and uses data in the order implied by the various data and control dependences; this is necessary to guarantee correctness of results. The material presented in this chapter requires some knowledge of data dependences and some associated concepts. Before we give a short introduction to data dependences however, we need to establish a basic notation.

A *program* is a list of $k \in N$ statements. S_i denotes the i-th statement in a program (counting in lexicographic order). I_j denotes a DO loop index, and i_j a particular value of I_j. N_j is the upper bound of a loop index I_j, and all loops are assumed to be normalized, i.e., the values of an index I_j range between 1 and N_j. The *stride* r_j of a loop index I_j is a positive constant by which I_j is incremented each time it is updated. We have two types of statements, *scalar* and *indexed* statements. An indexed statement is one that appears inside a loop, or whose execution is explicitly or implicitly controlled by an index (e.g., vector statements). All other statements are scalar. The *degree* of a program statement is the number of distinct loops surrounding it, or the number of dimensions of its operands. $S_i(I_1, I_2, \ldots, I_k)$ denotes a statement of degree k, where I_j is the index of the j-th loop or dimension. An indexed statement $S_i(I_1, \ldots, I_k)$ has $\prod_{j=1}^{k} N_j$ different *instances*, one for each value of each of I_j, $(j=1, \ldots, k)$. The first and last instance of a statement of degree k is $S_i(1,1, \ldots, 1)$ and $S_i(N_1, N_2, \ldots, N_k)$ respectively. S_i will be used in place of $S_i(I_1, \ldots, I_k)$ whenever the set of indices is obvious. The *order of execution* is defined between pairs of statements instances S_i, S_j as follows. For (scalar) statements with degree 0 we say that S_i is executed before S_j and denoted by $S_i \leq S_j$ if $i \leq j$, i.e., if S_i lexically precedes S_j. For S_i, S_j with degree k (if they have different degrees then scalar order of execution applies as well), we have the following three cases. If S_i and S_j do not have common indices, then $S_i \underset{o}{\leq} S_j$ if $i \leq j$. If they have the same k indices, then $S_i(i_1, \ldots, i_k) \underset{o}{\leq} S_j(j_1, \ldots, j_k)$ if $i \leq j$ and there is an $1 \leq m \leq k$ such that $i_1 = j_1$, $(l=1, \ldots, m)$, and $i_{m+1} < J_{m+1}$. If $i > j$, it is as above but with $m < k$. If S_i and S_j have $m < k$ common indices and $i_1 = j_1$, $(l=1, \ldots, m)$, then $S_i \underset{o}{\leq} S_j$ iff $i \leq j$. Otherwise the previous definition holds.

We also need to extend the definition of the $IN(S)$ and $OUT(S)$ sets (i.e., the sets of variables read and written by statement S respectively). We denote by $OUT(S_i(i_1, \ldots, i_k))$ the set of *variable instances* (not necessarily different) defined by statement instance $S_i(i_1, \ldots, i_k)$. Similarly, $IN(S_i(i_1, \ldots, i_k))$ is the set of variable instances used by the same statement instance.

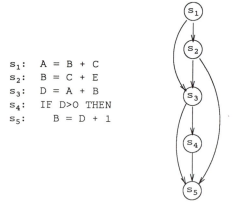

```
S₁:    A = B + C
S₂:    B = C + E
S₃:    D = A + B
S₄:    IF D>0 THEN
S₅:       B = D + 1
```

Figure 2.1. An example of data and control dependences.

Now we can proceed with the definition of data dependences. Two statements $S_i(I_1, \ldots, I_k)$ and $S_j(J_1, \ldots, J_k)$ are involved in a *flow* dependence $S_i \delta S_j$ if and only if there exist index values $(i_1, i_2, \ldots, i_k)$ and $(j_1, j_2, \ldots, j_k)$, such that $S_i(i_1, \ldots, i_k) \underset{\circ}{\leq} S_j(j_1, \ldots, j_k)$, and $\text{OUT}(S_i(i_1, \ldots, i_k)) \cap \text{IN}(S_j(j_1, \ldots, j_k)) \neq \varnothing$. An *antidependence* between S_i and S_j is defined as the flow dependence above, except for the last condition which now is $\text{IN}(S_i(i_1, \ldots, i_k)) \cap \text{OUT}(S_j(j_1, \ldots, j_k)) \neq \varnothing$. It is denoted by $S_i \bar{\delta} S_j$. An *output* dependence is again defined as above but with $\text{OUT}(S_i(i_1, \ldots, i_k)) \cap \text{OUT}(S_j(j_1, \ldots, j_k)) \neq \varnothing$, and it is denoted by $S_i \delta^\circ S_j$. In all three cases $S_i(i_1, \ldots, i_k)$ is called the dependence *source* and $S_j(j_1, \ldots, j_k)$ is called the dependence *sink*. Note that for a pair of statements S_i and S_j, $S_i \delta S_j$ denotes the *static dependence* and implies that a dependence exists at least between a pair of instances of the two statements. Clearly each static dependence may have several different *instances*.

For each data dependence involving statements $S_i(i_1, \ldots, i_k)$ and $S_j(j_1, \ldots, j_k)$ of degree k we define the r-th *distance* ϕ_r, or $\phi_r(\delta)$, to be $\phi_r = j_r - i_r$, $(1 \leq r \leq k)$. The k-tuple $<\phi_1, \phi_2, \ldots, \phi_k>$ is called the dependence distance vector. The *true* distance or simply distance Φ_{ij} is defined as

$$\Phi_{ij} = \sum_{r=1}^{k} \phi_r \prod_{m=r+1}^{k} N_m \qquad (2.1)$$

and gives the total number of iterations between the source and the sink of the dependence.

The program *data dependence graph* or DDG, is a directed graph $G(V, E)$ with a set of nodes $V = \{S_1, S_2, \ldots, S_n\}$ corresponding to statements in a program, and a set of arcs $E = \{e_{ij} = (S_i, S_j) \mid S_i, S_j \in V\}$ representing data dependences between statements. Figure 2.1 shows the DDG of a set of scalar statements.

The example of Figure 2.1 shows data dependences for scalar variables. The corresponding graph is called the *scalar* dependence graph. When vector elements are involved (usually inside loops) the computation of data dependences becomes more complex. We can no longer use the classical use–definition [AhSU86], [AlCo72] approach, since a nonempty intersection of the IN and OUT sets does not necessarily result to a true dependence. Subscript analysis is necessary in this case to determine whether the references in question are to the same vector elements. Consider for example the following loop.

```
        DO I = 1, N
s₁:         A(I+K) = ...
s₂:         ... = A(I)
        ENDO
```

where K is a nonnegative integer constant. Here $s_1 \leq s_2$ and $\text{IN}(s_1) \cap \text{OUT}(s_2) \neq \varnothing$, but we cannot determine yet whether a flow dependence from s_1 to s_2 exists. Several factors must be considered in this case. For a dependence to exist we must have two values of the index I, I_1 and I_2, such that

$$1 \leq I_1 \leq I_2 \leq N \text{ and } I_1 + K = I_2.$$

To test this we must know the values of K and N. In most programs the value of K is known at compile–time but this is not always true for loop bounds like N. If K$\leq$N then a dependence may exist. However if K>N no dependence between the two statements can exist. Frequently loop bounds are not known at compile–time but to be on the safe side they are assumed to be "large". In general, dependences can be computed by solving a Diophantine equation similar to the above. Algorithms for computing data dependences are given in [Bane79], [Wolf82].

In the previous example a dependence exists if I_2-I_1=K. This difference is said to be the *dependence distance* and gives the number of iterations that must be executed between a definition and a use of a particular element of array A (or equivalently, the number of iterations between the iteration containing the source and the iteration containing the sink of the corresponding dependence).

Several different transformations exist, that based on dependence information, can restructure serial programs into vector or parallel form, suitable for execution on SIMD and MIMD systems. In a restructured program, parallelism is usually explicitly specified via parallel constructs. In this chapter the only type of parallel constructs used are various types of parallel loops. A DO loop denotes an ordinary Fortran loop, which is serial. A loop whose iterations can execute in parallel and in any order is called DOALL. The dependences in certain loops may allow only partially overlapped execution of successive iterations. These loops are called DOACROSS and are mentioned in only a few cases in this chapter [Padu79], [Cytr84]. Of course, a loop is marked as being DO, DOALL, or DOACROSS after the necessary dependence analysis for that loop has been carried out.

Loop parallelization, discovering and packaging unstructured parallelism, interprocedural analysis, compile–time overhead analysis, and many other complex tasks can be carrier out automatically by a restructuring compiler. In many cases user assertions can be useful or necessary. Automating the parallelization process makes parallel program writing possible for nonspecialists, and in general, results to more efficient code.

After determining dependences and building the DDG, the compiler starts the process of optimizing and restructuring the program from a serial into a parallel form. During the optimization phase several architecture independent optimizations are applied to the source code to make it more efficient, more suitable for restructuring, or both. The restructuring phase which actually transforms the program into a vector and/or parallel form is also organized into architecture independent and architecture dependent subphases. In this chapter we look at program restructuring for SEA and MEA machine organizations.

2.2. COMMON OPTIMIZATIONS

Some standard and not so standard optimizations are useful independently of the organization of the machine on which we intend to run the program. In this section we discuss some of these optimizations but we cover in no way all of them.

2.2.1. Induction Variable Substitution

Induction variables are often used inside loops to simplify subscript expressions. An *induction variable* is a variable whose values form an arithmetic or geometric progression [AhSU86], [AlCo72], [PaWo86]. These variables are usually expressed as functions of the loop index. Their detection and elimination does not only reduce the number of operations inside the loop, but it may also allow vectorization of the loop that would be impossible otherwise due to dependence cycles. In the following loop

```
DO I = 1, N
    J = 2*I+1
    A(I) = (A(I) + B(J))/2
ENDO
```

the values of J form an arithmetic progression and thus J is an induction variable. The loop can be rewritten as

```
DO I = 1, N
    A(I) = (A(I) + B(2*I+1))/2
ENDO
```

If the values of an induction variable form a progression except at the first or last terms where there might be a discontinuity, then partial loop unrolling at the beginning or at the end of the loop may be necessary to remove the induction variable. This usually happens when the values of such a variable are a permutation of the terms of a progression. For example, in the loop

```
J = N
DO I = 1, N
    A(I) = (B(I) + B(J))/2
    J = I
ENDO
```

the values of J are $N, 1, 2, \ldots, N-1$. It is obvious however that J is an arithmetic progression shifted (with wrap around) once to the right. By unrolling the first iteration of the loop we get

```
A(1) = (B(1) + B(N))/2
DO I = 2, N
    A(I) = (B(I) + B(I-1))/2
ENDO
```

2.2.2. Index Recurrences

As is the case with induction variables, some times (less often) some loop-defined index variables are used to index array elements. Their values do not form progressions but they give for example, the sum of the first I terms of a progression, where I is the loop index. An example of a simple index recurrence is shown in the following loop.

```
J = 0
DO I = 1, N
    J = J + I
    A(I) = A(I) + B(J)
ENDO
```

In this case J is the sum $\sum_{k=1}^{i} k$ for each iteration I of the loop. In most cases these variables can be eliminated just like reduction variables. The above loop will become

```
DO I = 1, N
   A(I) = A(I) + B(I*(I+1)/2)
ENDO
```

2.2.3. Loop Unrolling

Loop unrolling can be applied in two forms. In the first, unrolling is done by peeling off one or more iterations at the beginning or at the end of the loop. In the second form unrolling happens inside the loop and results in changing the loop stride [AhSU86], [AlCo72], [PaWo86]. We already showed an application of loop unrolling in the previous section. Unrolling is useful in many other cases. For example, it is often the case where expensive intrinsic function calls such as MIN and MAX are part of DO statements (e.g., DO I=1, MAX(N,M)). If the relationship of N and M is known (which is often the case) the intrinsic function call can be eliminated by peeling off the last iteration of the loop. Consider the loop

```
DO J =1, N, K
   DO I = J, MIN(J+K, N)
      A(I) = B(I) + C(I)
   ENDO
ENDO
```

where $K \in Z^+$ is the outer loop stride. The intrinsic function call MIN(J+K,N) will be executed $\lceil N/K \rceil$ times. For N>>K this may introduce a large amount of unnecessary overhead. The compiler can eliminate automatically the intrinsic function call in the above loop by unrolling the last iteration of the outer loop, and produce the following equivalent code:

```
N1 = TRUNC(N/K)
N2 = N1 * K
N3 = N - N2
DO J = 1, N2, K
   DO I = J, J+K
      A(I) = B(I) + C(I)
   ENDO
ENDO
DO I = N3+1, N
   A(I) = B(I) + C(I)
ENDO
```

In its general form loop unrolling replicates the body of the loop inside the loop for K successive values of the loop index, and increments the loop stride by K-1.

2.2.4. Constant Propagation and Expression Evaluation

This is one of the most common optimizations found in almost any conventional compiler [AhSU86], [AlCo72], [PaWo86]. The idea here is to eliminate unnecessary run–time computation that can be easily done by the compiler. This requires the propagation of the value of program constants to all statements in the program that use them. For example, consider the following loop.

```
DO I = 1, N
   PI = 3.14
   PD = 2*PI
   A(I) = PD*R(I)**2
ENDO
```

After constant propagation, constant expression evaluation, and floating of loop invariants, the above loop will be transformed in the more efficient form:

```
PI = 3.14
PD = 6.28
DO I = 1, N
   A(I) = 6.28*R(I)**2
ENDO
```

Another useful application of constant propagation is to replace constants that appear in array index expressions with their actual values. This is a necessary step for computing accurate data dependences.

2.3. TRANSFORMATIONS FOR VECTOR/PARALLEL LOOPS

In this section we discuss some known and some new program transformation for discovering and exploiting parallelism in serial programs. There are several different program transformations in use, and each of them is applied to explore a particular type of parallelism, or to take advantage of specific properties of the code and the target machine. Many program transformations are unrelated to each other in the sense that the end–result is the same independently of the order in which they were applied. However, it is more frequently the case where the order in which different program transformations are applied is significant. Thus if we apply the same set of n transformations to the same program n! times, using a different order at each time, we may get n! programs (semantically equivalent but) syntactically different, with varying amounts of parallelism, that could possibly obtain different performance on the same machine. Finding the best order in which transformations should be applied is an open problem and the answer is known for only a few special cases.

The significance of the order of application becomes more evident with more complex machine architectures. For example, the problem is not as significant when we compile for purely vector (SEA) or parallel–scalar (MES) machines, as it is for parallel–vector (MEA) computers. Program restructuring for vector machines is referred to as *vectorization*. Similarly for parallel–scalar machines it is usually called *parallelization*. When the underlying architecture is parallel–vector, then vectorization as well as parallelization are equally important in a good compiler. However in this case we must face many tradeoffs between vectorization and parallelization.

In this section we focus on techniques for vectorizing and parallelizing serial programs without emphasizing the tradeoffs (except in a few cases). All material that follows assumes that a data dependence graph with all the necessary information has been constructed by the compiler for each specific case and example that is used.

2.3.1. Loop Vectorization and Loop Distribution

When compiling for a vector machine, one of the most important tasks is to generate vector instructions out of loops [Brod81], [Davi81], [PaWo86], [Wolf82]. To do this the compiler must check all dependences inside the loop. In the most simple case where dependences do not exist the compiler must *distribute* the loop around each statement of the loop and create a vector statement for each case. Vectorizing the following loop

```
DO I = 1, N
s₁:    A(I) = B(I) + C(I)
s₂:    D(I) = B(I) * K
ENDO
```

would yield the following two vector statements

```
s₁:    A(1:N) = B(1:N) + C(1:N)
s₂:    D(1:N) = K * B(1:N)
```

where $1:N$ denotes all the elements $1, 2, \ldots, N$. In the original loop one element of A and one element of D were computed at each iteration. In the latter case however all elements of A are computed before computation of D starts. This is the result of distributing the loop around each statement. In general loop distribution around two statements s_i and s_j (or around two blocks B_i and B_j) is legal if there is no dependence between s_i and s_j (B_i and B_j), or if there are dependences in only one direction. By definition, vectorization is only possible on a statement–by–statement basis. Therefore in a multistatement loop, loop distribution must be applied before vector code can be generated; if distribution is illegal vectorization of multistatement loops is impossible.

In nested loops only the innermost loop can be vectorized. For example, consider the following serial loop.

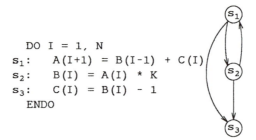

```
DO I = 1, N
s₁:    A(I+1) = B(I-1) + C(I)
s₂:    B(I) = A(I) * K
s₃:    C(I) = B(I) - 1
ENDO
```

The data dependence graph is shown on the right. A simple traversal of the dependence graph would reveal its strongly connected components (SCC). Those SCCs with single statements (that do not have self–dependences) can be vectorized. The result of vectorizing the above loop would be:

```
                DO I = 1, N
                  A(I+1) = B(I-1) + C(I)
                  B(I) = A(I) * K
                ENDO
                C(1:N) = B(1:N) - 1
```

2.3.2. Loop Interchange

Loop interchange is another transformation that can be very useful in many cases [PaWo86], [Wolf82]. It interchanges the (position) nest depth of a pair of loops in the same nest, and can be applied repeatedly to interchange more than two loops in a given nest of loops. As mentioned above, when loops are nested vectorization is possible only for the innermost loop. (Of course, by successive reductions of innermost loops to vector statements, more than one innermost loop can be reduced to vector notation.) Loop interchange can be used in such cases to bring the vectorizable loop to the innermost position. For example, the following loop

```
            DO I = 1, N
       s₁:   A(I) = B(I) + C(I)
       s₂:   D(I) = A(I-1) * A(I+1)
            ENDO
                  (a)

            DO I = 1, N
       s₁:   A(I) = B(I) + C(I)
       s₃:   TEMP(I) = A(I+1)
       s₂:   D(I) = A(I-1) * TEMP(I)
            ENDO
                  (b)

            DO I = 1, N
              TEMP(I) = A(I+1)
              A(I) = B(I) + C(I)
              D(I) = A(I-1) * TEMP(I)
            ENDO
                  (c)

          TEMP(1:N) = A(2:N+1)
          A(1:N) = B(1:N) + C(1:N)
          D(1:N) = A(0:N-1) * TEMP(1:N)
                  (d)
```

Figure 2.2. An example of node splitting and statement reordering.

```
DO I = 2, N
    DO J = 2, M
        A(I,J) = A(I, J-1) + 1
    ENDO
ENDO
```

is not vectorizable because the innermost loop (a recurrence) must be executed serially. But the outermost loop is parallel. By interchanging the two loops and vectorizing the innermost we get

```
DO J = 1, M
    A(1:N,J) = A(1:N, J-1) + 1
ENDO
```

Loop interchange is not always possible. In general a DOALL loop can be interchanged with any loop nested inside it. The inverse is not always true. Serial loops for example cannot always be interchanged with loops surrounded by them. Interchange is illegal for example in the following loop.

```
DO I = 2, N
    DO J = 1, M
        A(I,J) = A(I-1,J+1) + 1
    ENDO
ENDO
```

In general loop interchange is impossible when there are dependences between any two statements of the loop with "<" and ">" directions [Wolf82]. There is no unique way to determine the best interchange. The answer depends on what we want to achieve. The architecture of the target machine for example may dictate which possibility is the best. When we vectorize, interchange should be done so that the loop with the largest number of iterations is brought to the innermost position. This would create vector statements that will operate on long vector operands. For memory–to–memory systems (e.g., CDC Cyber 205) long vectors are particularly important. If on the other hand we compile for a scalar multiprocessor, bringing the largest loop (in terms of number of iterations) in the outermost position is more desirable, since that would allow the parallel loop to use more processors.

2.3.3. Node Splitting and Statement Reordering

Loop vectorization and parallelization is impossible when the statements in the body of the loop are involved in a dependence cycle [AhSU86], [AlCo72], [Wolf82]. Dependence cycles that involve only flow dependences are usually hard to break. There are cases however where dependence cycles can be broken resulting in total or partial parallelization of the corresponding loops. One case where cycle breaking is possible is with dependence cycles that involve flow and anti–dependences. Anti–dependences are "artificial" dependences that can usually be eliminated with simple techniques such as variable renaming.

Figure 2.2 shows an example of breaking a dependence cycle, and its effect on vectorizing the loop. The loop of Figure 2.2a cannot be vectorized since its statements are involved in a cycle. Node splitting can be employed here to eliminate the cycle by splitting the node (statement) which causes the anti–dependence. As shown in Figure 2.2b this is done by renaming variable A(I+1) as TEMP(I) and using its new definition in statement s_2. The corresponding dependence graph is shown on the right.

Now that the cycle is broken loop distribution can be used to distribute the loop around each statement. The loop of Figure 2.2b can be distributed around s_2 but not around s_1 and s_3, since there are dependences in both directions. Statement reordering can be used here to reorder the statements of the loop as in Figure 2.2c (reordering is not always legal). The loop of Figure 2.2c satisfies now the "one direction dependences" rule, and thus it can be distributed around each statement resulting in the three vector statements of Figure 2.2d.

2.3.4. Code Reordering for Minimizing Communication

In the previous section statement reordering was used to change the direction of dependences in order to make loop distribution possible. Statement (or in general code) reordering can be used in several cases to improve or make possible the application of a certain optimization. For example reordering can be used to improve the effectiveness of DOACROSS loops [Cytr86], [PoBa87]. Another application of code reordering is in the reduction of interprocessor communication in parallel computers [Poly87a].

The compiler can be used to partition the program into data dependent or independent tasks. Different tasks of a program can execute on different processors, even when there are data dependences across tasks. Is such cases data computed by one or more processors must be communicated to other processors that need them.

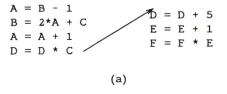

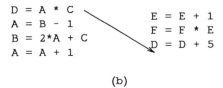

Figure 2.3. The impact of code reordering in the reduction of communication.

This communication takes place to satisfy the data dependences and it affects the execution time of the corresponding tasks in the form of processor delays. In certain cases code reordering can be used to reduce or minimize potential communication delays.

Consider for example the two basic blocks of Figure 2.3a, where each basic block forms a task. The arc in Figure 2.3a indicates the intertask data dependence. If these two tasks were scheduled to execute simultaneously on two different processors, the processor executing the second task would have to wait until the first task finishes execution. If we assume that each assignment statement takes a unit of time to execute, then the execution time of the two tasks on two processors will be 7 units; the same as if the two tasks were executed on a single processor. If the statements are reordered as in Figure 2.3b however, the execution time on two processors would be 4 units of time; the second processor will receive the new value of D by the time it will need it.

2.3.5. Loop Blocking

Loop blocking or *strip mining* is a transformation that creates doubly nested loops out of single loops, by organizing the computation in the original loop into chunks of approximately equal size [PaWo86]. Loop blocking can be useful in many cases. It is often used to "manage" vector registers, caches, or local memories with small sizes. Many vector computers for example have special vector registers that are used to store vector operands. Loop blocking can be used to partition vector statements into chunks of size K, where K is the length of the vector registers. The following loop

```
DO I = 1, N
    A(I) = B(I) + C(I)
ENDO
```

will become (after blocking)

```
DO J = 1, N, K
    DO I = J, MIN(J+K, N)
        A(I) = B(I) + C(I)
    ENDO
ENDO
```

In the same way blocking can be used to overcome size limitations of caches and local memories.

In parallel–vector machines (MEA) operations with long vector operands can be partitioned into shorter vectors, assigning each of the short vectors to a different processor. In this case loop blocking will introduce a parallel loop as in the following example. Consider the vector statement.

$$A(1:N) = B(1:N) * C(1:N)$$

In a system with P-processors (and if $N >> P$), this vector operation can be speeded up further by blocking it as follows.

```
K = TRUNC(N/P)
DOALL I = 1, P
    A((I-1)K+1:IK) = B((I-1)K+1:IK) *
                               C((I-1)K+1:IK)
ENDO
A(PK+1:N) = B(PK+1:N) * C(PK+1:N)
```

Notice that loop unrolling was implicitly used to eliminate the use of the intrinsic function MIN in the DOALL statement.

2.4. CYCLE SHRINKING

Some of the most important transformations are those that vectorize and parallelize serial loops. These transformations use the data dependence graph of a loop to determine whether the existing dependences allow the loop, or parts of it, to execute in parallel without violating the semantics. If no dependences exist this task is simple. In most cases however the dependence graph is complex, and appropriate tests are necessary to determine whether a pattern of dependences can allow vectorization or parallelization. Usually loops with dependence graphs that do not form strongly connected components can become fully or partially parallel. When the dependence graph forms a cycle node splitting can be used to break the cycle, assuming at least one of the dependences is an antidependence.

In many serial loops dependence cycles are impossible to break even after all known techniques are used. Such dependence cycles usually involve only flow dependences. In general, loops whose statements are involved in a dependence cycle are considered to be serial. *Cycle shrinking* can be used to extract any parallelism that may be (implicitly) present in a serial loop.

2.4.1. Simple Loops

Cycle shrinking is useful in cases where the dependence cycle of a loop involves dependences with distance greater than one. This scheme transforms a serial DO loop into two perfectly nested loops; an outermost serial and a parallel innermost loop. It is based on the observation that although there is a static flow dependence $S_1 \delta S_2$ between two statements S_1 and S_2 of a loop, there may be instances of S_1 and S_2 that are not involved in a dependence (since the dependence distance is greater than one). Cycle shrinking extracts these dependence-free instances of the statements inside a loop, and creates an inner parallel loop.

We can best describe cycle shrinking by considering initially dependence cycles where all dependences have the same distance $\lambda > 1$. In such cases cycle shrinking will speed up the loop by a factor of λ, called the *reduction factor*. First let us consider the case of singly nested serial loops with n statements $S_1, S_2, \ldots, S_n$ that are involved in a dependence cycle such that $S_1 \delta S_2 \delta \ldots S_n \delta S_1$. Furthermore assume that all n dependences have a constant distance $\lambda > 1$. For constant distance dependences, the array subscript expressions of elements that are involved in a dependence must be of the form $I \pm a$, where $a \geq 0$ and I is the loop index. Then (assuming loops are always normalized without loss in generality) we have the following.

Lemma 2.1. The iteration space $[1 \ldots N]$ of a loop whose dependences are of constant distance λ, can be partitioned into subintervals or *groups* $V_0 = [1 \ldots \lambda]$,

```
      DO I = 1, N
s₁:    A(I+K) = B(I) - 1
s₂:    B(I+K) = A(I) + C(I)
      ENDO
```

(a)

```
      DO I = 1, N, K
         DOALL J = I, I+K-1
            A(J+K) = B(J) - 1
            B(J+K) = A(J) +C(J)
         ENDO
      ENDO
```

(b)

Figure 2.4. (a) Example of loop with constant distance dependence cycle.
(b) The transformed loop of 2.4a.

$V_1=[\lambda+1\ldots2\lambda]$, ..., $V_r=[r\lambda+1\ldots N]$, so that the iterations of each group V_j are free of dependence sinks, assuming that groups $V_{1,V_2},\ldots,V_{j-1}$, ($j=1,2,\ldots,r$) have been executed. (For simplicity assume that the first dependence starts from the first iteration of the loop.)

Proof: First let us suppose that all dependence sources (for each instance of the static dependence cycle) belong to the same iteration of the loop. Then, since all dependences have the same distance λ, it follows that all dependence sinks also belong to the same iteration of the loop. Let i_1 and i_2 be two such iterations; i_1 involving the dependence sources of some instance of the dependence cycle, and i_2 involving the corresponding dependence sinks. Clearly such i_1 and i_2 should satisfy $i_2-i_1=\lambda$. Since no other dependences exist, it follows that all instances of statements in iterations $i_1, i_1+1, \ldots, i_1+\lambda-1=i_2-1$ contain no dependence sink and thus they are independent (assuming iterations $1, 2, \ldots, i_1-1$ have been executed). The statement of the lemma then follows directly.

Now let us consider the other extreme where the n dependence sources in a serial loop (and their corresponding sinks) belong to n different iterations of that loop. Without loss in generality assume that the first instance of $S_1\delta S_2$ corresponds to I=1, $S_2\delta S_3$ corresponds to I=2, ..., $S_n\delta S_1$ corresponds to I=n, where $n\leq N$. The cases of $n\leq\lambda$ and $n>\lambda$ are identical. Let us consider $n>\lambda$.

From the above hypothesis and since all dependences are of constant distance λ, it is clear that the sink of $S_1\delta S_2$ belongs to iteration $I=\lambda+1$, the sink of $S_2\delta S_3$ to iteration $I=\lambda+2$,..., and the sink of $S_n\delta S_1$ to iteration $I=\lambda+n$. Then, iterations

```
DO I = 3, N
   A(I) = B(I-2) - 1
   B(I) = A(I-3) * K
ENDO
      (a)

DO J = 3, N, 2
   DOALL I = J, J+1
       A(I) = B(I-2) - 1
       B(I) = A(I-3) * K
   ENDOALL
ENDO
      (b)


I = 3:   A(3) = B(1) - 1
         B(3) = A(0) * K
I = 4:   A(4) = B(2) - 1
         B(4) = A(1) * K
         ---------------
I = 5:   A(5) = B(3) - 1
         B(5) = A(2) * K
I = 6:   A(6) = B(4) - 1
         B(6) = A(3) * K
         ---------------
I = 7:   A(7) = B(5) - 1
         B(7) = A(4) * K
I = 8:   A(8) = B(6) - 1
         B(8) = A(5) * K
         ---------------
I = 9:   A(9) = B(7) - 1
         B(9) = A(6) * K
I =10:   A(10) = B(8) - 1
         B(10) = A(7) * K
         ---------------
I =11:   A(11) = B(9) - 1
         B(11) = A(8) * K
I =12:   A(12) = B(10) - 1
         B(12) = A(9) * K
         ---------------
      (c)
```

Figure 2.5. (a) A serial loop. (b) The transformed loop. (c) The unrolled version of (b).

$I=1, 2, \ldots, \lambda$, are free of dependence sinks and thus independent. Therefore iterations $V_0 = [1 \ldots \lambda]$ can be executed in parallel satisfying the first instance of the n dependences in the cycle. Then group $V_1 = [\lambda+1 \ldots 2\lambda]$ can be constructed in the same way and so on. The general case is identical. ∎

Lemma 2.1 indicates that serial loops with dependences that have equal (constant) distances can be partially parallelized. This can be done by transforming the serial loop into two perfectly nested loops. The innermost loop is a DOALL and at each time its index runs over the iterations of a group V_j, $(j=1, 2, \ldots, r)$, where $r = \lceil N/\lambda \rceil$. The outer loop is a serial DO loop whose index runs across groups V_j, $(j=1, 2, \ldots, r)$.

Consider for example the loop of Figure 2.4a. The dependence graph is shown next to it. Such loop would be treated as serial by the existing compilers. However, if cycle shrinking is applied the same loop will be transformed to that of Figure 2.4b. The transformed loop can now be executed $\lambda = K$ times faster. The larger the distance λ, the greater the speedup. Values of $\lambda = 2$ or 3 occur in numerical programs. Another example is shown in Figure 2.5 where the loop has been unrolled to clearly show the effect of cycle shrinking. Two iterations at a time can be executed in parallel in this case.

Let us consider now the case where the distance of each dependence (in the static dependence cycle) is constant, but distances between different static dependences are different. In this case we have a cycle $S_1 \delta_1 S_2 \ldots S_k \delta_k S_1$ where ϕ_i is the distance of the i-th dependence. Without loss in generality assume that $\phi_1 \geq \phi_2 \geq \ldots \geq \phi_n$. Then we have the following.

Corollary 2.1. If $\lambda = \min(\phi_1, \phi_2, \ldots, \phi_n) \equiv \phi_1$, then Lemma 2.1 holds true.

```
DO I = 1, N
    X(I) = Y(I) + Z(I)
    Y(I+3) = X(I-4) * W(I)
ENDO
        (a)

DO J = 1, N, 3
    DOALL I = J, J+2
        X(I) = Y(I) + Z(I)
        Y(I+3) = X(I-4) * W(I)
    ENDOALL
ENDO
        (b)
```

Figure 2.6. Another application of cycle shrinking.

Proof: The proof follows directly from Lemma 2.1. For example if $I=i_1$ is the iteration that contains the source of the static dependence $S_1\delta_1S_2$, then iterations $I=i_1$, i_1+1, ..., $i_1+\phi_1-1$ $(=i_1+\lambda-1)$ contain no dependence sink and are thus independent. By definition then it follows that iterations $I=i_1+\lambda, i_1+\lambda+1, ..., i_1+2\lambda-1$ contain sinks whose corresponding sources have been executed. The proof is identical for the other cases. ■

An example of a serial loop whose dependence cycle involves dependences with different distances is shown in Figure 2.6a. In this case $\phi_1=4$ and $\phi_2=3$. According to Corollary 2.1 the cycle can be reduced by a factor of $\lambda=\min(3,4)=3$ resulting in the loop of Figure 2.6b.

The next case to be examined is when the distance of each static dependence is different for different instances of the dependence. In singly nested loops this happens when we have array subscripts of the form $aI\pm b$ where $a\geq 1$ or $a\leq -1$. An example of such case is shown in Figure 2.7a. Here the distance of each static flow dependence varies between different instances of the dependence. The minimum distance between all instances of both dependences in the example is $\lambda=2$. (Actually distances are monotonically increasing between successive iterations.) Corollary 2.1 can be applied in this case to transform the loop as in Figure 2.7b. Even though cycle shrinking extracts some parallelism from this loop, it is still a rather conservative solution in the sense that it leaves some parallelism unexploited. A more general and powerful approach will be discussed in Section 2.4. Lemma 2.1 and Corollary 2.1 can be summarized in the following.

Corollary 2.2. A sufficient condition for a loop dependence cycle $S_1\delta_1S_2\delta_2...\delta_{n-1}S_n\delta_nS_1$ to be reduced by a factor of λ is

```
DO I = 4, N
   A(4I-1) = M * B(3I-1)
   B(4I-1) = C(I) + A(3I-1)
ENDO
      (a)

DO J = 4, N, 2
   DOALL I = J, J+1
      A(4I-1) = M * B(3I-1)
      B(4I-1) = C(I) + A(3I-1)
   ENDOALL
ENDO
      (b)
```

Figure 2.7. Cycle shrinking with varying dependence distances.

$$\lambda = \min_{1 \leq i \leq n} \{ \phi(\delta_i) \}. \tag{2.2}$$

Allen and Kennedy stated Corollary 2.2 in [AlKe87] where they use it in a similar transformation for blocking and vectorizing loops.

Theorem 2.1. Consider a DO loop with k statements which are all involved in a dependence cycle. If the reduction factor of the cycle is λ, then cycle shrinking increases the total parallelism in the loop by a factor of $\lambda *k$.

Proof: Since cycle shrinking creates λ independent iterations, the parallelism is increased by a factor of λ. Furthermore, all statement instances (in a group with λ independent iterations) are also independent. This is true because all k statements are involved in the cycle, and according to Lemma 2.1, each λ–iteration group is free of dependence sinks. Thus within each group all $\lambda *k$ statement instances can execute in parallel. ∎

2.4.2. Complex Loops

In this section we discuss cycle shrinking for complex nested loops. There are three versions of cycle shrinking that can be used for nested loops. They differ in the way individual and true distances are used to compute the reduction factor, and they are discussed below.

Simple Shrinking: In this version the dependence cycle is considered separately for each individual loop in the nest. For a loop at nest–depth 1 only the 1-th elements of the distance vector are considered. For each loop in the nest, cycle shrinking is applied separately as in the single loop case.

True Dependence Shrinking (or TD–Shrinking): In this version only true distances are used. Each dependence in the dependence cycle is labeled by its true distance computed by (2.1). Cycle shrinking is then applied as if the nested loop was a single loop. In this case a multidimensional iteration space is treated as a linear space. It will be shown later that, as a result of this, loops are blocked by cycle shrinking in an "irregular" fashion.

Selective Shrinking: Here we consider each component of the distance vectors separately as in the case of simple cycle shrinking. In a loop nest of depth k we thus have k different dependence cycles, one for each individual loop. Each dependence in a cycle is labeled with the corresponding element of its distance vector. Next, selective shrinking computes the reduction factor λ_i, ($i = 1, 2, \ldots, k$) (using (2.2)) for each loop in the nest starting with the outermost loop. The process stops when for some $1 \leq j \leq k$, $\lambda_j \geq 1$. Then the j–th loop in the nest is blocked by a factor of λ_j. In addition, all loops nested inside the j–th loop are transformed to DOALLs.

One can make a number of interesting observations at this point:

  1) The true distances depend on the loop size. This is not true with the individual distances. Thus, in general, the larger the loop sizes the

longer the true distances, and therefore the more the potential parallelism.

2) An implication of the previous observation is that more parallelism can potentially be exploited by blocking the loops in an "irregular" fashion.

3) In general, the loop upper bounds must be known in order to compute and compare the true distances. The values of the distances per se are not needed, but determining the minimum true distance in a cycle is essential for cycle shrinking to work in this mode.

It is also clear that, by definition, selective shrinking is always better than simple shrinking. In addition we have the following theorem.

Theorem 2.2. Let $S_1 \delta_1 S_2 \delta_2 \ldots S_k \delta_k S_1$ be a dependence cycle with k statements that are nested inside m loops of sizes $N_1, N_2, \ldots, N_m$ respectively (counting from the outermost to the innermost loop). Let also $<\phi_1^1, \ldots, \phi_m^1>$ and Φ_i be the distance vector and the true distance of δ_i, $(i=1, \ldots, k)$ respectively. The reduction factor obtained by TD–shrinking is greater than or equal to the total reduction factor obtained by simple shrinking. Or, equivalently,

$$\min(\Phi_1, \ldots, \Phi_k) \geq \prod_{i=1}^{m} \min(\phi_i^1, \phi_i^2, \ldots, \phi_i^k) .$$

Proof: Without loss in generality assume that $\Phi_1 = \min(\Phi_1, \Phi_2, \ldots, \Phi_k)$, and let $\phi_i^{r_i} = \min(\phi_i^1, \phi_i^2, \ldots, \phi_i^k)$, $(i=1, 2, \ldots, m)$. By definition we have $\Phi_1 = \sum_{i=1}^{m} \phi_i^1 \prod_{j=i+1}^{m} N_j$, and

$$N_1 \geq \phi_1^1 \geq \phi_1^{r_1}$$

$$N_2 \geq \phi_2^1 \geq \phi_2^{r_2} \qquad (2.3)$$

$$\cdot \quad \cdot \quad \cdot$$

$$N_m \geq \phi_m^1 \geq \phi_m^{r_m} .$$

From (2.3) we have $\prod_{i=2}^{m} N_i \geq \prod_{i=2}^{m} \phi_i^{r_i}$ and thus,

$$\phi_1^1 \prod_{i=2}^{m} N_i \geq \phi_1^{r_1} \prod_{i=2}^{m} \phi_i^{r_i} = \prod_{i=1}^{m} \phi_i^{r_i} \qquad (2.4)$$

and from (2.4) it follows directly that

$$\Phi_1 = \sum_{i=1}^{m} \phi_i^1 \prod_{j=i+1}^{m} N_j \geq \prod_{i=1}^{m} \phi_i^{r_i} = \prod_{i=1}^{m} \min(\phi_i^1, \phi_i^2, \ldots, \phi_i^k)$$

which proves the theorem. ∎

It remains to compare TD–shrinking to selective shrinking. Consider the true distance Φ of a dependence as defined by (2.1), and let $\mu_r = \phi_r \prod\limits_{m=r+1}^{k} N_m$. Then we have the following.

Lemma 2.2. If ϕ_r is positive, then

$$\mu_r \geq \sum_{i=r+1}^{k} \mu_i, \ (r=1, 2, \ldots, k-1) . \tag{2.5}$$

Proof: For simplicity and without loss in generality let us assume that loops are normalized. By definition we have

$$N_{r+i} - 1 \geq \phi_{r+i}, \ (i=0, 1, 2, \ldots, k-r) . \tag{2.6}$$

Relation (2.5) can be rewritten as

$$\phi_r \prod_{i=r+1}^{k} N_i \geq \phi_{r+1} \prod_{i=r+2}^{k} N_i + \phi_{r+2} \prod_{i=r+3}^{k} N_i + \ldots + \phi_{k-1} N_k + \phi_k .$$

By using (2.6) it is enough to show that

$$\prod_{i=r+1}^{k} N_i \geq (N_{r+1}-1) \prod_{i=r+2}^{k} N_i + (N_{r+2}-1) \prod_{i=r+3}^{k} N_i + \ldots + (N_{k-1}-1) N_k + N_k - 1$$

$$\text{or, } \prod_{i=r+1}^{k} N_i \geq \prod_{i=r+1}^{k} N_i - \prod_{i=r+2}^{k} N_i + \prod_{i=r+2}^{k} N_i - \ldots - N_k + N_k - 1$$

and by canceling out the corresponding terms we have $0 \geq -1$. Thus (2.5) is always true. ∎

Based on Lemma 2.2, we can now derive the condition under which TD–shrinking is more effective than selective shrinking. This condition is stated in the following theorem.

Theorem 2.3. Let $\Phi_m = \sum\limits_{r=1}^{k} \phi_r \prod\limits_{i=r+1}^{k} N_i$ be the minimum true distance in a dependence cycle of a nested loop of nest–depth k. Let also λ_T and λ_S be the reduction factors obtained for this loop by TD–shrinking and selective shrinking respectively. Then we have the following:

i) If there exist r_1, r_2 with $1 \leq r_1 < r_2 \leq k$ such that $\phi_{r_1} > 0, \phi_{r_2} < 0$, and $\phi_j = 0, (j=r_1+1, r_1+2, \ldots, r_2-1)$, and $\phi_i \leq 0, (j=1, 2, \ldots, r_1-1)$, then $\lambda_T < \lambda_S$.

ii) In all other cases $\lambda_T \geq \lambda_S$.

Proof: i) If such r_1 and r_2 exist, then from Lemma 2.1 it follows immediately that

$$\lambda_T = \sum_{i=1}^{k} \phi_i \prod_{j=i+1}^{k} N_j \leq \phi_{r_1} \prod_{j=r_1+1}^{k} N_j + \sum_{i=r_2}^{k} \phi_i \prod_{j=i+1}^{k} N_j \leq \phi_{r_1} \prod_{j=r_1+1}^{k} N_j \leq \lambda_S .$$

ii) Again using Lemma 2.1, this statement is proved in the same way. ∎

```
DO I = 3, N₁
    DO J = 5, N₂
        . . .
        A(I, J) = B(I-3, J-5)
        B(I, J) = A(I-2, J-4)
        . . .
    ENDO
ENDO
        (a)



DO I₁ = 3, N₁, 2
    DO J₁ = 5, N₂, 4
        DOALL I = I₁, I₁ + 1
            DOALL J = J₁, J₁ + 3
                . . .
                A(I, J) = B(I-3, J-5)
                B(I, J) = A(I-2, J-4)
                . . .
            ENDOALL
        ENDOALL
    ENDO
ENDO
        (b)



DO I₁ = 3, N₁, 2
    DOALL I = I₁, I₁ + 1
        DOALL J = 5, N₂
            . . .
            A(I, J) = B(I-3, J-5)
            B(I, J) = A(I-2, J-4)
            . . .
        ENDOALL
    ENDOALL
ENDO
        (c)
```

Figure 2.8. Simple and selective shrinking for multiply nested loops.

Thus TD–shrinking and selective shrinking are always superior to simple shrinking. Theorem 2.3 gives us the condition for selecting between the other two schemes, depending on the distance vector.

Let us consider the application of the three versions of cycle shrinking to the loop of Figure 2.8a. Here the two statements are involved in a dependence cycle $S_1 \delta S_2$ and $S_2 \delta S_1$. The distance vectors for the two dependences are $<\phi_1^1, \phi_2^1> \geq <2,4>$, and $<\phi_1^2, \phi_2^2> = <3,5>$.

Simple shrinking considers the dependence graph with respect to indices I and J individually. For the loop of Figure 2.8a both graphs are cycles. Cycle shrinking can then be applied on each cycle separately. For the cycle corresponding to the outer loop the distances are 2 and 3. Cycle shrinking will shrink the outer loop by a factor of $2=\min(2,3)$. Similarly the innerloop will be shrunk by a factor of $4=\min(4,5)$. The resulting loop is shown in Figure 2.8b. The transformed loop can execute 8 iterations at a time in parallel, resulting in a speedup of 8.

The loop of Figure 2.8a will be transformed to that of Figure 2.8c if selective shrinking is used. Since the outermost loop has a reduction factor of 2, it is blocked as in Figure 2.8c and the inner loop becomes a DOALL. In this case $\lambda = 2N_2 - 8$.

Now let us compute the true distance for each dependence in the cycle and compare it to the individual distances. The true distances give us the *total* number of loop iterations (irrespectively of which loop) over which a dependence travels. Here we have

$$\Phi_{12} = \phi_1^1 (N_2 - 4) + \phi_2^1$$

$$\Phi_{21} = \phi_1^2 (N_2 - 4) + \phi_2^2$$

In the case of our example the value of N_2 need not be known. By symbolic comparison of Φ_{12} and Φ_{21} it is easy to determine that

$$\Phi_{12} = \min(\Phi_{12}, \Phi_{21}) = 2N_2 - 4.$$

Thus the reduction factor $\lambda = 2N_2 - 4$ gives us the total number of loop iterations that can be executed in parallel during each step. For this example TD–shrinking works better than selective shrinking for any integer N_2.

Let us see now how the loop of Figure 2.8a can be transformed under TD–shrinking, assuming that the reduction factor λ is known (which is the case for our example). Since the λ iterations within each group form a DOALL, we are not concerned in what order they execute. However, the $\lceil \prod_{i=1}^{m} N_i / \lambda \rceil$ different groups must be executed in the order implied by the original loop. That is, if a group runs up to (I=i, J=j), the next group must start from (I=i, J=j+1) or (I=i+1, J=1). For our example let $N=N_1-3+1$ and $M=N_2-5+1$.

The transformed loop is shown in Figure 2.9. The temporary variables T1 through T4 are used to mark the coordinates of the initial and the final points in the iteration space. The iteration space has a total of NM iterations. The transformed loop will sweep the iteration space by executing λ iterations in parallel at a time. $\lceil NM / \lambda \rceil$ barrier synchronizations are enforced by the outer loop which sees the iteration space as a linear. If the index expressions in the loop body are to be preserved by cycle

```
DO K = 1, NM, λ

    T1 = (K DIV M) + 1
    T2 = ((K + λ) DIV M) + 1
    T3 = K MOD M
    T4 = M - ((K + λ) MOD M) + 1

    DOALL I = T1, T2
            IF I <> T1 THEN L1 = 5
            ELSE L1 = T3
            IF I <> T2 THEN L2 = N₂
            DOALL J = L1, L2
                    .  .  .
                    A(I, J) = B(I-3, J-5)
                    B(I, J) = A(I-2, J-4)
                    .  .  .
            ENDOALL
    ENDOALL
ENDO
```

Figure 2.9. TD–cycle shrinking for the loop of Figure 2.8a.

shrinking, the value of the outer serial loop must be decomposed into two coordinates, an I and a J coordinate. Alternatively, we could linearize the corresponding arrays (i.e., A and B) in the loop body, and collapse the two DOALLs into a single DOALL with λ iterations. This would eliminate the extra statements inserted by TD–shrinking. Linearizing arrays is straightforward and we will not discuss it further [AhSU86].

The most serious overhead may arise from the two conditional statements that were inserted between the two DOALLs in Figure 2.9. These conditionals set the initial and the final value of the J coordinate. They can be easily eliminated by unrolling the first and last iterations of the outer DOALL. The resulting loop is shown in Figure 2.10. Note that the three DOALLs in Figure 2.10 are completely independent. Thus, these three DOALLs can execute concurrently, in addition to executing each of them in parallel. The case of nonconstant distances is treated similarly.

The next case is non–perfectly nested loops. This case however is similar to the perfectly nested loop case, since only the common outer loop(s) is considered. The individual loops at the same nest–level in such a non–perfectly nested loop can be processed separately. Consider for example the loop of Figure 2.11a. Cycle shrinking can be applied to the two innerloops separately if necessary (not in this case of course since both loops are DOALLs). The outer loop is serial because the two DOALLs are involved in a flow dependence cycle. Distances for the two dependences need only be computed with respect to index I. In this case the distances are 2, and 3, and thus

$\lambda=2$. After cycle shrinking the loop is transformed to that of Figure 2.11b.

Notice that according to Theorem 2.1 the improvement is not just a factor of $\lambda=2$. In addition to executing every two iterations of the outer loop in parallel, the two innermost DOALLs can also execute in an overlapped fashion since they are completely independent. Therefore the available parallelism is increased by a factor of 4, assuming the inner loops are of equal size.

```
DO K = 1, NM, λ

    T1 = (K DIV M) + 1
    T2 = ((K + λ) DIV M) + 1
    T3 = K MOD M
    T4 = M - ((K + λ) MOD M) + 1

    DOALL J = T3, M
          . . .
          A(T1, J) = B(T1-3, J-5)
          B(T1, J) = B(T1-2, J-4)
          . . .
    ENDOALL

    DOALL I = T1+1, T2-1
        DOALL J = 5, N₂
              . . .
              A(I, J) = B(I-3, J-5)
              B(I, J) = A(I-2, J-4)
              . . .
        ENDOALL
    ENDOALL

    DOALL J = 5, T4
          . . .
          A(T2, J) = B(T2-3, J-5)
          B(T2, J) = B(T2-2, J-4)
          . . .
    ENDOALL

ENDO
```

Figure 2.10. A more efficient version of the loop of Figure 2.9.

In general, all the (simple or compound) statement instances which belong to a single group (as defined by Lemma 2.1) are independent. This offers the potential of exploiting more parallelism at the statement level. Whether this parallelism can be utilized or not depends on the system as well as the processor architecture. For example, if "statement" means an assignment statement, then independent statements can execute concurrently on different functional units (under the assumption that we have multifunctional processors).

In an MES system (multiple execution scalar), different statements can execute on different processors. This is not always possible in reality however, due to the overhead involved with the processor assignment process. As explained in Chapters 3 and 4, parallelism at the statement level (fine grain) is difficult to exploit. Even if the assignment of statements to processors is done deterministically before program execution, the processor/process initialization and other run–time activities (which are unavoidable with present architectures) may be too costly to allow effective concurrency at this level.

If the statements are compound (e.g., themselves loops), then high level spreading is possible. The larger the statement size (task size) the more effective the concurrent execution. Of course one can force tasks to be of coarse granularity by merging smaller tasks together (Chapter 6). This merging cannot proceed beyond a point since task merging reduces the available parallelism in a program. As shown in Chapter 3, for a given parallel machine–program combination, there are ways for computing the minimum number of statements which need to be merged into a single task. A sophisticated compiler should be able to derive conservative estimates and obtain a good grouping of independent statements together.

Recall that the three versions of cycle shrinking differ only in the way dependence distances are computed (and interpreted). If the dependences are forward pointing with respect to each dimension of a matrix, then TD shrinking is clearly better than simple of selective shrinking. Nevertheless, a loop transformed under TD shrinking would incur more overhead during execution, than selective shrinking. Soon it becomes evident that even for a simple loop it is not easy for the casual programmer to perform the appropriate (inexact) analysis and choose the most efficient version. Such questions arise frequently in program restructuring. Based on the defacto complexity of manual restructuring, one may argue similarly about the complexity of parallel programming itself. We will return to this issue in Chapter 3.

The next section discusses heuristic approaches to computing dependence distances. A complete presentation on data dependences and dependence distances is out of the scope of this book. However, it should be pointed out that exact distance calculation is expensive even for simple index expressions. Thus, fast and less exact schemes are desirable in certain cases. Moreover, symbolic dependence and distance calculation may succeed in cases where exact schemes are not applicable.

2.4.3. Computing Dependence Distances

The effectiveness of cycle shrinking depends on how accurately we can compute dependence distances. In particular, what is of interest to us is how accurately we can compute the minimum distance for each static dependence in a cycle. This becomes more difficult as the complexity of array index expressions increases. Fortunately, in

```
DO I = 3, N₁
    DOALL J = 1, N₂
        . . .
        A(I, J) = B(I-2, J)
        . . .
    ENDOALL

    DOALL K = 1, N₃
        . . .
        B(I, J) = A(I-2, J-4)
        . . .
    ENDOALL
ENDO
        (a)


DO L = 1, N, 2
    DOALL I = L, L+1
        DOALL J = 1, N₂
            . . .
            A(I, J) = B(I-2, J)
            . . .
        ENDOALL

        DOALL K = 1, N₃
            . . .
            B(I, K) = A(I-3, K)
            . . .
        ENDOALL
    ENDOALL
ENDO
        (b)
```

Figure 2.11. Cycle shrinking for non–perfectly nested loops.

real programs array index expressions are usually simple expressions like the ones used so far. A common index expression is of the form I±a, where a is an integer constant. For such simple cases the *difference* of the index expressions can actually give us the *distance* of the corresponding dependence (if it exists). For example, the distance of a hypothetical dependence between two array elements A(I±a) and A(I±b) is |a±b|. The distance of all instances of such a dependence is obviously constant. Other fast heuristic schemes for computing the minimum dependence distance can be applied to certain special cases.

In the forthcoming example dependence distances can be computed (and cycle shrinking can be applied) even when *no* information on data dependences is available. Consider the following loop.

```
DO I = 1, N
    A(3I+1) = ...
        ... = A(2I-4)
ENDO
```

Suppose that there is a dependence from the first to the second assignment statement. We can define the *increment factor* ρ of the second index expression 2I-4 to be the value by which the value of that expression is incremented for successive values of I. The increment factor of 2I-4 is obviously $\rho=2$. It is easy to observe that for each I, a flow dependence may develop if $3I+1 \geq 2I-4$. Let us define the difference D = 3I+1-2I+4 = I+5. It can be seen now that for each value of I, the element A(3I+1) defined by that iteration cannot be consumed before

$$\left\lceil \frac{D}{\rho} \right\rceil = \left\lceil \frac{I+5}{2} \right\rceil$$

iterations later. This indicates that the previous loop can be transformed to the following set of DOALLs.

```
        J = 1
L1:     INC = MIN(N-J, CEIL((J+5)/2) - 1)
        DOALL I = J, J+INC
            A(3I+1) = ...
                ... = A(2I-4)
        ENDOALL
        J = J + INC + 1
        IF J<N GOTO L1
```

No dependence is violated by the transformed loop. Of course this particular loop could be transformed directly into a single DOALL if appropriate synchronization was used. Whether synchronization could make the loop execute more efficiently than the one shown above depends on several factors such as size of the loop, efficiency of synchronization instructions of a particular machine, the size of D and ρ, etc.

In general, however, distance computation must be done as part of the data dependence analysis phase. This is so because only in this case we can accurately compute distances (at a higher cost), or can we check whether distances are computable at all. A detailed presentation on dependence analysis is given in [Bane79], [Wolf82], [AlKe87]. Let us outline here the basic steps for single loops and linear index expressions of the form aI±b. In particular, let us answer the existence question of a flow dependence between the two statements of the following loop.

```
DO I = 1, N
   A(aI+b) = ...
        ... = A(cI+d)
ENDO
```

For a flow dependence to exist we must have values i and j of index I such that $1 \leq i \leq j \leq N$ and $ai+b = cj+d$ or $ai-cj = d-b$. This Diophantine equation has a solution iff $\gcd(a,c)$ (i.e., the greatest common divisor of a, c), divides $d-b$. If (i_0, j_0) is any solution, then all solutions (i, j) of the equation are given by

$$i = i_0 + \frac{tc}{\gcd(a,c)}$$

$$j = j_0 + \frac{ta}{\gcd(a,c)}.$$

Acceptable solutions are those for which $1 \leq i \leq j \leq N$. In [Bane79] it is shown how to compute the set $S = \{ (i, j) \mid (i, j) \text{ a solution and } 1 \leq i \leq j \leq N \}$. From the set S we can then obtain the distance vector as $< (j-i) \mid (i,j) \in S >$. The procedure for multiply nested loops and index expressions with more than one variable is similar. For non-linear index expressions (that rarely occur in real programs) there is not known algorithm that solves the general problem efficiently.

In Section 2.4 we examine a run–time data dependence testing scheme that can be applied to complex loops for which cycle shrinking is not very effective.

2.4.4. Cycle Shrinking vs. Partition

In its purpose cycle shrinking is similar to partial loop partition, another scheme for extracting parallelism from seemingly serial loops, which is described in [Padu79]. In this section we briefly outline the partition method, and then we prove that cycle shrinking is always superior to partition (at least theoretically). Some examples that compare the effectiveness of the two schemes are also given.

Consider the following DO loop.

```
DO I = 1, N
   S₁
   S₂
    · · ·
   Sₖ
ENDO
```

with k statements that are involved in a dependence cycle $S_1 \delta_1 S_2 \ldots \delta_{k-1} S_k \delta_k S_1$, and let ϕ_i be the distance of δ_i, $(i=1, 2, \ldots, k)$ Partition transforms the above loop to the following equivalent.

```
        DOALL J = 1, g
            DO I = J,  J+⌊(N-J)/g⌋
                S₁
                S₂
                 . . .
                Sₖ
            ENDO
        ENDOALL
```

where g≡gcd$(\phi_1, \phi_2, \ldots, \phi_k)$ is the greatest common divisor of all k distances in the dependence cycle. For the sake of completeness, the same loop will be transformed by cycle shrinking to the following one.

```
        DO J = 1, N, λ
            DOALL I = J,  J + λ - 1
                S₁
                S₂
                 . . .
                Sₖ
            ENDOALL
        ENDO
```

where $\lambda = \min(\phi_1, \phi_2, \ldots, \phi_k)$. The following well–known lemma gives us the first comparison of the two schemes.

Lemma 2.3. If $\phi_1, \phi_2, \ldots, \phi_k$ are positive integers, then

$$\min(\phi_1, \phi_2, \ldots, \phi_k) \geq \gcd(\phi_1, \phi_2, \ldots, \phi_k) \text{ or,} \lambda \geq g.$$

Thus the size of the DOALL created by cycle shrinking is always greater than or equal to the size of the DOALL created by partition. Partition tries to group together all iterations of a DO loop that form a dependence chain. Each such group is executed serially, while different groups can execute in parallel. Dependences are confined within the iterations of each group and dependences across groups do not exist. In contrast, cycle shrinking groups together independent iterations and executes them in parallel. Dependences exist only across groups and are satisfied by executing the different groups in their natural order.

The second advantage of cycle shrinking over partition stems from the above difference and from Theorem 2.1. Since all iterations of a group formed by cycle shrinking are dependence sink–free (in addition to executing them in parallel) all statements inside each iteration can also execute in parallel. For a loop with k statements this gives us another speedup factor of k. This is not true however for partition, since all iterations within each group (and thus all statement instances) form a dependence chain. Thus the speedup obtained by cycle shrinking for a loop with k statements is $S_{cs} = \lambda * k$, while the speedup due to partition for the same loop would be $S_{pa} = g$, where $\lambda \geq g$ and $k \geq 1$.

Let us consider a particular example. The following loop,

```
DO I = 3, N
    A(I) = B(I-2)
    B(I) = A(I-3)
ENDO
```

has $\lambda=2$ and $g=1$. Thus partition is unable to discover any parallelism. Cycle shrinking will transform this loop to the following equivalent.

```
DO J = 3, N, 2
    DOALL I = J, J + 1
        A(I) = B(I-2)
        B(I) = A(I-3)
    ENDOALL
ENDO
```

In addition to executing every two iterations in parallel, the two statements inside the DOALL are also independent. We thus have a total speedup of 4. Clearly selective and TD–shrinking are always better than both simple shrinking and partition. In cases where both latter schemes fail, TD–shrinking can still improve parallelism. Consider the following loop.

```
DO I = 1, N
    DO J = 1, N
        A(I,J) = A(I-1,J-1) + 1
    ENDO
ENDO
```

Cycle shrinking and partition will fail to transform the above loop. TD–shrinking however will transform the loop to a form similar to that of Figure 2.9 or Figure 2.10, by forming a DOALL with N+1 iterations.

2.4.5. The Cost of Barriers in Cycle Shrinking

For an "ideal" parallel machine (one that incurs zero overhead) shrinking is always preferable over partition. In reality however overhead is an important factor. The disadvantage of cycle shrinking is that it needs $\lceil N/\lambda \rceil$ barrier synchronizations as opposed to only 1 required by partition. When λ is very small and the loop contains very few statements, the overhead involved may outweight the benefit of the resulting parallelism.

To avoid applying cycle shrinking in such cases the compiler can perform approximate tests to evaluate the potential gain in performance. These tests are described below for simple loops with N iterations; their generalization to multiply nested loops is straightforward. Let λ, g, and k be as defined above. Moreover let β, T_1, T_s, and T_p be the execution time of a single loop iteration, the serial execution time of a loop, and the execution time of the transformed loops after shrinking and partitioning respectively. In general, the overhead associated with barrier synchronization in multiprocessor systems is not constant. However, for our purpose we can assume a worst–case overhead of γ. For simplicity, let us also assume that our base–unit is the execution time of a program "statement". This gives us $\beta=k$.

For serial loops of the type discussed so far, the compiler must compute λ and g and make the appropriate selection between cycle shrinking, partitioning, or none of the above (in which case the loop remains serial). Two cases are of interest: $\lambda > g = 1$ and $\lambda k > g > 1$.

Case 1: $\lambda > g = 1$. In this case cycle shrinking is the only alternative for parallelizing the loop. The question that must be answered at this point is whether the overhead due to barrier synchronization can potentially outweight the parallelism introduced by shrinking. The loop can be transformed if

$$T_1 = N\beta > T_s = \frac{N\beta}{\lambda k} + \frac{N\gamma}{\lambda} .$$

If we use $\beta = k$ and simplify the inequality we get

$$\lambda k > \gamma + 1 . \tag{2.7}$$

The worst–case barrier overhead γ, (which is architecture and machine dependent), can be supplied by the compiler. λ and k are computed as part of the transformation. Since this is only a rough test, it is conceivable that even though (2.7) may hold true, in reality $T_1 < T_s$. However, γ can be chosen conservatively so that the error margin can be negligible.

Case 2: $\lambda k > g > 1$. In this case a performance improvement of at least g is secured. The question is whether shrinking is potentially better than partitioning. Again an approximate test can be formulated as follows. If

$$T_p = \frac{N\beta}{g} > T_s = \frac{N\beta}{\lambda k} + \frac{N\gamma}{\lambda}$$

then shrinking is preferred, otherwise partitioning is chosen. After simplification we arrive at

$$\lambda k > g (\gamma + 1) . \tag{2.8}$$

Tests (2.7) and (2.8) do not always guarantee correct selection between the two methods, but they do provide the compiler with a simple test for avoiding gross errors.

2.5. LOOP SPREADING

Loop spreading can be used to extract limited parallelism out of loops in sequence (which individually may have to be executed sequentially) by obtaining a partial overlap of their iterations. In addition, we assume dependences across loops. This inhibits independent and concurrent execution of the individual loops. Our presentation is based on the case of two loops. However, loop spreading can be applied iteratively to a chain of several loops in the same manner. This and other generalizations are handled similarly and are considered later in this section.

2.5.1. The Transformation for Chains of Loops

We will consider the body of a loop as a block. Let us denote the body of the k–th loop in a program by $\beta_k (*)$ and let $\beta_k (i)$ denote the loop body of the i–th iteration of that loop. We will assume for convenience that the index variable of the k–th loop varies from 1 to N_k. Obviously, $\beta_k (*) = \bigcup_{i=1}^{N_k} \beta_k (i)$. We will first consider the transformation for two loops in sequence. Let B_1 and B_2 be two serial loops in sequence and let $\beta_i(j)$ denote the j-th iteration of B_i. The transformation will produce a new serial loop such that each iteration of the new loop will execute one iteration of B_1 (say $\beta_1(i)$) and one iteration of B_2 (say $\beta_2(i-k)$) in parallel. Thus the two following loops

```
DO I=1, N₁
    β₁(I)
ENDO
```

```
DO I=1, N₂
    β₂(I)
ENDO
```

will be transformed to

```
DO I=1, N₁
    COBEGIN
        β₁(I);
        IF I>K THEN β₂(I-K);
    COEND
ENDO
```

```
DO I=N₁₋ₖ₊₁, N₂
    β₂(I)
ENDO
```

Since the original iterations of B_1 (B_2) are still executed in sequence, violations may arise from loop across dependences only. Thus if iterations $\beta_1(i)$ and $\beta_2(i-k)$ are to be executed in parallel we must verify that no flow, anti, or output dependences exist for all i such that $1 \leq i \leq N$. This translates to

$$\bigcup_{p=1}^{N} OUT(\beta_1(p)) \cap IN(\beta_2(i-k)) = \emptyset \tag{F.1}$$

$$\bigcup_{p=1}^{N} OUT(\beta_1(p)) \cap OUT(\beta_2(i-k)) = \emptyset \tag{F.2}$$

$$\bigcup_{p=1}^{N} IN(\beta_1(p)) \cap OUT(\beta_2(i-k)) = \emptyset \tag{F.3}$$

We will try to choose a value of k such that the above equations are satisfied. It is clear that for maximum parallelism we must choose the minimum value of k.

The IN/OUT set for the iteration i will typically consist of scalars and arrays indexed by subscript expressions. Determining scalar intersection is quite easy and obvious methods will suffice. For arrays, to get a better idea of the intersection set we need to study the functions of loop variables which appear in their subscript expressions. When these functions are non-linear little can be done except taking a conservative approach and assuming dependence. Hence we assume that the functions are linear which is the most common case in real programs. Let $f_1, \ldots, f_n$ $(g_1, \ldots, g_m)$ be the functions appearing in the subscript expressions for an array, say X, in iterations $\beta_1(i)$, $(\beta_2(j))$ respectively. We will first consider the case when n=m=1. In this case let f (g) be the only functions in the subscript expression. Hence, we have simplified the problem to finding when we can do the following conversion:

```
        DO I=1, N₁
            X(f(I))= · · ·
        ENDO

        DO I=1, N₂
                · · · =X((g(I))
        ENDO
```

to

```
        DO I=1, N₁
            COBEGIN
                X(f(I))= · · · ;
                IF (I>K) THEN  · · · =X(g(I-K));
            COEND
        ENDO

        DO I=N₁-K+1, N₂
                · · · =X(g(I-K))
        ENDO
```

Let $f(i)=ai+b$ and let $g(j)=cj+d$. Then the problem reduces to checking whether there are values i_0 and j_0 within loop bounds such that $f(i_0)=g(j_0)$. If there are no such values or if $i_0<j_0$ then the dependence is not hard to satisfy, indeed, any non–negative value of k will satisfy it. If $i_0>j_0$ then the value of k chosen must be greater than i_0-j_0. If either a or c is equal to zero then the process of checking dependence and computing the value of k is trivial. In what follows, we assume that neither a nor c is zero. First, we can check the existence of i_0, j_0 (maybe not within loop bounds) by the g.c.d. test. If that is passed then we can do the following to obtain the value of k. The problem has been reduced to choosing the value of k such that for all $i, 1 \leq i \leq N$, if $f(i)=g(i-k+1)$ then $1>0$. Substituting we get $f(i)=g(i-k+1)$, or $ai+b=ci-ck+cl+d$, or finally

$$1 = \frac{(a-c)i+(b-d)}{c} + k.$$

Since we must have $1>0$, we get

$$k > \frac{(c-a)i+(d-b)}{c}.$$

Also, since $1 \leq i \leq N$, we know that the maximum value of $((c-a)i+(d-b))/c$ must occur at i=1 or i=N depending on the sign of $(c-a)/c$. In either case we see that the following must hold.

$$k > \left(\frac{c-a}{c}\right)^+ (N-1) + \frac{c-a+d-b}{c}$$

where x^+ is defined [Bane76] as

$$x^+ = \begin{cases} x & \text{if } x > 0 \\ 0 & \text{otherwise.} \end{cases}$$

Notice that $a, b, c,$ and d are (in practice) compiler constants. The loop bound N must also be known. This may not necessarily be the case. When N is unknown, only the cases where $a/c < 1$ are affected and (for these cases) a conservative estimate of N can be used.

2.5.2. Generalizations

Let us consider now the application of loop spreading to more general cases, including multidimensioned arrays, chains of loops, and multiple interloop dependences. The principle is always the same as indicated above, the main difference is the calculation of the best value of k. Let us consider each of these cases.

The example above cites only flow dependences. The case of anti and output dependences can be handled similarly. If k_1, k_2, k_3 are the minimum values of k such that the three feasibility equations (F.1–F.3) are satisfied respectively, then choosing $k=\max(k_1, k_2, k_3)$ will satisfy all three equations.

The example above cites just a single array. The case of many arrays can be handled by a repetition of the method for all arrays and choosing the maximum value of k over all arrays.

In the example the array X is one–dimensional. If it was multidimensional we would apply the above method in each dimension and then choose the minimum value of k as the appropriate value. This is because if two references to a multidimensional array X are to reference the same memory location, the subscript functions must agree on all dimensions.

There is only one reference to X in each loop body. When there are many references this method must be applied to each pair of such references, and then the appropriate value of k must be chosen to be the maximum over all such pairs of references.

In the example there are only two loops in sequence. When there are n loops in sequence the following method can be applied to compute k_j for the j-th loop, $2 \leq j \leq n$.

```
k₁=0
for j=2 to n do
  for i=1 to j-1 do
    Compute k'ᵢⱼ with respect to the loops Bᵢ and Bⱼ
    using the above method.
  endfor
  kⱼ=max{k'ᵢⱼ+kᵢ | 1 ≤ i ≤ j-1}
endfor
```

Let us now look at an example. Consider the two loops:

```
DO I=1, 10
    X(3I+4)=A(I-1)+1
    A(I)=Y(-2I+25)
ENDO

DO I=1, 10
    D(I)=X(4I+2)
    X(I+1)=D(I)**2+D(I-1)
    E(I)=Y(-2I+23)
ENDO
```

There are possible dependences from the first statement of the first loop to the first and second statement of the second loop because both could conceivably reference the same locations of the array X. Similarly, there could be dependences from the second statement of the first loop to the last statement of the second loop because of the array Y.

Then for the array X we have the following pairs of functions $(3i+4, 4i+2)$ and $(3i+4, i+1)$. For array Y we have $(-2i+25, -2i+23)$. In the pair $(3i+4, 4i+2)$, $a=3, b=4, c=4, d=2$. Since $N=10$, we get

$$k > \left\lceil \frac{4-3}{4} \right\rceil^+ (10-1) + \frac{4-3+2-4}{4} > 2.$$

Similarly, from the other two pairs we get $k>-5$ and $k>1$. Choosing the minimum value of k satisfying the above inequalities, we get $k=3$. Hence the parallel version of the above loop is

```
DO I=1, 10
    COBEGIN
        β₁(I);
        IF (I>K) THEN β₂(I-3);
    COEND
ENDO

DO I=8, 10
    β₂(I)
ENDO
```

Assuming $\beta_{1(I)}$ and $\beta_{2(I)}$ take the same time, τ, to execute, the total execution time of the original loops is 20τ, while that of the transformed loop is 13τ. This is the best possible overlap for the above example.

2.6. LOOP COALESCING

As shown in Chapter 4, compile–time scheduling is a simple problem when we deal with singly nested loops where all loop iterations have equal execution times. In that case, the obvious one–step processor assignment is also the optimal one: the optimal distribution of N iterations to P processors is clearly the one that assigns $\lceil N/P \rceil$ iterations to each processor. It would be therefore desirable to have, if possible, parallel programs with singly nested parallel loops.

DOALL 1 I=1,15
DOALL 2 J=1,7

. . .
. . .
. . .

2   ENDOALL
1 ENDOALL

For P=27 the optimal processor allocation (Chapter 4) assigns 3 processors to outer loop and 7 processors to inner loop which results in 5 iterations. The corresponding superoptimal allocation assigns 27 processors to 105 iterations which results in a total of only 4 parallel iterations.

Figure 2.12. Scheduling with coalescing.

In this section we discuss a compiler transformation called *loop coalescing* that restructures certain types of multiply nested loops into single parallel loops. Thus, for those loops that can be restructured, the optimal processor assignment problem becomes simple. In addition, processor assignments for the transformed loops are generally better than the optimal assignments to the original loops generated by an algorithm which is discussed in Chapter 4. This is true assuming all iterations of a loop have equal execution times. When this last condition is not satisfied the optimal processor assignment becomes a complex problem even for singly nested loops. In Chapter 4 we show how loop coalescing can be used to achieve optimal or near-optimal static and dynamic schedules for general parallel loops. This transformation is also used in Chapter 4 to reduce (and minimize in certain cases) the number of synchronization points needed during the execution of hybrid loops. We start from the perfectly nested loop case and generalize the concepts and results as we proceed.

Let $L = (N_m, N_{m-1}, \ldots, N_1)$ be a perfectly nested DOALL and P the number of available processors. Let $N = \prod_{i=1}^{m} N_i$, B is the execution time of the innermost loop body, and

$$T_P^o = \left\lceil \frac{N}{P} \right\rceil B \qquad (2.9)$$

where T_P^o represents the minimum execution time of loop L on P processors. Consider now any allocation ω of the P processors to the component loops of L, and let ω_0 be the optimal such allocation. If T_P^ω and $T_P^{\omega_0}$ denote the parallel execution time of L for the allocations ω and ω_0 respectively, then

```
DO 1 I=1,N
   DO 2 J=1,M                              DO 1 J=1,N*M

      A(I,J)=B(I,J)        →                 A(J,1)=B(J,1)

 2   ENDOALL                             1   ENDOALL
 1 ENDOALL
```

Figure 2.13. Example of loop collapsing.

$$T_P^\omega = \prod_{i=1}^m \left\lceil \frac{N_i}{q_i} \right\rceil B$$

for some distribution of q_i, ($i=1,2,\ldots,m$) processors to the component–loops N_i, ($i=1,2,\ldots,m$) of L respectively, such that $\prod_{i=1}^m q_i \leq P$. From Lemma 4.3 (Chapter 4) it then follows that

$$T_P^o \leq T_P^{\omega o} \leq T_P^\omega.$$

An allocation ω of P processors to a multiply nested loop L is said to be *superoptimal* if and only if

$$T_P^\omega = T_P^o. \tag{2.10}$$

Obviously (2.10) holds true for all singly nested loops, but in general, is not true for multiply nested loops which are assigned processors deterministically. It becomes evident therefore that transforming arbitrarily complex loops into single loops, not only simplifies the processor assignment problem, but it also improves the resulting schedules.

Loop coalescing transforms a series of nested DOALLs to a single DOALL with an iteration space equal to the product of the iteration spaces of the original loop. Then the superoptimal allocation is accomplished in a single step by allocating all P processors to the transformed loop. In order to apply loop coalescing to a nest of DOALLs, all dependence directions must be "=" [Wolf82]. Consider for example the loop of Figure 2.12 that is to be executed on a P=27 processor system. The optimal deterministic assignment to the original loop allocates 3 (clusters of) processors to the outer loop and 7 processors to the inner loop. This results in a total of 5 iterations per processor. If the original loop is coalesced into a single DOALL with 105 (=15*7) iterations, all processors are assigned to that single loop which results in 4 iterations per processor.

Loop coalescing resembles loop collapsing, another well–known transformation. Loop collapsing though is different than coalescing in both its purpose and mechanism. The former is a memory related transformation that collapses doubly nested loops only, to single loops by transforming two dimensional arrays into vectors.

DOALL 1 J=1,N
    DOALL 2 K=1,N

        A(J,K) = ...

2   ENDOALL
1 ENDOALL

becomes

DOALL 1 I=1,N^2

    A($\lceil I/N \rceil$, I - N$\lfloor$(I - 1)/N$\rfloor$) = ...

1 ENDOALL

Figure 2.14. Loop coalescing in two dimensions.

Figure 2.13 shows an example of loop collapsing. The purpose of this transformation is to create long vectors for efficient execution on memory–to–memory SEA systems (e.g., CDC Cyber 205). No subscript manipulation is attempted by loop collapsing.

Loop coalescing should be applied so that the original and the transformed loops are semantically equivalent. This means that the transformation should manipulate loop subscripts so that there always exists a one–to–one mapping between the array subscripts of the original and the transformed loop. Moreover, the resulting loop should be scheduled such that each processor knows exactly which iterations of the original loop it has been assigned. Since the resulting loop has a single index, we must find mappings that correctly map subscript expressions of the original loop (which are multivariable integer functions) to expressions involving a single subscript (corresponding to the index of the restructured loop).

Before we describe the general transformation let us look at two examples of loop coalescing. Figures 2.14 and 2.16 show the cases of coalescing perfectly nested DOALLs of nest depth two and three. Consider first the loop of Figure 2.14 and its coalesced equivalent. Figure 2.15 shows the index values for the two cases in the order they are assumed. Clearly the first subscript J of A(J,K) should be transformed into an expression involving I, i.e.,

$$J \longrightarrow f(I)$$

where f is an integer–value function and such that the value of f(I) is incremented by one each time I assumes a value of the form wN+1, for w$\in$ Z$^+$. Similarly we must determine a mapping g such that

$$K \quad \longrightarrow \quad g(I)$$

and such that $g(I)$ assumes the successive values $1, 2, \ldots, N$, but its values wrap around each time $f(I)$ becomes $wN+1$, as it becomes evident from Figure 2.15. For the case of the loop of Figure 2.14 it can be seen that

$$J \quad \longrightarrow \quad f(I) = \left\lceil \frac{I}{N} \right\rceil \qquad (2.11)$$

$$K \quad \longrightarrow \quad g(I) = I - N \left\lfloor \frac{I-1}{N} \right\rfloor.$$

The mappings in (2.11) satisfy the properties mentioned above. In the case of the triply nested DOALLs of Figure 2.16 the corresponding mappings are defined by,

$$J \quad \longrightarrow \quad f(I) = \left\lceil \frac{I}{N^2} \right\rceil$$

$$K \quad \longrightarrow \quad g(I) = \left\lceil \frac{I}{N} \right\rceil - N \left\lfloor \frac{I-1}{N^2} \right\rfloor$$

J	K	I
1	1	1
1	2	2
1	3	3
.	.	.
1	N	N
2	1	N+1
2	2	N+2
.	.	.
2	N	2N
.	.	.
.	.	.
.	.	.
N	1	(N-1)N+1
N	2	(N-1)N+2
.	.	.
N	N	NN

Figure 2.15. Index values for original and coalesced loop – two dimensions.

```
    DOALL 1 J=1,N
      DOALL 2 K=1,N
        DOALL 3 L=1,N

          A(J,K,L) = ....

    3         ENDOALL
    2     ENDOALL
    1 ENDOALL
```

becomes

```
    DOALL 1 I=1,N³
```

$$A(\lceil I/N^2\rceil , \quad \lceil I/N\rceil - N\lfloor (I-1)/N^2\rfloor, \quad I - N\lfloor (I-1)/N\rfloor) = \ldots.$$

```
    1 ENDOALL
```

Figure 2.16. Loop coalescing in three dimensions.

$$L \quad \longrightarrow \quad h(I) = I - N\left\lfloor \frac{I-1}{N}\right\rfloor.$$

It is clear that the mappings f, g, and h follow a regular pattern. As it is shown below, loop coalescing can be applied to a much wider range of nested loops with unequal loop bounds. The following theorem defines the general array subscript transformation for loop coalescing. Let $L=(N_m, N_{m-1}, \ldots, N_1)$ be any m–way (non–perfectly) nested loop, and $L'=(N=N_m N_{m-1}\ldots N_1)$ be the corresponding coalesced (single) loop. Let also $J_m, J_{m-1}, \ldots, J_1$ denote the indices of the loops in L, and I the index of the transformed loop L'. Then we have the following.

Theorem 2.4. Any array reference of the form $A(J_m, J_{m-1}, \ldots, J_1)$ in L can be uniquely expressed by an equivalent array reference
$A(f_m(I), f_{m-1}(I), \ldots, f_1(I)) = A(I_m, I_{m-1}, \ldots, I_1)$ in L', where

$$I_k = f_k(I) = \left\lfloor \frac{I}{\prod\limits_{i=1}^{k-1} N_i}\right\rfloor - N_k \left\lfloor \frac{I-1}{\prod\limits_{i=1}^{k} N_i}\right\rfloor, \qquad (k=m,m-1,\ldots,1) \tag{2.12}$$

or for the case of equal loop bounds,

$$I_k = \left\lfloor \frac{I}{N^{k-1}}\right\rfloor - N\left\lfloor \frac{I-1}{N^k}\right\rfloor, \qquad (k=m,m-1,\ldots,1).$$

Proof: Consider an m–level nested loop L that is transformed into a single loop L$'$ with index I, as above. Any array reference of the form $A(J_m, \ldots, J_i, \ldots, J_1)$ will be transformed into $A(I_m, \ldots, I_i, \ldots, I_1)$, where I_i, (i=m, ..., 1) are functions of I. We will derive the mapping for $J_i \rightarrow I_i$ and prove that it is given by (2.12).

A *step* is defined to be one execution of the loop–body of the innermost (1st) loop. It is clear that the 1st index I_1 is incremented by one at each step. The second index I_2 is incremented at steps of size N_1, I_3 at steps of size $N_1 N_2$, ..., I_i is incremented at steps of size $N_1 N_2 \cdots N_{i-1}$, and so on. At each moment the total number of steps (iterations) that have been completed is given by I. It is clear therefore that the expression

$$\left\lceil \frac{I}{N_1 N_2 \cdots N_{i-1}} \right\rceil \tag{2.13}$$

is incremented by one at steps of size $N_1 N_2 \ldots N_{i-1}$. However, all indices (but the outermost) wrap around and assume repeatedly the same values for each iteration of their outermost loops. Each index assumes a maximum value which is its corresponding loop upper bound. This value is reached after N_1 steps for I_1, after $N_1 N_2$ steps for I_2, ..., after $N_1 N_2 \cdots N_i$ steps for I_i and so on. Therefore the mapping defined by (2.13) for I_i is correct as long as $I \leq N_1 N_2 \ldots N_i$ but not for later steps. Thus we have to "compensate" (2.13) for the wrap around of the values of I_i. This can be done by subtracting from (2.13) the multiples of N_i at the steps at which I_i repeats its values. In other words we should subtract from (2.13) the multiples of N_i which are given by,

$$N_i \left\lceil \frac{I-1}{N_1 N_2 \ldots N_i} \right\rceil. \tag{2.14}$$

From (2.13) and (2.14) it follows that the correct mapping for I_i is given by,

$$I_i \rightarrow \left\lceil \frac{I}{N_1 N_2 \ldots N_{i-1}} \right\rceil - N_i \left\lceil \frac{I-1}{N_1 N_2 \ldots N_i} \right\rceil. \quad \blacksquare$$

For the last iteration, index I_k, (k = m, m-1, ..., 1) should more precisely be defined by

$$I_k = \min (N_k, \ f_k(I)).$$

From (2.12) we also observe that for the outermost index I_m, the transformation is $\left\lceil I / \prod_{i=1}^{m-1} N_i \right\rceil$ since the second term in (2.12) is always zero.

2.6.1. Processor Assignment and Subscript Calculation

From a first observation, it seems that loop coalescing introduces expensive operations in the subscript expressions and hence, one may question its practicality. The rather complicated subscript expressions do not pose any serious performance problem because, as shown later in this section, these expressions need only be evaluated once per processor, and each processor is assigned blocks of consecutive iterations. Each subscript calculation consists of two division operations, one

```
    DOALL 1  J=1,2
       DOALL 2  K=1,3
          DOALL 3  L=1,6

          A(J,K,L)= ....

3      ENDOALL
2      ENDOALL
1 ENDOALL
       (a)
```

becomes

```
    DOALL 1  I=1,36
```

$$A\left(\left\lfloor\frac{I}{18}\right\rfloor,\ \left\lceil\frac{I}{6}\right\rceil-3\left\lfloor\frac{I-1}{18}\right\rfloor,\ I-6\left\lfloor\frac{I-1}{6}\right\rfloor\right)= \ldots.$$

```
1 ENDOALL
       (b)
```

becomes

```
DOALL 1  p=1,56
```

$$A\left(\left\lceil\frac{(p-1)r+1}{18}\right\rceil \cdots \left\lceil\frac{pr}{18}\right\rceil,\ \left\lceil\frac{(p-1)r+1}{6}\right\rceil-3\left\lfloor\frac{(p-1)r}{18}\right\rfloor \cdots \left\lceil\frac{pr}{6}\right\rceil-3\left\lfloor\frac{pr-1}{18}\right\rfloor,\right.$$

$$\left.(p-1)r+1-6\left\lfloor\frac{(p-1)r}{6}\right\rfloor \ldots pr-6\left\lfloor\frac{pr-1}{6}\right\rfloor\right)= \ldots.$$

```
1 ENDOALL
       (c)
```

Figure 2.17. Coalescing for block scheduling.

multiplication and one subtraction.

Considering again a loop of the form $L = (N_m, \ldots, N_1)$ all partial products $\prod_{i=1}^{j} N_i$, $(j=1,2,\ldots,m)$ are obtained (and stored for later use) at no extra cost during the evaluation of $\prod_{i=1}^{m} N_i$ which involves m multiplications.

Now let us see what happens when the coalesced loop L' is scheduled on P processors. Each processor will be assigned to execute $r = \lceil N/P \rceil$ successive iterations of L'. More specifically, processor p, $(p = 1, 2, \ldots, P)$ will execute iterations $(p - 1)r + 1$ through pr of the coalesced loop.

Suppose next that an array reference of the form $A(\ast, \ldots, \ast, f_1(I), \ast, \ldots, \ast)$ exists in the code of L'. Then from the previous paragraphs it follows that processor p will access those elements in the i-th dimension of A that are included in

$$A(\ast, \ldots, \ast, f_1((p-1)r+1) : f_1(pr), \ast, \ldots, \ast)$$

(where the notation $i:j$ denotes all increments of 1 from i to j inclusive). In general, from (2.12) it follows that the subscripts in the k-th dimension referenced by processor p are in the following interval,

$$I_k \in \left[\left[\frac{(p-1)r+1}{\prod\limits_{j=1}^{k-1} N_j} \right] - N_k \left[\frac{(p-1)r}{\prod\limits_{j=1}^{k} N_j} \right] \cdots \left\lfloor \frac{pr}{\prod\limits_{j=1}^{k-1} N_j} \right\rfloor - N_k \left\lfloor \frac{pr-1}{\prod\limits_{j=1}^{k} N_j} \right\rfloor \right].$$

In order to see in more detail how the subscript computation is performed after processors have been assigned, consider the following example. Let us suppose that we have the loop of Figure 2.17a that is coalesced into the single DOALL of Figure 2.17b, which is to be executed on P=5 processors. In this case $N_3=2$, $N_2=3$, $N_1=6$ and therefore $r=\lceil N_3 N_2 N_1/P \rceil = \lceil 36/5 \rceil = 8$.

Since the coalesced loop is executed on 5 processors, as far as array A is concerned, it is equivalent to the pseudo–vector loop of Figure 2.17(c). Thus, for each processor we only need to compute the value range for each subscript. Since each subscript depends only on p, all subscript ranges can be evaluated in parallel. For

Processor 1	Processor 2	Processor 3	Processor 4	Processor 5
A(1,1,1)	A(1,2,3)	A(1,3,5)	A(2,2,1)	A(2,3,3)
A(1,1,2)	A(1,2,4)	A(1,3,6)	A(2,2,2)	A(2,3,4)
A(1,1,3)	A(1,2,5)	A(2,1,1)	A(2,2,3)	A(2,3,5)
A(1,1,4)	A(1,2,6)	A(2,1,2)	A(2,2,4)	A(2,3,6)
A(1,1,5)	A(1,3,1)	A(2,1,3)	A(2,2,5)	
A(1,1,6)	A(1,3,2)	A(2,1,4)	A(2,2,6)	
A(1,2,1)	A(1,3,3)	A(2,1,5)	A(2,3,1)	
A(1,2,2)	A(1,3,4)	A(2,1,6)	A(2,3,2)	

Figure 2.18. Distribution of array elements (and iterations) among 5 processors.

p=3 for example, the range of A that is referenced by the 3rd processor is given by,

$$A\left(\left\lceil\frac{17}{18}\right\rceil \cdots \left\lceil\frac{24}{18}\right\rceil, \quad \left\lceil\frac{17}{6}\right\rceil - 3\left\lfloor\frac{16}{18}\right\rfloor \cdots \left\lceil\frac{24}{6}\right\rceil - 3\left\lfloor\frac{23}{18}\right\rfloor, \quad 17 - 6\left\lfloor\frac{16}{6}\right\rfloor \cdots 24 - 6\left\lfloor\frac{23}{6}\right\rfloor\right)$$

or   A(1:2, 3:1, 5:6)   (2.15)

Since we know the upper bounds for each index, (2.15) uniquely determines the elements of A that will be accessed by the 3rd processor (A(1,3,5), A(1,3,6), A(2,1,1), A(2,1,2), A(2,1,3), A(2,1,4), A(2,1,5), A(2,1,6)). The detailed access pattern of the elements of A by each processor in our example is shown in Figure 2.18.

Therefore the subscript expressions that are superficially introduced by loop coalescing should not degrade performance significantly, especially when P is small compared to the number of iterations of the coalesced loop.

```
        DOALL 1 J=1,N
          DOSERIAL 2 K=1,N
          DOALL 3 L=1,N

              A(J,K,L) = ...

3       ENDOALL
2       ENDOSERIAL
1 ENDOALL
            (a)
```

becomes

```
        DOSERIAL 1 K=1,N
          DOALL 2 I=1,N²

              A(⌈I/N²⌉,  K,  I - N⌊(I-1)/N⌋) = ...

2       ENDOALL
1 ENDOSERIAL
            (b)
```

Figure 2.19. Coalescing of a hybrid loop.

Even though we have considered the most simple subscript expressions so far, it is easy to observe that loop coalescing can be applied in the same way for any polynomial subscript expression. In the following sections we generalize the transformation and show how it can be applied to hybrid and non–perfectly nested loops.

2.6.2. Hybrid Loops

Loop coalescing may be applied selectively on hybrid loops. A loop is hybrid when it contains combinations of DOALLs, DOACRs, and serial loops. An example of a hybrid loop is shown in Figure 2.19a. In such cases loop coalescing can be applied to transform only the DOALLs of the hybrid loop. Only the subscripts of array references that correspond to the DOALLs are transformed in this case. The indices (subscripts) of any serial or DOACR loop are left unchanged. The coalesced version of the loop in Figure 2.19a is shown in Figure 2.19b.

2.6.3. Non–Perfectly Nested Loops, One Way Nesting

Coalescing can also be applied to non–perfectly nested loops. The subscript transformations remain the same, but care must be taken to assure correct execution of code segments that appear in different nest levels. Such code segments must be executed conditionally in the transformed loop. Let us consider for the moment only one–dimensional nesting as in the example of Figure 2.20a, where S_1 and S_2 denote straight line code segments. Obviously if the DOALLs of the example are coalesced, segment S_1 should be executed conditionally in the transformed loop. The compiler must insert a conditional statement before the first statement of S_1. Fortunately this is an easy task for the compiler to do and the conditionals are always straight forward to compute.

The coalesced version of the example loop of Figure 2.20a is shown in Figure 2.20b. Scalar t is a compiler generated temporary variable that is used to test the value of I and is reset each time code segment S_1 is executed. The extension to multiple nonperfectly nested loops is also straightforward.

2.6.4. Multiway Nested Loops

A loop is multiway nested if there are two or more loops at the same nest level. The loop in Figure 2.21a is a multiway (2–way) nested loop. Figure 2.21b shows the corresponding coalesced loop. However, extra care should be taken with multiway nested loops. As it can be observed from Figure 2.21, in this case coalescing alters the execution order of the two statements in the example. In the loop of Figure 2.21a all elements $A(J, *)$ are computed before any element of $B(J, *)$ is computed. In the coalesced loop the order of execution changes and ordered pairs $(A(J, i), B(J, i))$ are computed for each J instead. Thus, coalescing in this case can be applied as long as the second component of the direction vector of (any) flow dependences from DOALL 2 to DOALL 3 is ">".

2.7. RUN–TIME DEPENDENCE TESTING

Most techniques that have been developed so far to analyze array subscripts and determine loop dependences, solve this problem at compile–time. This of course is desirable because there is no run–time overhead. Another alternative would be to determine data dependences dynamically at run–time. In this section we consider the

```
        DOALL  1  J=1,N
              }S₁
        DOALL  2  K=1,N
              }S₂
     2     ENDOALL
     1  ENDOALL
                    (a)
```

becomes

```
     t=0
     DOALL  1  I=1,N²
           IF (⌈I/N⌉ .NE. t)  THEN
               S₁
               t = ⌈I/N⌉
           ENDIF
               S₂
     1  ENDOALL
                    (b)
```

Figure 2.20. Coalescing of a non–perfectly nested loop.

problem of *run–time dependence checking* or RDC, and propose a hybrid solution.

Resolving data dependences at run–time is certainly not a new idea. One could say that this is the main purpose behind the concept of dataflow [ArNi87]. Tomasulo in [Toma67] introduced the tagged–token scheme that allowed dynamic detection of dependences by the hardware. Other hardware mechanisms were discussed in [Uht85],[Uht87]. All these schemes make little or no use of compile–time information to aid the solution of the problem. Nicolau in [Nico84] discusses run–time disambiguation (RTD), a compiler solution to some restricted instances of the problem. RTD is rather limited in scope and specificly suited for trace–scheduling. The main idea behind RTD is to have the compiler introduce assertions about the relationship of different program variables (typically loop indices). These assertions are associated with probability estimates that need to be supplied by the user or the compiler.

The RDC transformation proposed here is a new scheme that relies on precise information obtainable at compile or run–time, as opposed to relying on probabilistic assertions. Also, RDC targets dependences different than those resolved by RTD. RDC is important for many reasons. The first and most obvious reason is that in many loops there exist array subscripts that are not amenable to compile–time analysis. In such cases subscript expressions are complex integer functions or even unknown functions about which the compiler cannot draw any conclusions. Another

```
        DOALL 1  J=1,N
          DOALL 2  K=1,N

            A(J,K) = ....

    2     ENDOALL

          DOALL 3  L=1,N

            B(J,L) = ....

    3     ENDOALL
    1 ENDOALL
              (a)
```

becomes

```
        DOALL 1  I=1,N²
```

$$A(\lceil I/N \rceil \,,\ I - N \lfloor (I - 1)/N \rfloor) = \ldots.$$
$$B(\lceil I/N \rceil \,,\ I - N \lfloor (I - 1)/N \rfloor) = \ldots.$$

```
    1 ENDOALL
              (b)
```

Figure 2.21. Coalescing of a 2–way nested loop.

reason (which we consider even more important) for using RDC is the following. Even when the compiler can accurately determine loop dependences, not all instances of the statements may be involved in a dependence, or the distances of the same static dependence may vary between its different instances. This means that even when static dependences indicate that a particular loop is serial, we may still have several iterations of that loop that are dependence free and which could execute in parallel. RDC detects such cases and exploits all parallelism in loops that would otherwise be considered serial. Only iterations that are involved in a dependence are executed in a restricted manner in order as to satisfy these dependences.

The main idea behind RDC is to exploit the information about the program available to the compiler, and based on that information, have the compiler generate code that resolves dependences (not amenable to compile–time analysis) at run–time. Even though the principle is the same for different types of array subscripts, the mechanisms of the transformation vary for different cases. A transformation for RDC of array variables with subscripted subscripts is discusses in detail in [Poly86a],[Poly87a]. In the next section we consider RDC for linear subscript

---

```
DO I = 1, N
   A(2I-1) = B(I-1) + 1
   B(2I+1) = A(I+1) * C(I)
ENDO
```

Figure 2.22. A serial loop.

---

expressions. In the first part of this section we consider RDC for singly nested loops that contain array subscripts which cannot be analyzed with the existing compile-time techniques, or serial loops with varying dependence distances which can indeed have some parallelism. RDC can be extended for multiply nested loops following the same procedure.

2.7.1. The RDC Transformation for Nonsubscripted Subscripts

Cycle shrinking can be used to partially parallelize serial loops when the dependence cycles involve dependences with constant distances. When the dependence distances vary between different iterations, cycle shrinking can still be applied as it was shown in Section 2.3.2. In such cases however shrinking is rather conservative. RDC is a more suitable technique since it sequentializes only those iterations that are involved in a true dependence. All remaining iterations can execute in parallel.

Consider for example the loop of Figure 2.22. The distance of the flow dependence $S_1 \; \delta \; S_2$ can take the values 1, 2, 3,.... If cycle shrinking is applied, a distance of 1 must be assumed. That amounts to a purely serial loop. In reality however the loop of Figure 2.22 is not totally serial. Figure 2.23 shows the unrolled version of this loop for the first 10 iterations, and the corresponding data dependences. It is clear that some of the iterations (e.g., iterations 1, 2, 3, 5, 7, 9) could be executed in parallel. RDC can detect such "unstructured" parallelism in statically serial loops.

The basic steps of the transformation are shown in Figure 2.24. The transformation which is carried out by the compiler has two phases. An *implicit* and an *explicit* phase. The implicit part involves computations performed by the compiler which are transparent to the user. The explicit phase transforms the loop itself.

The *scalar dependence graph* or SDG of a loop is a dependence graph which shows dependences based on the name of the variables involved and not on the subscripts. Many dependences in an SDG may be superfluous. The *name* of a dependence is the name of the variables involved in that dependence. Index expressions in array references are assumed to be 1-to-1 functions. Also loops are assumed to be normalized for simplicity in notation.

The basic idea is to be able to determine at run-time whether a particular iteration of a loop depends on one or more previous iterations. This requires some recording of relevant information from previous iterations. For a loop DO I = 1, N and for a dependence $S_j \; \delta_j \; S_{j+1}$ in that loop, we define the *dependence source vector* (or

DSV) R_j to be a vector with N elements, where non–zero elements indicate the values of I for which S_j is a dependence source, and zero elements in R_j correspond to values of I for which S_j is not involved in a dependence.

The first step of the transformation is to create a DSV R_j for each flow dependence $S_j \; \delta \; S_{j+1}$ in a cycle. If $e_j(i)$ is the index expression of the left hand side of S_j, then DSV R_j has subscripts in the range $[e_j(1)\ldots e_j(N)]$, assuming index expressions are monotonically increasing/decreasing functions. (If the latter assumption is relaxed, the range is given by $[\min\limits_{1\leq i\leq N} e_j(i) \; \ldots \; \max\limits_{1\leq i\leq N} e_j(i)]$.) The compiler initializes all elements of S_j to zero. A single bit–vector V with subscripts in the range $[1\ldots N]$ is also created and is initialized to zero. Vector V is called the *synchronization vector*. Then for all values of j the compiler initializes the elements of R_j and V as follows:

```
DOALL I = 1, N
       DOALL (for all values of j)
             R_j(e_j(I)) = I
       ENDOALL
       V(I) = 1
ENDOALL
```

Notice that only a *single* synchronization vector is needed for all dependences. This constitutes the implicit phase of the transformation. It creates a vector R_j for each dependence δ_j and stores in it the values of the original loop index I, for which we may have a potential dependence source. For each such dependence δ_j the explicit phase of RDC inserts the statement

$$\text{IF } (1 \leq R_j(h_j(I)) < I) \text{ THEN WAIT ON } V(h_j(I))$$

at the beginning of the target loop, where $h_j(I)$ is the index expression of the dependence sink at the right hand side of statement S_{j+1}. When checking the value $R_j(h_j(I))$, we can have an out–of–bound condition if $h_j(I)$ lies outside the interval $[e_j(1) \; \ldots \; e_j(N)]$. In this case however, no dependence is possible. At the end of the target loop the compiler also inserts the statement

$$\text{CLEAR } V(I) \quad .$$

The effect of this is to detect possible unsatisfied dependences at run–time, and synchronize the execution of loop iterations that are involved in a dependence. Iterations which are not possibly involved in a dependence are executed in parallel without any constraints. The `clear` statement resets the elements of V which correspond to statements with dependence sources that have completed execution. This in effect frees the statements (iterations) with the corresponding dependence sinks, to execute at any time. It is also worth noting that all the `IF` tests can be carried out in parallel as shown in Figure 2.24 by the `cobegin/coend` clause. An iteration of the transformed loop is blocked if one or more of the tests fail.

The transformed loop of Figure 2.22 is shown in Figure 2.25. The appropriate declarations of vectors R and V are omitted. When the transformed loop is executed as a DOALL, only those iterations that are involved in a dependence will be sequentialized. All other iterations will be executed in parallel. For example, if $N=10$ in Figure 2.25, iterations 1, 2, 3, 5, 7, and 9 will be free to execute in parallel

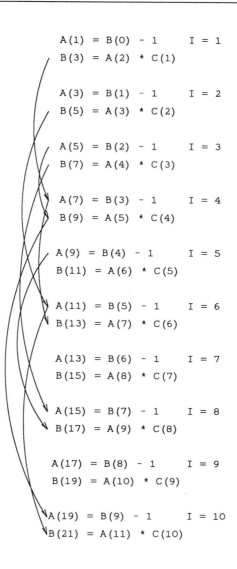

```
A(1)  = B(0)  - 1      I = 1
B(3)  = A(2)  * C(1)

A(3)  = B(1)  - 1      I = 2
B(5)  = A(3)  * C(2)

A(5)  = B(2)  - 1      I = 3
B(7)  = A(4)  * C(3)

A(7)  = B(3)  - 1      I = 4
B(9)  = A(5)  * C(4)

A(9)  = B(4)  - 1      I = 5
B(11) = A(6)  * C(5)

A(11) = B(5)  - 1      I = 6
B(13) = A(7)  * C(6)

A(13) = B(6)  - 1      I = 7
B(15) = A(8)  * C(7)

A(15) = B(7)  - 1      I = 8
B(17) = A(9)  * C(8)

A(17) = B(8)  - 1      I = 9
B(19) = A(10) * C(9)

A(19) = B(9)  - 1      I = 10
B(21) = A(11) * C(10)
```

Figure 2.23. The unrolled version of the loop of Figure 2.22.

RUN–TIME DEPENDENCE CHECKING

Input:
A cycle of static dependences $S_1 \; \delta \; S_2 \; \delta \; \cdots \; \delta \; S_n \; \delta \; S_1$.

IMPLICIT PHASE

Step 1:
For each static dependence i create the source vector $R_i(1:N)$ and initialize
it to zero. Assuming that array subscripts are 1–to–1 mappings the
compiler executes the following loop:

```
DOALL I=1, N
    COBEGIN
            R₁(e₁(I))=I;
            R₂(e₂(I))=I;
                . . .
                . . .
                . . .
            Rₙ(eₙ(I))=I;
    COEND
    V(I)=1
ENDO
```

where $e_j(i)$ is the value of the index expression of the *source* of the
j-th static dependence when the loop index is i.

EXPLICIT PHASE

Step 2:
For the j-th static dependence insert at the beginning of the target loop
the following statement.

```
        IF  (1 ≤ Rⱼ(hⱼ(I))< I)  THEN WAIT ON V(hⱼ(I))
```

where $h_j(i)$ is the value of the index expression of the *sink* of the
j-th static dependence when the loop index is i.

Step 3:
For each static dependence j insert at the end of the target loop the
following statement

```
                CLEAR V(I)
```

Figure 2.24. The RDC transformation.

```
DOALL I = 1, N
    COBEGIN
        IF (1 ≤ R₁(I+1) < I) WAIT ON V(I+1);
        IF (1 ≤ R₂(I-1) < I) WAIT ON V(I-1);
    COEND
    A(2I-1) = B(I-1) + 1
    B(2I+1) = A(I+1) * C(I)
    CLEAR V(I)
ENDO
```

Figure 2.25. The loop of Figure 2.22 after the RDC transformation.

---

immediately. Iterations 4, 6, and 8 must wait for iterations 3 and 5 to complete. Finally iteration 10 must wait for iteration 6 to complete. In a system with 6 processors the transformed loop will take only 3 cycles to complete as opposed to 10 cycles that would be required for the original serial loop.

Finally, let us consider the extra storage requirements introduced by the transformation. For each dependence handled by RDC we need to maintain a dependence source vector. For all practical purposes we can assume that the size of these vectors is equal to the number of iterations of the loop. Therefore, for a loop with N iterations and k dependences, the storage requirements of RDC grow as $O(kN)$, i.e., linearly on the size of the loop.

2.8. SUBSCRIPT BLOCKING

There are many cases where parallelism can be found neither by the user nor by the compiler. We can distinguish these cases into feasible and non–feasible. Feasible cases usually cover problems that are very complex, and parallelism at low levels is difficult to specify of uncover. The non–feasible cases are those in which parallelism depends directly on the input and computed data, or a particular data structure makes it impossible for the compiler to extract parallelism. In such cases parallelism can only be detected and utilized at run–time. There are two possibilities for detecting and exploiting parallelism that occurs during program execution. We can either use

- the compiler, or
- explicit synchronization.

Using the compiler means having the compiler generate appropriate code that will detect and exploit parallelism when it occurs. The second alternative would be to force the task execute in parallel by synchronizing all its components. This however may involve high overhead since synchronization is used even where it is not needed [ZhYL83]. In this section we consider another transformation which is based on run–time dependence checking to partially parallelize loops with subscripted subscripts.

2.8.1. The Problem of Subscripted Subscripts and its Application

The term *subscripted subscript* refers to a variable reference of the form A(f(i)) where A is the identifier of an array and its subscript f(i) is itself a vector. When statements with subscripted subscripts appear in scalar code there is nothing we can do at compile–time but to assume a data dependence chain, that involves all subscripted references of the same variable. This conservative assumption would disallow potential high or low level spreading. A similar assumption is used when subscripted subscripts appear inside loops. In such cases we assume that cross–iteration dependences of unit distance exist. This in effect serializes the corresponding loop. In such cases the potential loss in performance that results by serializing a loop could be very significant.

Examples of loops with subscripted subscripts are shown in Figure 2.26. In each case A denotes an array identifier and f and g subscript vectors. Dependences in scalar code are straightforward to detect. When we have array references with complicated subscripts however, (that usually occur inside loops) a Diophantine equation (that involves the subscript expressions in the two references) must be solved to determine whether a dependence exists [Bane79]. Depending on the complexity of the subscript expressions, such a Diophantine equation may or may not have a solution. For the latter case tests exist that, although do not compute dependences, can give us an affirmative or negative answer as to whether a dependence exists.

With loops that involve subscripted subscripts, as are the examples of Figure 2.26, the above approach obviously cannot be applied. Only in the case where the subscript f(i), for example, is specified by a closed form expression a Diophantine equation can be formed. In real cases however f(i) is simply a vector of integer values that is input to the program or computed as part of the program. In such cases exact dependence analysis is impossible and all loops of this type are serialized. None of the existing commercial or experimental optimizing compilers parallelize general loops with subscripted subscripts (even though vectorization is possible for certain cases).

Subscripted subscripts are used often in numerical programs that solve sparse systems, and in general manipulate sparse matrices, as well as in Fortran programs that implement combinatorial problems. In sparse matrices only a fraction of the matrix elements are non–zero numbers. Storing the entire matrix would be wasteful. For a 1K×1K matrix for example 8 Mbytes of physical memory would be needed if double precision is used. The common approach used for storing sparse matrices is to compact the matrix and store only the non–zero elements. This is usually done by keeping three vectors, A, R, and C. Vector A holds the non–zero elements of a sparse matrix M, and R and C hold the row and column subscripts for each element in A. Two vectors are also used in some cases. A widely–used numerical package that solves systems of sparse equations is HARWELL. Many subroutines in this package contain loops with subscripted subscripts of the type shown in Figure 2.26. During operations with sparse matrices many zero elements become non–zero. This is commonly referred to as *fill–in*. Since the pattern of fill–in is unpredicatable an expandable data structure should be used to store new elements. The most popular data structures in such cases are linked lists, which are implemented in Fortran by means of two unbounded vectors.

$$
\begin{array}{l}
\rule[-3em]{0.5pt}{5em}\quad 1, \ N \\[1em]
s_1: \quad f(i) \ = \quad \cdot \ \cdot \ \cdot \\[1em]
s_2: \quad A(f(i)) \ = \quad \cdot \ \cdot \ \cdot
\end{array}
$$

Figure 2.27. Example of definition–use of f(i).

In graph–theoretic problems a similar approach is used to store graphs which are typically represented by their adjacency matrix. An adjacency matrix is sparse if the number of edges is very small compared to the number of vertices. Large combinatorial problems are often coded in Fortran for efficiency reasons, and their sparse matrices are store in a similar way. Parallelizing loops with subscripted subscripts would amount to a significant gain in performance for many applications. In this section we discuss a compiler transformation which can be used to parallelize in part loops with subscripted subscripts. As shown later some overhead is introduced during the parallelization of such loops. This overhead may be nontrivial for certain loops.

Subscript blocking works by examining the values of the subscript vector, (f(i) in Figure 2.26 for example) and extracting the parallel iterations repeatedly. In general we distinguish two cases: 1) the subscript vector f(i) is known at compile–time, and 2) f(i) is computed at run–time. When f(i) is known at compile–time subscript–blocking can be implicitly applied to transform the corresponding loop(s) into DOALL(s) with zero overhead. This is because the part of the transformation that checks the pattern of f(i) is done by the compiler and it is "charged" to compilation time. For the second case where f(i) is computed and it is not known at compile–time the checking of f(i) must be done at run–time which may introduce significant overhead. If the original loop is large enough, this overhead is amortized and can be small compared to the benefits of the extracted parallelism. An example of subscript blocking that can be implicitly applied in the compiler is when a sparse matrix is known and f(i) holds for instance, the row indices of its non–zero elements. In this case the values of f(i) are available to the compiler and can be used to compute exact dependences. On the other hand if f(i) is associated with fill–in elements which are generated during program execution, the values of the subscript vector are not available to the compiler.

Let us consider the dependence relation between the definition of a subscript vector $f(i)$ and its use in an array reference of the form $A(f(i))$. Consider for example the loop of Figure 2.27. If $f(i)$ is computed outside the loop which uses or assigns $A(f(i))$, subscript–blocking always works. If $f(i)$ is computed inside the loop as shown in Figure 2.27, a dependence always exists from s_1 to s_2. If there is no backward dependence from s_2 to s_1, then s_1 and s_2 belong to different π–blocks and loop distribution can thus be applied to separate the definition of $f(i)$ in s_1 and its use in s_2. If there is a hypothetical dependence from s_2 to s_1 then both statements are involved in a dependence cycle and cannot be separated. This however does not happen very often in practice. For instance, in all HARWELL subroutines that we examined, the definitions and uses of vector subscripts could always be distributed. Therefore, the definitions of vector subscripts are of no concern to the following discussion.

2.8.2. The Transformation

A set of successive iterations of a loop is said to form a *domain*. A *sink–domain* is a domain in which one or more statements are sinks. A domain that does not contain any sinks is called a *source–domain*. It is obvious that all source domains of a loop can be executed in parallel.

Let us consider for example the case of Figure 2.26a which involves output dependences. In this case an output dependence may exist from $A(f(i)) \longrightarrow$

```
V(1:N) = 0;
S(1) = 1;
j = 1;

DO   i=1, N
     if V(f(i))=0 then V(f(i))=1
     else  j = j+1;
           S(j) = i;
ENDO

DO   k=1,j
     DOALL   i=S(k),  S(k+1)-1

         A(f(i)) = ...

     ENDOALL
ENDO
```

Figure 2.28. The subscript blocking transformation for the loop of Figure 2.26a.

A(f(j)) for i>j. If the loop involves only a single statement, we may execute it automatically as a vector statement. If we assume that memory writes are always performed in the order they are issued then the loop can be forced to execute as a vector statement without violating any dependences; only the most recent assignment for each element of A will be valid. The above assumption may be valid for SEA systems but not necessarily for MES or MEA machines. In addition the loop of Figure 1a may be parallel but not a vector loop. In general even though the loop of Figure 1a can be vectorized for SEA machines, it should be executed serially on MES machines.

To parallelized loops of this type we can proceed as follows. Before we enter the loop where the vector subscript f(i) is used, we examine the values of f(i) and construct the "free-runs" or source domains. In other words we find subsets of successive iterations none of which contains a statement which is a dependence sink. To perform the construction of source domains we use two auxiliary vectors V and S. V is a binary vector and S a vector with integer elements. Vector V is used to detect dependences (conflicts) as explained below and S holds the indices of the subscript–vector f(i) that correspond to loop iterations that are involved in a conflict.

Specifically after f(i) is generated, its elements are read and the corresponding elements of the bit–vector V are set to 1. For each f(i), if V(f(i))=0, it is then set V(f(i))=1. If it is found that V(f(i))=1, this indicates a previous occurrence of the value f(i) for another j>i. Since this implies a dependence from some f(j) to f(i), j<i, index i is saved in S(k). All iterations up to S(k)-1 can therefore be executed in parallel. This procedure is performed by an extra loop that is inserted by the compiler before the source loop. The transformed loop of the example in Figure 2.26a is shown in Figure 2.28. Obviously the size of vectors f, V and S is equal to the size of array A. As shown in Figure 2.28 the original serial loop is transformed into a series of DOALL loops. If β is the number of times a conflict was detected, then we have a total of $\beta + 1$ DOALLs created out of the original loop.

Let us consider the example of Figure 2.29. Only output dependences are considered. The values of the subscript–vector f(i) are given in the top vector of Figure 2.29. After the first 3 iterations of the first loop of Figure 2.28 are executed, the 4–th, 5–th and 7–th bits of V will be set. During the next iteration for i=4, a conflict occurs since V(f(4)) $\neq$ 0. The current index (i=4) is then stored in the next (2nd) empty position of S. The same process is repeated until i=10. The final configuration of vectors V and S is shown in Figure 2.29. The asterisks next to V indicate positions where conflicts (output dependences) were detected. The original loop is then transformed into a series of DOALLs by the second loop of Figure 2.28. In this case 4 DOALLs were created each corresponding to one of the four domains {1-3}, {4-5}, {6-9}, {10-11} of the original loop respectively.

In the above example we can observe that the creation of DOALLs was performed in a conservative manner. That is, a dependence was assumed whenever a conflict occurred, without taking into account the possibility of eliminated dependences due to the completion of earlier domains. For example, in Figure 2.29, a dependence pointing to the sixth element of f(i) was assumed. However the source of this dependence belongs to a previous DOALL and thus the dependence should be considered eliminated. We can solve this problem by using extra storage as follows.

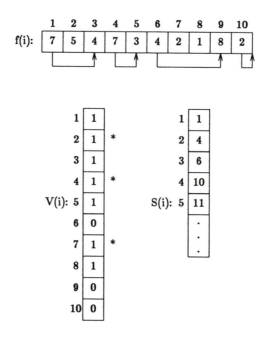

Figure 2.29. Example of computing vectors V and S.

Vector V is defined now as an integer–valued vector. Instead of setting bits in V, we store the index i in position f(i) of V. Whenever a conflict occurs at V(f(j)) we store the corresponding index j in the next free slot of S as previously, and overwrite the old value of V(f(j)) with j. Dependences that should be ignored are specified by the test of the following lemma.

Lemma 2.4. Let m be the last index value inserted in vector S. If a conflict occurs at position x=f(i) of V and y=V(x), then the dependence is discarded if y<m. Otherwise the dependence is saved in vector S. In either case, set V(f(i)) ← i.

Proof: We need to show that if a dependence is discarded by the test of the lemma, then the source of the dependence does not belong to the current domain. Let j be the position of the most recent value inserted in S, and let i be the current index of f. The current domain includes elements from m=f(j) to f(i) inclusive. The conflict occurs at position f(i) of V whose old value is y. Then it is obvious that the source of the dependence, i.e., y belongs to the current domain if and only if y ≥ m, which proves the lemma. ■

The version of the example of Figure 2.29, where vector V is a vector of integers is shown in Figure 2.30. The result now is three DOALL loops. The transformation results in a series of DOALL loops as shown by the second loop of Figure 2.28. The serial loop however in this case is slightly different and is shown in Figure 2.31.

2.8.3. Recurrences with Subscripted Subscripts

The case of flow and anti–dependences e.g., Figure 2.26c, or recurrences, e.g. Figure 2.26d, is very similar to the case of output dependences that we discussed above. Let us consider in this section the case of subscript blocking for recurrences (Fig. 8.1d), and ignore for the moment output dependences. In this case we have two subscript vectors f(i) and g(i). Two vectors V_f and V_g are used to carry out the tests, and a vector S to record the independent domains. As shown later the two vectors V_f and V_g are necessary only if we want to detect both data (or flow) dependences and anti–dependences. The tests in this case are similar to those of the previous section. Vector V_f is used to store the definitions of a variable and V_g to store its uses. Initially, vector V_f is set to zero. Then starting from i = 1 we examine the

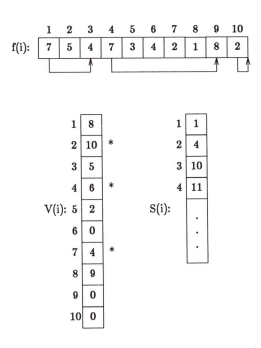

Figure 2.30. The example of Figure 2.29 when V is not a bit–vector.

```
DO   i=1,  N

    if V(f(i))  >= S(j-1) then
        S(j)  = i;
        j = j+1;
    V(f(i))  = i;

ENDO
```

Figure 2.31. The set–up loop for V and S when V is an integer vector.

```
V_f(1:N)  = 0;
S(1)  = 1;
j = 1;

DO   i=1,  N
    if V_f(g(i))  > S(j) then
            j = j+1;
            S(j)  = i;
        V_f(f(i))  = i;
ENDO

S(j+1)  = N;

DO   k=1,  j
    DOALL   i=S(k),  S(k+1)-1

            A(f(i))  = A(g(i));

    ENDOALL
ENDO
```

Figure 2.32. The transformed loop of Figure 2.26d.

pairs of elements $(f(i), g(i))$ of the two subscript vectors, storing the corresponding indices to locations $V_f(f(i))$ and $V_g(g(i))$. A data dependence is found when for some i, $V_f(g(i)) \neq 0$. The corresponding dependence is $V_f(g(i)) \longrightarrow i$, and i is stored in the next free location of vector S. However as in the previous section, if the source of a flow dependence does not belong to the current domain, that dependence is correctly ignored as stated in the following lemma.

Lemma 2.5. Let j be the index of the last element of S, and $m = S(j)$. If for some i, $k = V_f(g(i)) \neq 0$ and $k < m$, the data dependence $k \rightarrow i$ is correctly discarded.

Proof: The previous domains include all loop iterations up to $(m - 1)$. Since k is the source of the data dependence and $k \leq m - 1$, it belongs to a previous domain and therefore has been eliminated due to the order of execution enforced by subscript

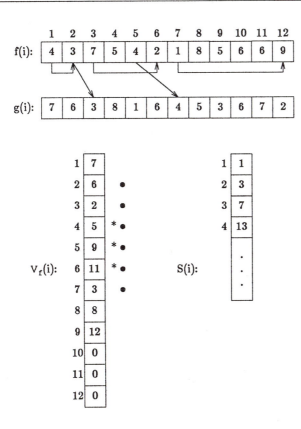

Figure 2.33. Example of subscript blocking for recurrences.

blocking. ■

As mentioned above the flow dependences are detected using only vector V_f, and the corresponding domains are stored in vector S. The transformed loop of Figure 2.26d is shown in Figure 2.32. Figure 2.33 gives the vectors f(i) and g(i) for an application of subscript blocking using the loop of Figure 2.26d. Output dependences were ignored so far but are computed exactly as described in the previous section. The flow dependences in this example are shown in Figure 2.33 by arrows from f(i) to g(i). Dependences that were discarded by Lemma 2.5 are not shown. Asterisks and bullet–marks next to V_f indicate output and flow dependences respectively. As it can be seen, only two out of the six flow dependences defined disjoint domains (DOALLs). The domains defined by data dependences alone are {1–2}, {3–6}, and {7–12}.

Anti–dependences are found in the same way using vectors V_f and V_g in the reverse order. For a given i, if $V_g(f(i)) > 0$ and $V_g(f(i))$ belongs to the current domain, an anti–dependence $A(V_g(f(i))) \rightarrow A(i)$ exists. Output dependences can be computed here without extra storage for their corresponding domains. In fact flow and output dependences may define different domains but they can be combined to form domains that satisfy both types of dependences as shown in Figure 2.34. If an output domain lies entirely within a single flow domain, a new domain is created otherwise output domains are ignored. If in the example of Figure 2.33 both

```
DO   i=1, N
     if (V_f(g(i)) or V_f(f(i)) > S(j)) then
                    j = j+1;
                    S(j) = i;
     V_f(f(i)) = i;
ENDO
```

Figure 2.34. The set–up loop of Figure 2.32 for data and output domains.

```
DO 1 i = 1, N
   DO 2 j = 1, M
          .  .  .
        A(f_1(i,j), f_2(i,j)) = A(g_1(i,j), g_2(i,j))
          .  .  .
2      ENDO
1 ENDO
```

Figure 2.35. An example of multidimensional recurrence with subscripted subscripts.

output and flow dependences are taken into consideration, the corresponding domains (DOALLs) are $\{1-2\}$, $\{3-6\}$, $\{7-10\}$, and $\{10-12\}$.

The overhead introduced by the set–up loop can be reduced by executing the set–up loop itself in parallel. For instance this can be done by using synchronization instructions to synchronize the write operations in V_f and S by each iteration. Those iterations that access different elements of V_f will be executed in parallel, while the writes to the same element will be done serially. Depending on how we use synchronization instructions to execute the set–up loop in parallel, we may have to order the elements of S. This can also be done in parallel.

2.8.4. Multiply Nested Loops

Subscript blocking works in precisely the same way for multiply nested loops, as it does for singly nested loops. However the auxiliary vector V now becomes a multidimensional table with a number of dimensions equal to the number of loops in the nest, plus one. Or more precisely, equal to the maximum number of subscripted subscripts in an array reference (inside the loop). Vector S can always be stored in a 2–dimensional table. If we have m nested loops for example, V will be organized as an (m+1)–dimensional table and S will be a 2–dimensional table with rows of size m, where each row holds values of the m indices.

```
V_f(1:N, 1:M) = (0,0);
k=1;
S(k) = (1,1);

DO  i=1, N
      DO  j=1, M
              if (V_f(g_1(i,j),g_2(i,j)) or V_f(f_1(i,j), f_2(i,j)) > S(k)) then
                      k = k+1;
                      S(k) = (i,j);
              V_f(f_1(i,j), f_2(i,j)) = (i,j);
      ENDO
ENDO
S(k+1) = (N, M);
DO  l = 1, k
      n1 = S(l).1; n2 = S(l+1).1;
      m1 = S(l).2; m2 = S(l+1).2;
      if m2>1 then m2 = m2-1
      else n2 = n2-1; m2 = M;
      DOALL  i = n1, n2
              DOALL  j = m1, m2
                      . . .
                      A(f_1(i,j), f_2(i,j))=A(g_1(i,j), g_2(i,j));
                      . . .
              ENDOALL
      ENDOALL
ENDO
```

Figure 2.36. The loop of Figure 2.35 after the transformation.

The rows of S define the boundaries of successive source domains. The result of the transformation in this case will be again two disjoint loops. The first will consist of m perfectly nested   DO loops and will be functionally identical as in the single loop case (Figure 2.34). The second loop will consist of m+1 loops; a serial outermost loop which defines the source domains, and m DOALL loops.

Let us consider an example. For simplicity we consider the case of a 2–dimensional recurrence with subscripted subscripts as the one shown in Figure 2.35. We will apply the transformation to the loop of Figure 2.35 taking into consideration flow and output dependences only. As mentioned above, the auxiliary vector V_f is set up in this case using the same algorithm as in the previous section. Vectors V_f and S will be represented by a 3–dimensional and a 2–dimensional table, respectively. To simplify our notation and drawings we represent V_f with a 2–dimensional table where each entry can store an ordered pair of the form (a,b), $a,b \in Z^+$. The same representation is used for S. In general, for a nested loop $L = (N_1, N_2, \ldots, N_m)$ the size of the i–th dimension of V_f will be N_i and the size of the m+1–st dimension will be m. S will always be represented by a set of rows of size m.

To compare elements of V_f and S in our example we use the following rule. If (a_v, b_v) is an element of V_f, and (a_s, b_s) an element of S, then

$$(a_v, \ b_v) \ \geq \ (a_s, \ b_s)$$

if and only if $a_v \geq a_s$, or $a_v = a_s$ and $b_v \geq b_s$. If $(a_s, \ b_s)$ is the i–th element (row) of S then $a_s = S(i).1$, and $b_s = S(i).2$. The transformed loop of Figure 2.35 is shown in Figure 2.36.

A detailed example for N=3, and M=4 is shown in Figure 2.37. Figure 2.37 shows the unrolled version of the example loop with arcs illustrating flow and output dependences. After the set–up loop of Figure 2.36 is executed the final configuration of table V_f and the resulting domains in S are also shown in Figure 2.37. The four domains that were created by subscript blocking in this case are $\{(1,1), (1,2), (1,3)\}$, $\{(1,4), (2,1)\}$, $\{(2,2), (2,3), (2,4)\}$, and $\{(3,1), (3,2), (3,3), (3,4)\}$. Note that from a total of six flow and output dependences only three were used to define the source domains.

2.8.5. Expected Speedup

The set–up loops created by subscript blocking can be executed in parallel using some sort of synchronization. In case the subscript vector is known at compile–time the transformation can be applied without the set–up loop, in which case the extra overhead is zero. We believe that this rarely happens in real code and therefore the set–up loop is needed to define the domains at run–time. The body of the set–up loop will always contain three to four statements, and in general it is independent of the body size of the original loop.

Let C and B be the execution time of the loop body (i.e., one iteration) of the set–up loop, and the original loop respectively. If we assume that each statement takes a unit of time to execute, then we always have C=3, or 4. Consider the case of a perfectly nested serial loop $L = (N_1, \ N_2, \ldots, \ N_m)$ (B) of nest depth m, where N_i is the number of iterations of the i–th loop and B is the execution time of the loop

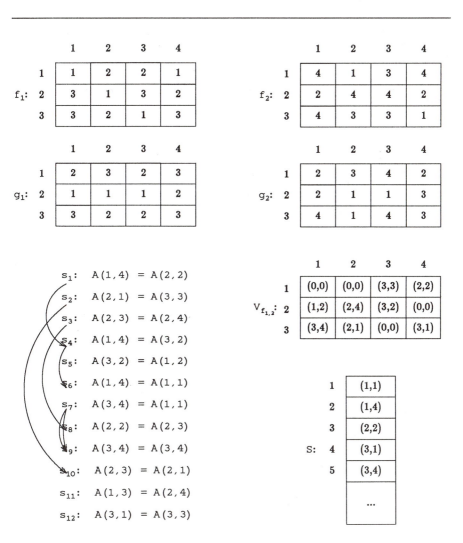

Figure 2.37. The unrolled loop of Figure 2.35 with its subscript values and the V_f and S tables.

body. Subscript blocking will transform this loop into two loops $O = (N_1, N_2, \ldots, N_m)$ (C) and $R = (\beta, N_1, N_2, \ldots, N_m)$ (B). O is the set-up loop and R is a set of m DOALL loops nested in a serial outermost loop with β iterations. β is the number of domains. Let T_p^O, T_p^R be the parallel execution times of O and R on p processors, respectively. Also let $N = \prod\limits_{i=1}^{m} N_i$. Since the execution time of the original loop is NB, the expected speedup of the transformed loop on p processors would be

$$S_p = \frac{NB}{T_p^O + T_p^R}. \qquad (2.16)$$

Let α_i be the number of writes (conflicts) to the i-th element of V_f, and $\alpha = \max\limits_{i} \{\alpha_i\}$. Since the updates to the same element of V_f are serialized, the parallel execution time of O with unlimited processors will be determined by the maximum number of conflicts in each element of V_f, i.e., $T_\infty^O = \alpha C$. On p processors, each processor will execute an average of $\lceil N/p \rceil$ iterations of O. Therefore for the limited processor case,

$$T_p^O = \begin{cases} \lceil N/p \rceil C & \text{if } \alpha \leq \lceil N/p \rceil \\ \alpha C & \text{otherwise} \end{cases} \qquad (2.17)$$

T_p^R is computed as follows. Let β be the number of domains and m_i be the number of iterations in the i-th domain, $(i=1, 2, \ldots, \beta)$. Obviously $\sum\limits_{i=1}^{\beta} m_i = N$. Then we have

$$T_p^R = \sum_{i=1}^{\beta} \left\lceil \frac{m_i}{p} \right\rceil B \qquad (2.18)$$

and since by definition

$$\frac{m_i}{p} \leq \left\lceil \frac{m_i}{p} \right\rceil \leq \frac{m_i}{p} + 1, \qquad (i=1, 2, \ldots, \beta) \qquad (2.19)$$

from (2.18) and (2.19) it follows that

$$\frac{NB}{p} \leq T_p^R \leq \frac{NB}{p} + \beta B \qquad (2.20)$$

If we assume $T_p^O \approx NC/p$ in (2.17), we finally have from (2.16) and (2.20) that

$$\frac{NB}{(NB)/p + (NC)/p} \geq S_p \geq \frac{NB}{(NB)/p + (NC)/p + \beta B} \qquad \text{or,}$$

$$p\left(\frac{B}{B + C} \right) \geq S_p \geq p\left(\frac{B}{B + C + (\beta B p)/N} \right). \qquad (2.21)$$

When N is large relative to β and p, the speedup converges to the upper limit in (2.21). As an example, for a loop with N=100, B=50, C=3, p=16 and β=8, the speedup range (depending on the size of the domains) is

$$15 \geq S_{16} \geq 7.$$

If all eight domains have 16 or fewer iterations, then $S_{16} \approx 12.5$. If the set-up loop is executed serially, then the expected speedup would be

$$S_p = \frac{NB}{NC + NB/p} = p\left(\frac{B}{B + pC}\right).$$

Assuming that $B = kC$, we have $S_p = pk/(k+p)$ and the speedup is greater than one when $k \geq 2$.

2.9. FUTURE DIRECTIONS

The restructuring compilers of the future will undoubtly need to possess many properties that we do not find in today's most sophisticated parallelizing compilers. So far, the attention has only focused on optimization and restructuring techniques. However, the complexity of the new parallel machines requires the compiler to perform many additional functions than just restructuring. These functions include memory management in a memory hierarchy environment. Good memory management requires knowledge of the program which the operating system is unable to know. Scheduling is also a candidate for the compilers of the near future. Memory management, minimization of interprocessor communication, synchronization and various other types of overhead are important issues that could be tackled by the compiler. Another important aspect of the near future compilers for parallel machines is ease of use and interaction with the user. There are many cases where the user's assistance (in the form of assertions for example) is necessary for parallelizing a program and exploiting the resulting parallelism.

It is very likely that in the next few years we will see a transfer of many run-time activities (that are now considered the operating system's responsibility), to the compiler. This will become necessary as performance becomes more of a critical factor. Any activity involving the operating system is known to involve a large overhead. This overhead cannot be tolerated above a certain point. Also, in time-sharing, systems knowledge of specific program characteristics is not necessary to achieve high throughput. In parallel processor environments however, knowledge of program characteristics is necessary for minimizing program turnaround time. Thus the shift of operating system functions to the compiler will be a logical consequence. Compilers will become highly interactive and far more complex than modern restructurers, while the software layer between the user and the hardware called the operating system will become thinner, at least in high performance computer systems.

Parallelism in algorithms and programs may be implicit, or may be explicitly specified at several different levels. When parallelism exists in fixed-size "quantums", it is rather easy to understand and exploit. The unstructured nature of parallelism makes its efficient exploitation and parallel programming to be very complex tasks. Devicing methods and tools that automatically perform these tasks is thus a very important research subject.

CHAPTER 3

A COMPREHENSIVE ENVIRONMENT FOR AUTOMATIC PACKAGING AND SCHEDULING OF PARALLELISM

3.1. INTRODUCTION

The state of the art in vectorizing and parallelizing compilers has overcome the language barrier and offers a viable (and not necessarily exclusive) alternative to parallel programming. The evolution of parallel programming languages has not kept up with the evolution of parallel architectures [KDLS86], [GGKM83], [Chen83], [MiUc84]. Even though this may change in the future, currently we are confined to using enhanced versions of existing languages which do not provide either the power or the flexibility for programming modern parallel supercomputers [ANSI86], [GuPL88], [MeRo85]. Under this reality parallel programming remains still a highly complex and empirical art, even for the skillful programmer. Parallelizing compilers offer a solution to both of these problems. A serial program can be automatically vectorized and/or parallelized, and in many cases automatic concurrentization can proceed to the maximum possible degree.

Given that a program has been written or transformed into a vector–parallel form the next issue is packaging and scheduling of the parallelism present in that program. This issue is the focus of this chapter which attempts to address program partitioning (or parallelism packaging) and scheduling in a comprehensive manner. We propose a general framework that we call an *auto–scheduling compiler* (ASC) and which offers an efficient yet practical alternative to partitioning and scheduling. The basic idea is to have the compiler generate drive–code as part of the object code for each program. This will result in some sort of self–driven parallel programs. The drive–code does not necessarily imply replication of the functions of the operating system at selective points in a program. It rather implies extending run–time libraries and reducing (or even eliminating) the responsibilities of operating systems in dedicated parallel environments. Before focusing on auto–scheduling compilers in Sections 3.2 and 3.3 we give a general discussion on the various aspects of the problem by comparing alternatives and existing approaches. Throughout this chapter our machine model is a shared memory parallel processor system with scalar, vector, or VLIW processors. Nevertheless, most of the discussion and the schemes presented here are applicable to message passing or other types of parallel systems.

3.1.1. Previous Approaches & Current Parallel Machines

The problem of scheduling is an old problem that has been studied by several researchers in a theoretical context [Coff76], [CoGr72], [Grah72] [Sahn84], [Ston77]. Even in its most simplified formulations scheduling is NP–complete [GaJo79]. Unfortunately, most of the models that have been used in theoretical studies of the problem are of little use in the case of parallel programming. The non–applicability of these models is obvious but some justification is given in Section 3.2.2. As a result of the weakness of these models, simple heuristic approaches became more appealing. However, even in these cases too restrictive assumptions are often used [ScGa85].

By turning to existing parallel machines, one can easily verify the fact that very little of our theoretical knowledge is in use. For example, no existing general-purpose parallel computer supports automatic scheduling at the task level. In fact, the state of the art is manual creation and elimination of tasks whose effectiveness depends solely on the programmer's abilities. Worse yet, there is a wide–spread disagreement on a more basic issue, namely, dedicated vs. multiprogramming on parallel processor systems. In the following section we briefly consider the latter issue but the focus of this work is on dedicated environments where a single parallel program executes at a time reserving all machine resources. Thus our goal is minimizing the execution time for each program while keeping machine utilization high. From now on, a dedicated environment is assumed unless stated otherwise.

Let us consider parallel execution of programs on existing machines such as the Cray X–MP, Alliant FX/8, Sequent, etc. It is safe to say that, excluding vectorization, the only other type of parallelism that is often exploited by these systems is that of singly nested parallel loops. Cray through microtasking and Alliant through its hardware–based concurrency control mechanism [Cray85], [Alli85]. Nested parallel loops and nested parallel constructs in general are not supported by any of the existing systems. High–level spreading, that is, parallel execution of independent tasks is at best supported through manual and rather primitive schemes (e.g., macrotasking [Cray85]). The user is responsible for creating and synchronizing the execution of parallel tasks through run–time library calls, which in turn, make invocations to the kernel for allocating stack space and performing various initialization tasks. The cost involved with operating system calls is such that parallel tasks need to be significantly large to justify it. However, the user is left to guess the appropriate task size.

3.1.2. Modes of Operation and Importance of Scheduling

Let us return briefly to the dedicated vs. multiprogramming issue. There is no question that the main goal of parallel programming is to achieve minimum execution time for a given parallel program, and not necessarily maximum machine utilization. Yet, many existing systems (e.g., Sequent, Encore) are routinely used as time–sharing computers. If time–sharing is of prime concern, then one might wonder whether many serial machines are a better solution to a single parallel system (with comparable cost/performance ratio). In the former case utilization will most likely be higher since unnecessary contention (e.g., memory and bus conflicts) is not present as is the case in a parallel machine which operates in a multiprogramming mode. Of course, cost considerations make utilization also an important issue. In this aspect, we share the belief of many that parallel machines and software should be designed and optimized around the goal of minimizing execution time. Only under the above assumption scheduling of parallel programs becomes an important issue.

An ideal parallel machine should be one which can switch automatically between dedicated and multiprogramming modes. When parallel programs or real–time applications are running, dedicated (batch) mode is most appropriate. Otherwise multiprogramming is the most cost–effective mode of operation. One can envision an self–adapting operating system which can switch between the two modes automatically. Even in a single user mode "slave" jobs may be executing periodically whenever physical processors are not used by a "master" job, to keep utilization high.

Of course, even in a multiprogramming mode there might be several serial and/or parallel programs running with different priorities, different resource requirements and so on. A sophisticated operating system should be able to accommodate each user according to its demands. For example, *variable size* time–quantums can be used to thrust large parallel jobs.

In the rest of this chapter we focus on purely dedicated environments. In such cases a primitive operating system (e.g., batch) might be a better solution as far as performance is concerned. The drrive–code generated through an auto–scheduling compiler would allow the program to spread itself across many processors without external help. Thus, run–time scheduling overhead can be kept very low. As a result, we can afford finer granularity parallel tasks.

3.1.3. Sophisticated vs Simple & Static vs Dynamic

There are many approaches to program scheduling. Most can be classified as static or dynamic. In static schemes scheduling is done before program execution based on knowledge of global program information. Most of these schemes attempt to predict execution time of different parts of the program and, in general, are based on other parameters which are usually unknown at compile–time. Thus we try to "optimize" a parameter based on approximate information and idealized models. Static schemes are usually complex and time consuming where as compilation time should not be considered less important than execution time. The advantage of static scheduling is in that run–time overhead with respect to scheduling is minimal.

Dynamic schemes are typically based (if at all) on local information about the program. Scheduling decisions are made at run–time which incur a penalty or overhead. Thus by necessity dynamic approaches should be less "sophisticated" and rather simple. This overhead is the main disadvantage of dynamic scheduling. Excluding the overhead, it is not clear whether a dynamic scheme would be less effective than an even optimal static one (since the latter is based on approximate information to obtain an "optimal" schedule).

It has been shown that in many cases of random task graphs optimal static schedules can be achieved by deliberately keeping one or more processors idle in order to better utilize them at a later point. This and other scheduling anomalies are reported in [Grah72]. Detecting such anomalies however requires processing of the entire task graph in advance. Since this is not possible at run–time the luxury of deliberately keeping processors idle (with the hope that we may better utilize them later) should not be permitted.

It is not unrealistic to say that the following guideline for any run–time scheduling scheme should always be applied: Make simple and fast scheduling decisions at run–time. This principle implicitly forbids asking questions of the form: "How many processors should we allocate to this task?"; this means, in general, that we are willing to hold up idle processors until they become as many as the number of processors requested by that task. This is exactly what we want to avoid.

Since deliberate idling of processors is to be avoided as much as possible, any dynamic scheduling scheme should be designed to answer questions of the following type: "How much work should be given to this processor?" In other words, when a processor becomes idle try to assign it a new task as soon as possible, making the best possible selection. It has been shown that this policy is guaranteed to result in an execution time which, theoretically speaking, is never more than twice the optimal [Coff76]. In real cases however, the resulting execution time is very close to the optimal, assuming no overheads. Thus the overhead factor is the crucial optimization parameter in dynamic scheduling.

Our goal is to design a dynamic scheduling scheme that is efficient, realistic, and involves as low an overhead as possible. Since scheduling is done in a non deterministic way in this case, we should design our scheme such that processors are scheduled automatically and select the "best" task to execute next by going through a simple and fast procedure. To achieve this we design our scheme around the following two objectives:

- Keep all processors as busy as possible.
- Run–time overhead should be kept minimal.

Dynamic scheduling can be done through centralized or distributed control. In the former case a global control unit is responsible for selecting and dispatching tasks to idle processors. In the latter case no single control unit makes global decisions for allocating processors, but rather the processors themselves are responsible for determining what task to execute next.

One may argue against global control units in a parallel processor machine, stating as an argument that a single control unit may constitute a bottleneck. We do not necessarily share this view point at least with respect to scheduling. If bottleneck is the issue rather than cost, we can argue that a sophisticated global control unit can be designed such that it never becomes the scheduling bottleneck. The rationale behind this argument is the nature of the dynamic scheduling problem itself: No matter how many control units we have, there is always a bottleneck. Even in a fully distributed–control parallel processor system, where each processor makes its own scheduling decisions, processors must access a common pool of ready tasks. That common pool becomes the bottleneck, since it is a critical region, and each processor has to lock and unlock semaphores to enter the critical section and grasp a task. Worse yet, there is little hope that this bottleneck can be overlapped with execution, which is possible with centralized control. One can also argue that instead of a common pool of ready tasks, we can use multiple pools of ready tasks. Even in this case (unless each processor has its own pool of ready tasks) someone must make the decision on which processors access which pool at run–time. Moreover since the tasks are spawned from the same program, we should have a way of distributing them to the common pools. This argument can go on recursively but the conclusion is that due to the nature of the parallel execution of a single program, there is always some kind of bottleneck with run–time scheduling. We choose a parallel machine with distributed control for the following discussion.

Dynamic scheduling should not be blindly enforced. This can be as bad as the other extreme of static scheduling. Although precise information (especially with respect to execution time) is not known at compile–time, less precise information about the program can be used by a dynamic scheme to achieve better results. We return to this subject in Section 3.2.2.

3.1.4. Scheduling Goals: Overhead & Load Balancing

Load balancing refers to the finish time of all processors that execute a parallel program. Assuming that all processors start execution at the same time, the latest to finish is the one which determines the parallel execution time. In an ideal situation where all processors finish at the same time, one may consider that as the optimal execution time. Unless static scheduling was used, this optimality is fallacious. In dynamic scheduling, both load balancing and run–time overhead are equally important and neither can be optimized without considering the other.

Consider for instance the following two scenarios. A program is scheduled using a sophisticated approach which ignores overhead, and then a naive scheduling algorithm, which disregards load balancing but focuses on minimizing overhead. In the first case we may have a perfectly balanced load with all processors finishing at time t_b. In the second case we may have a very unbalanced load (i.e., processors finishing at varying times) but the last processor finished at time t_u with $t_u < t_b$. This may be due to significant overhead incurred by the sophisticated scheme. Even though the naive scheme achieves an overall better execution time there is still room for improvement. A better algorithm would be one that incurs little overhead and achieves a better load balance. The tradeoff between load balancing and run–time overhead is one of the critical aspects of dynamic scheduling.

This is particularly true in the presence of barrier synchronization. Typically, a barrier is set at the end of every parallel loop in a program and all processors must clear the barrier before they can proceed to other tasks. Unbalanced load can thus occur several times during the execution of a single program.

Scheduling overhead depends mainly on machine organization. So far most of the existing parallel processor systems have not addressed this issue adequately nor have they taken it into account either in the compiler or the hardware. On the Cray

X–MP for example multitasking can be applied at any level, although it has been shown that below a given degree of granularity multitasking results in a slowdown. The responsibility of multitasking a program is in addition left entirely to the user. This is also a disadvantage since the average user must know the details of the machine and the code to determine the best granularity. If the code is complex enough, e.g., containing several nested branching statements, finding the minimum size of code for multitasking would be a difficult procedure even for the most skillful programmer. In real systems where scheduling is done by the compiler or the hardware (e.g., Alliant FX/8) the critical task size is also ignored. So we may have the case where a programmer or a compiler schedules a single statement parallel loop on several processors with successive iterations executing on different processors. This would most likely result in a performance degradation.

3.1.5. Granularity and Partitioning

Another important question in parallel programming is the task granularity issue. Also, should tasks be defined at compile time (program partitioning) or should they be formed at run–time? These issues are not independent of load balancing and overhead. For example, the larger the task granularity, the more significant becomes the balancing of load. If tasks are of small granularity, and since by definition, dynamic scheduling is performed on a task–by–task basis, balancing becomes less of an important factor. At the same time, if the overhead associated with dispatching a task is significant, then tasks should be of large granularity in order to shadow this overhead with gains in execution time.

Our approach to program partitioning and task granularity is a hybrid one which allows for task formation both at compile and at run–time. Our goal is to use effectively information about the program in the initial phase of partitioning, and then allow these statically defined tasks to be decomposed into smaller size tasks at run–time, if that can help in balancing the load.

In what follows we assume that a compiler can partition a program into a set of *tasks*. A task is *serial* or *parallel*. At run–time parallel tasks are decomposed into a (predefined or undefined) number of *processes*. A process is a serial entity and executes on a single processor. Thus processes can be formed statically (e.g., serial tasks) or dynamically. Section 3.2.1 discusses possible approaches to static partitioning.

3.1.6. Synchronization and Precedence Relations

In a shared memory parallel machine communication between tasks is done by means of synchronized reads/writes to a shared memory location. Synchronization is necessary to communicate data between parts of a program executing on different processors. Put in other words, synchronization is necessary to guarantee the enforcement of data dependences. Since a parallelizing compiler is fully aware of the data dependences in a program, it can generate automatically synchronization instructions before or after each pair of statements that are involved in a dependence. The problem of generating and eliminating redundant synchronization instructions is an active area of research and more can be found in [MiPa87].

Given that each dependence in a program is synchronized, one might wonder why not let the entire program execute in a dynamic environment without additional scheduling restrictions. In some sense this argument is similar to the dataflow vs.

control flow controversy [GPKK82]. In addition, the overhead of fine granularity tasks on real machines makes this "dataflow" like approach very inefficient. A large amount of program information that can be used to our advantage would otherwise be wasted. Therefore, given that tasks are of medium to large granularity and that several intertask dependences may exist between pairs of tasks, the next question is how precedence relations, data dependences, and synchronization relate to each other.

If simultaneous execution of dependent tasks is not allowed in a given model, then explicit synchronization is unnecessary. Multiple intertask dependences can be summarized to a single precedence constraint which is enforced during execution. However, the hardware should provide mechanisms to guarantee that all reads/writes done by a given task are complete by the time a successor task starts execution. Below we show that this restriction does not reduce the degree of exploitable parallelism in a program, assuming that a powerful parallelizing compiler is available.

If simultaneous execution of dependent tasks is allowed by a model, then explicit synchronization is necessary. However, additional precedence constraints are still useful. The use of precedence relations (e.g., summary of interask dependences) will eliminate the overhead of manipulating at run–time tasks which are not ready to start. In what follows we assume that dependent tasks cannot execute simultaneously without any loss in parallelism. Nevertheless, the proposed framework can accommodate both approaches; and the latter approach by selectively eliminating precedence relations and keeping explicit synchronization. However, we believe that this assumption is more pragmatic for eliminating run–time overhead.

Another aspect of synchronization which is of significance here is barrier synchronization. We have two types of barriers, *blocking* and *non–blocking*. In the former case, all processors associated with a barrier must update (in/decrement) the barrier, and then wait until the barrier is cleared. In the latter case a processor is responsible for updating its barrier, but after the update it is allowed to proceed with other tasks. The wait phase in blocking barriers can be quite significant especially if the processor loads are very unbalanced. In the framework of auto–scheduling compilers only non–blocking barriers are used. This is true since, by definition, only tasks that are ready to execute are queued at any given time.

3.2. A COMPREHENSIVE APPROACH TO SCHEDULING

There are advantages and disadvantages to each scheduling approach. With the growing variety and complexity of parallel architectures monolithic approaches to program scheduling become obsolete. Both compilers and run–time systems need to cooperate in order to achieve desirable results. Pure static schemes are too unrealistic to be practical. Similarly, pure dynamic schemes that ignore useful program information are bound to fail badly in certain cases. An ideal scheduler should use to its advantage information about a program, but it should also operate in the "obvious and least expensive" mode whenever information is inadequate.

Our approach to the parallelism packaging and scheduling problem is a blend of compiler and run–time schemes. Figure 3.1 shows the different components of our framework as parts of an auto–scheduling compiler. In this chapter we address the problem with a shared memory parallel architecture in mind, but the general concepts are valid for any parallel architecture. Below we discuss briefly the main

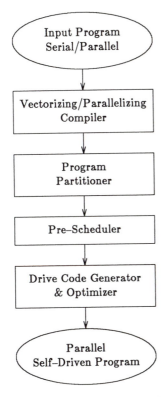

Figure 3.1. The major modules of an auto–scheduling compiler.

components of an auto–scheduling compiler and expand on each of them in the following sections.

Partitioning (or packaging of parallelism): This phase is responsible for partitioning the code (and/or data structures) of a program into identifiable modules which are treated as units when it comes to firing. For example, compiling vector or VLIW instructions, or grouping a set of instructions into a unit is part of partitioning. Program partitioning can be done statically by the compiler. In a fully dynamic environment (e.g., dataflow) partitioning is implicit and depending on our execution model, an allocatable unit can range from a single instruction to a set of instructions. Static (explicit) partitioning is desirable because it exploits readily available information about program parallelism and can consider overhead and other performance factors. In our case we use a semi–static partitioner: the formation of tasks is based on the syntax of the language and other program information, but a task is allowed to be decomposed into subtasks dynamically during program execution. The result of the partitioner is a program task graph with nodes corresponding to tasks (instruction modules) and arcs representing data and control dependences. Partitioning is discussed in Section 3.2.1.

Pre-scheduling: After a program is partitioned into a set of identifiable tasks, the compiler can insert certain scheduling suggestions based on its knowledge about the program. In Section 3.2.2 we shown why pre-scheduling is useful within the proposed framework.

Dynamic task scheduling (nested parallel tasks): Scheduling at the task level is then performed dynamically during execution. At this level tasks are treated as units of execution. Tasks which are ready to execute are queued in a ready-task queue. Each idle processor tries to dispatch the next available task from the queue (if any). Also, tasks are queued and thus are qualified for execution as soon as they become "ready". This environment can be realized through an auto-scheduling compiler which generates control code to implement the above procedure. Section 3.3 discusses possible implementations of auto-scheduling compilers.

Loop (or parallel task) scheduling: Upon queueing, a serial task is dispatched at once as soon as a processor becomes idle. However, a parallel task can draw several processors to execute it and thus it remains queued until exhausted. As shown below, in our case it is safe to assume that the only type of parallel tasks are parallel loops. In Section 3.2.4 we discuss three main approaches to dynamic scheduling of parallel loops. These are self-scheduling, chunk-scheduling, and guided self-scheduling. They differ in the number of iterations that they allocate to each processor. One can view this as dynamic partitioning of a loop into a set of allocatable units.

Within a basic block (or within a processor): Finally, we briefly address the question of scheduling within a processor at the fine granularity level in Section 3.2.5. Packaging of parallelism and scheduling at this level is more architecture dependent than any of the earlier phases of program scheduling.

3.2.1. Partitioning

The role of the partitioner is to break a program down to a set of tasks, define a summary of data and control dependences between tasks, and perform certain architecture dependent optimizations. Traditionally, partitioning has been studied in a context which is almost identical to scheduling [Bokh88], [Ston77]. Our approach is different in the sense that grouping of tasks and allocating goups to processors is not considered but only in special cases. Also, for certain cases (e.g., loops) partitioning of tasks into allocatable units is postponed until run-time.

Let us discuss the first phase of partitioning, namely the definition of tasks. Our approach to this is based entirely on the syntax of the underlying language. If we consider imperative languages such as C, Fortran, and Pascal, then we choose to use the "natural" boundaries in defining tasks. Thus an *outer loop* is considered to be a single task. So do *subroutine calls* and finally *basic blocks*. This approach gives the impression that nested parallel tasks are not allowed in our model. As explained later this is not the case, but nevertheless, it is always possible to work without nested tasks without missing any parallelism in a given program. This can be done by applying the following techniques in a specified order. First, subroutines can be expanded in line. Then, loop distribution can be applied wherever possible, loop interchange can be used to bring parallel loops to adjacent nest levels, and finally loop coalescing can be used to transform a set of nested parallel loops into a single parallel loop [PaWo86], [PoKu87], [Poly87]. Also, recursion can be automatically or manually converted to iteration. Thus a single level of parallelism can capture all the parallelism in a program. It is not clear however that this process is better, in terms of efficiency of implementation, than having arbitrarily nested parallel tasks. What is important is that both approaches are feasible without loosing any parallelism. In order to complete the picture we discuss later how our proposed framework deals with nested parallelism.

In fact, our approach to partitioning as defined above is recursive. A first–level subroutine call defines a task which in turn consists of other tasks that result by the explicit partitioning of the corresponding subroutine body. Similarly, an outer loop defines a task which consist of a set of other tasks (e.g., other loops or basic blocks at deeper nest levels). By assuming that only structured programming is allowed, the result of partitioning will be a directed acyclic graph. The subroutine call graph of an application will also be an acyclic graph.

Nodes in the task graph correspond to tasks. An arc implies the existence of one or more data dependences between the two tasks. During execution, a task cannot start unless all preceding tasks on which it depends have completed execution. One might wonder whether this is a restrictive model since parallel execution of dependent tasks is not allowed. However, compiler transformations such as cycle shrinking [Poly88a], and loop spreading [GiPo88] can be used to overlap execution of dependent tasks while the above "restriction" is still enforced. This is not possible only in cases where the density of dependences (and thus run–time communication during concurrent execution) is too high to justify any overlap of execution.

The next step of our partitioner is to traverse the call graph bottom–up and check the size of each task against the *critical process size* or CPS. Intuitively, the CPS is the minimum size of a process whose execution time is equal to the overhead that it incurs during scheduling (dispatching) at run–time. The compiler can roughly estimate the CPS for each task in the program as shown in [Poly88b]. The effect of this pass is to merge small tasks into larger ones and serialize certain loops. For example, it is very unlikely that spreading the iterations of a parallel loop (with a single statement and very few iterations) across an equal number of processors will result in any speedup. The purpose of this is to at least avoid spreading that would slowdown execution. The most obvious candidate tasks for merging are basic blocks.

3.2.2. Pre–Scheduling

As mentioned earlier, most of the results from the classical scheduling theory are of little value in practical situations. Let us consider a central result from classical scheduling, namely the *critical path* algorithm and its many variations [Coff76]. Scheduling based on the critical path approach works only if the following two assumptions hold true: there are only serial tasks in a program, and the exact execution time is known. In general, neither assumption is valid in practice. We can

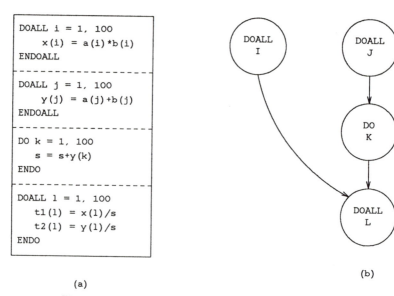

```
DOALL i = 1, 100
    x(i) = a(i)*b(i)
ENDOALL
- - - - - - - - - - - - - - - - - -
DOALL j = 1, 100
    y(j) = a(j)+b(j)
ENDOALL
- - - - - - - - - - - - - - - - - -
DO k = 1, 100
    s = s+y(k)
ENDO
- - - - - - - - - - - - - - - - - -
DOALL l = 1, 100
    t1(l) = x(l)/s
    t2(l) = y(l)/s
ENDO
```

(a)

(b)

Figure 3.2. An example of a program fragment and its task graph.

conform to the first assumption by, for example, fully unrolling DOALL loops and considering one iteration as a serial task. This is not a practical solution for two reasons. First, in order to unroll a loop we need to know the exact number of its iterations. Often, this information is not available at compile–time. Secondly, unrolling parallel tasks (loops) may result in the creation of thousands of serial nodes in the task graph. Scheduling such a graph using an even linear heuristic may be forbiddenly expensive in time. Certainly we do not want to pay the execution time that could possibly be saved (through an efficient schedule) with the same or more amount of preprocessing (compilation) time. Moreover, the second assumption about knowledge of execution time is seldom applicable. Hence, fully static scheduling (which always requires perfect knowledge of program parameters) is not a good and general solution.

On the other hand, our previous discussion implies that fully dynamic scheduling is a viable and practical solution, since (as long as the run–time overhead is kept low) the resulting execution times should not be far from "optimal". We believe that this position is true with one exception which is analyzed in this section. This exception stems from the fact that dynamic scheduling ignores global program information and the general topology of the task graph. We can better illustrate this weakness of dynamic scheduling through the use of a specific example.

Let us consider the program fragment of Figure 3.2a consisting of four parallel and serial loops. Figure 3.2b shows its task graph with precedence (dependence) relations. One can easily see the potential performance "threat" here: DOALL loops I and J may execute to completion before serial loop K is scheduled. Let us consider first how a critical path algorithm could schedule these loops. If the critical path is the I-to-L loop, DOALL I would execute to completion, then loop J and then loop K would run on a single processor. Even though this may not be true for the code of Figure 3.2a, one can easily make DOALL I large enough to demonstrate the above point. Let us turn now to dynamic scenarios which are of interest here.

During dynamic scheduling loops I and J will be queued and executed before loop K. Whether loop I executes to completion followed by loop J (or vice versa), or whether their execution in intermixed does not matter in this case. What is of significance is that in the worst case, a hypothetical parallel machine will be fully utilized during the execution of the two DOALLs and only one of its processors will be busy during the execution of the serial loop K. Alternatively, one could detect the potential bottleneck and force loop I to execute in parallel with the serial loop.

Such bottlenecks can be avoided by a simple, yet effective and general prepro-cessing of the task graph which can be carried out by the compiler, and it is termed *pre-scheduling*. Before we describe how such problems can be avoided let us drama-tize the extend of performance degradation in the above example by analyzing its worst case. It is clear to see that the worst case happens for small J and L loops but let us derive the asymptotic value for the sake of completeness.

Let t_i, t_j, t_k and t_l denote the serial execution time of the four loops of Figure 3.2b which are to be executed on a p-processor machine. For simplicity assume that p divides exactly the number of loop iterations. Let t_{best} and t_{worst} denote the execution times for the best and the worst scenarios as they were described above. Then $\alpha = t_{best}/t_{worst}$ is an indicator of the performance degra-dation due to the bottleneck. After substitution we have

$$\alpha = \frac{t_j/p + \max(t_i/(p-1), t_k) + t_l/p}{t_i/p + t_j/p + t_k + t_l/p}. \tag{3.1}$$

Clearly $0 < \alpha \leq 1$ and α is maximized when $t_k = t_i/(p-1)$. After substitution and simplification in the above equation we get

$$\alpha = \frac{t_j + t_l + pt_k}{t_j + t_l + (2p-1)t_k}. \tag{3.2}$$

We can express t_j and t_l as functions of t_k with $t_j = c_1 t_k$ and $t_l = c_2 t_k$ where c_1, c_2 are arbitrary positive constants. After yet another substitution and simplification in (3.2) we finally get

$$\alpha = \frac{c_1 + c_2 + p}{c_1 + c_2 + (2p-1)}.$$

Hence, α reaches the worst value asymptotically which is

$$\alpha \rightarrow \frac{p}{2p-1}$$

when loops J and L are very small compared to I and K. Therefore, performance can degrade asymptotically by as much as 100% depending on the particular case.

Many different cases like the above can arise in a program graph. Worse yet, the effect of these bottlenecks is clearly cumulative. Fortunately, this type of bottlenecks (which is the only serious case) can be easily detected and eliminated by the compiler through a simple preprocessing of the task graph.

The partitioning phase gives us a graph representation of the program, $G(N, E)$, where N is the set of tasks (nodes) and E is the set of arcs representing precedence relations. A node in G is called *entry* node if it has no predecessors (or an indegree of 0). An *exit* node is one without successor nodes. G can be transformed to a graph with a single entry node n_{ent} by adding an empty node connected to all entry nodes, and an exit node n_{ext} connected from all exit nodes respectively.

Next, the nodes of G are labeled such that all nodes with the same label are independent and they form a layer. Since G is acyclic this can be done with a modified breadth-first-search (MBFS) traversal. The MBFS labeling algorithm is shown in Figure 3.3. The number of different node groups or layers is m and nodes within a layer are independent and thus can execute simultaneously without any restrictions.

After the layered representation of G is derived we compute the *maximum descend factor* or MDF for each node as follows. Let $L(n_i)$ be the label of node n_i, and $n_i^1, n_i^2, \ldots, n_i^k$ be the successor nodes of n_i. Then the *distance* of arc

---

Procedure MBFS
```
        Q ← empty;                start with empty queue
        1 ← 0;              label value 0
        for i←1 to n do
               L(n_i) ← 1;
        endfor
        Q ← Q ∪ {n_ent};
        L(n_ent) ← 1;
        while (Q not empty) do
                1 ← 1+1;
                q ←  a node from Q with indegree=0;
                Q ← Q-{q};
                for (all nodes n adjacent to q) do
                    L(n) ← max(L(n), 1);
                    Q ← Q ∪ {n};
                    Erase all arcs incident to this node;
                endfor
        endwhile
        m ← 1;
endMBFS
```

Figure 3.3. A modified BFS algorithm for labeling.

$e_i^j = (n_i, n_i^j)$ is defined to be

$$d(e_i^j) = L(n_i^j) - L(n_i)$$

and the maximum descend factor $\delta(n_i)$ of n_i is defined as

$$\delta(n_i) = \min_{1 \leq j \leq k} \{d(e_i^j)\}.$$

The descend factor gives an estimate of how much the execution of a task can be postponed. Delaying the execution of ready parallel tasks is the key to avoiding bottlenecks of the type described above. In fact there are two simple rules that eliminate the possibility of inefficient schedules:

- Give priority to serial (over parallel) tasks.
- Delay the execution of parallel tasks as long
  as machine utilization is kept at maximum levels.

The enforcement of these rules would forbid, for example, two large loops (i.e., large enough for each of them to fully utilize the system) from executing simultaneously. Thus in the example used earlier, loop I will not execute before loop J completes; but the potential problem still remains since I may execute to completion before loop K is scheduled. However, as shown below, serial tasks are given priority over parallel ones at the same layer. Therefore, in the same example, loop K will be initiated before I.

This delaying of parallel tasks is achieved by descending them to lower levels in the layered representation of G. Each node in n_i is pushed $\delta(n_i)$ layers down. Procedure **Descend** of Figure 3.4 shows how this is performed. Since the descend of a task may free other tasks to be delayed, the routine is recursively applied to parent nodes. Initially, the routine is applied to all nodes with an MDF greater than one. At completion all tasks in the graph have an MDF of one. An example is shown in Figure 3.5. Task T_4 is the only one with a $\delta_4 > 1$ and is pushed to level 4 (Figure 3.5b). As a result, T_2 is also pushed down one level to level 3 (Figure 3.5c). Parallel tasks that descend to lower levels serve as "work reservoirs" for cases where there is not enough work to fully utilize the machine. At some point during execution these tasks become free to run, but their execution is deliberately delayed as long as utilization is kept at maximum levels, and they are scheduled only if there are idle processors. It should be pointed out that the above procedure is equivalent to the latest–scheduling approach [Coff76].

Delaying of parallel tasks can be implemented by means of two ready-to–execute task queues, SQ and PQ. Serial tasks are queued in SQ while parallel tasks are queued in PQ. During execution, idle processors first check SQ for ready tasks. Only if SQ is empty a processor would try to dispatch a task from PQ. A software switch can be used to turn incoming processors to either queue. When a processor finds an empty SQ it sets the switch (displacement) so that idle processors are directed to PQ. The first processor to queue a new serial task in SQ is the one which resets the switch. Thus further execution of a parallel task which may be in progress, can be delayed temporarily in favor of newly arriving serial tasks.

Notice that the only information needed by the pre–scheduling phase is the type of tasks (serial/parallel), which is always known to the compiler. Let us take up

Procedure Descend (n_i^1)
        push node n_i^1 at level
        1 down δ_i^1 levels
if $(\delta_i^1 = 1)$ or $(n_i^1$ is serial$)$ **then** exit;
push down node n_i^1 to level $1+\delta_i^1-1$;
for (all predecessors $n_j^{1'}$ of n_i^1) **do**
        if $(\delta_j^{1'}=1-1')$ **then**
                    Recompute $\delta_j^{1'}$;
                    Descend $(n_j^{1'})$;
        endif
    endfor
EndDescend

Figure 3.4. The procedure for delaying the execution of parallel tasks.

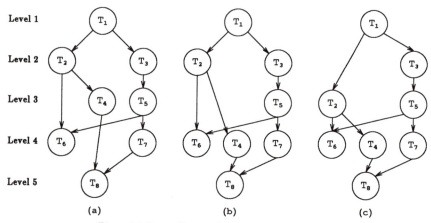

(a)   (b)   (c)

Figure 3.5. Descending parallel tasks at pre–scheduling.

again on the previous example. Suppose that loop J executes alone in the system, but at some point before its completion one processor becomes idle. That processor is directed to PQ and starts execution of loop I. However, as soon as loop J completes, the serial loop K is immediately queued in SQ. Then, according to the scheme described above, the next idle processor to come around will dispatch the serial loop from SQ while (presumably) the execution of I is in progress. Thus we achieve the desired overlap of I and K.

For the sake of completeness let us consider the only case under the above scheme during which loop K executes alone. This can happen under the following condition: Some processors of the machine become idle while the execution of I is still progressing on some other processors. This can happen due to two possibilities. Either the number of iterations of J is less than p and therefore the remaining processors are thrown to I, or some processors (previously busy on J) become idle and start on I. In either case (and since we assumed that K executes alone) it follows that the execution time is dominated by loops J and K while the parallelism of J is fully utilized. Thus the execution time of I is totally masked any way, and no performance gain can result from any overlap between the execution of I and K. In the following sections we see how the compiler can generate code to queue and execute tasks without the intervention of the operating system.

3.2.3. Run–Time Task Scheduling

After the partitioning and the pre–scheduling phases have been completed by the compiler, the next issue is the scheduling of the tasks which have been defined statically. This issue is the focus of this chapter and we discuss our approach in detail in Section 3.3. The choice here is either dynamic or static scheduling. Many arguments were given so far to justify our belief that at this level, dynamic scheduling is the most pragmatic approach. Therefore, our focus on this question is mostly on implementation. In dynamic scheduling the critical aspect is run–time overhead which dictates program and machine performance as well as the allowable level of task granularity.

Very few existing machines support dynamic scheduling of the tasks of a parallel program, and in these cases dynamic scheduling is implemented through the operating system. Motivated by the need to reduce or eliminate run–time overhead, we have proposed to implement dynamic scheduling through the compiler instead. This can be done by having the compiler generate drive–code for each task in a program, as part of the object code itself. The drive–code can keep track and update precedence relations, influence the allocation of processes at run–time, perform memory allocation and other bookkeeping operations. This does not necessarily imply elimination of the operating system or replication of operating system code in the user's program. However, during the parallel execution of a program invocations to the operating system can be eliminated. As illustrated in Section 3.3 the drive code is fairly simple and easy to generate. Thus for now, we assume that tasks are scheduled dynamically somehow and processors may be idle only when there are no ready–to–execute tasks in the queue.

3.2.4. Loop Scheduling

Since tasks are scheduled in a fully dynamic fashion, the next question of interest is what happens within a task. Serial tasks are treated as units of allocation and upon dispatching they are executed to completion. Hence the only type of tasks that allow for more manipulation are parallel tasks. In this section we consider specific aspects of scheduling the components (processes) of a parallel task. Of course parallelism can be exploited even within a single process in the form of low level spreading, vector instructions, etc. We will touch upon the issue of fine granularity parallelism exploitation in the next section.

Without loss in generality we can assume that a parallel task is always an arbitrarily complex nest of vector, parallel, and serial loops. In a parallel machine with vector processors it is always appropriate to have vectorizable innermost loops. Compiler transformations exist to interchange loops and create vector innermost loops [Wolf82]. Also, loop distribution [PaWo86] and loop coalescing [Poly87] can be used to breakdown a nest of loops to a set of one-way nested loops with a single DOALL component. Therefore nested parallelism can be exploited in all cases. The above process is not necessary but it justifies our approach of considering only a single DOALL at a time which in turn simplifies our discussion.

Even though task scheduling is performed dynamically, there are several ways of scheduling the iterations of a parallel loop, including static and dynamic approaches. In a static scheme the user or the compiler decides which iterations are allocated to a given processor. The only advantage offered by static allocation is the elimination of the run-time overhead associated with dynamic dispatching of iterations. However, the drawbacks of static scheduling are too many to consider it as a practical and general solution. It is efficient in cases where the number of processors and the number of loop iterations are known at compile-time, and all loop iterations have equal execution times. These parameters are rarely known simultaneously in practice.

Loops in numerical programs can be fairly complex with conditional statements and subroutine calls. A general solution should distribute iterations to processors at run-time based on the availability of processors and other factors. However, the overhead associated with run-time distribution must be kept very low for dynamic scheduling to be practical. We consider here three possible schemes for scheduling of loops. The first two are well-known and one or the other is used by most modern parallel machines. The third is a more efficient approach which was introduced in [PoKu87]. The three schemes differ in the number of loop iterations that they assign to each idle processor, and thus in the balancing of load and the total execution time. We consider each approach below.

3.2.4.1. One Iteration at a Time (Self–Scheduling)

This scheduling scheme is commonly referred to as *self-scheduling*. An idle processor picks a single iteration of a parallel loop by incrementing the loop indices in a synchronized way [Smit81], [TaYe86]. Thus if N is the total number of iterations of a loop, self-scheduling involves N dispatch operations. Roughly speaking, if p processors are involved in the execution of the loop, then each processor gets N/p iterations. Let B be the average iteration execution time and σ the overhead involved with each dispatch. Then self-scheduling is appropriate if $B \gg \sigma$ and there is a large variation of the execution time of different iterations. Because self-scheduling assigns one iteration at a time, it is the best dynamic scheme as far as load balancing is concerned. It was pointed out earlier however that a perfectly balanced load is meaningless if the overhead used to achieve it exceeds a certain threshold. Overall, self-scheduling may be appropriate for loops with relatively small number of iterations which have variable execution times and only if σ is small compared to B.

3.2.4.2. Chunk–Scheduling

A *chunk–scheduling* scheme is the same in principle as self–scheduling. But in this case, a fixed number of iterations (chunk) is allocated to each idle processor (as opposed to a single iteration). By doing so one can reduce the overhead by compromising load balancing. This is clear since the unit of allocation is of higher granularity now, and thus the potential variation of finish time among the processors is also higher. There is a clear tradeoff between load balancing and overhead. At one extreme, the chunk size is roughly N/p and each processor performs only one dispatch per loop. The variation of finish time is also the highest in this case. At the other extreme, the chunk size is one and we have self–scheduling with perfect load balancing and maximum overhead. Intermediate values of the chunk size in the range $[1 \ldots \lceil N/p \rceil]$ will produce results that are better or worse than either of the extreme cases. The main drawback of chunk–scheduling is the dependence of chunk size on the characteristics of each loop which are unknown even at run–time. Worse yet, even for the same loop, the execution time is not monotonous with monotonically increasing or decreasing chunk size. This makes the derivation of an optimal chunk size almost impossible even on a loop–by–loop case. To emphasize this weakness of chunk–scheduling let us consider the simplest case of a DOALL loop with N constant execution time iterations (B), which is to be executed on a system with p processors. Assuming all processors start at the same time, its parallel execution time T_p will be approximately

$$T_p = \frac{N}{kp}(kB + \sigma)$$

where k is the chunk size. The first derivative of T_p is $T_p' = -(N\sigma)/(k^2 p)$, which has neither global nor local extremes. Therefore, even for the simplest cases one cannot compute an "optimal" chunk size. A somewhat arbitrary approximation to T_p can yield an optimal chunk size. For example, let us rewrite T_p as

$$T_p = \left\lceil \frac{N}{kp} + 1 \right\rceil (kB + \sigma) . \tag{3.3}$$

Depending on the values of N, k, and p (3.3) can be exact or approximate. However, in this case $T_p' = (k^2 pB - N\sigma)/(k^2 p)$ which has a global extreme at

$$k = \sqrt{(N\sigma)/(pB)} .$$

One can easily verify that this extreme is a global minimum. But even these approximations may give us values which are far from the optimal one. We believe that chunk–scheduling should be avoided as a general loop scheduling policy.

Depending on the relative values of B, p, and σ chunk–scheduling may result in a slowdown (i.e., a parallel execution time which is greater than the serial) if k assumes values below some threshold. We call this threshold the *critical process size* or CPS. A conservative estimate of the CPS can be derived in general assuming we know a conservative value of the average iteration execution time B [Poly88b]. Then we can compute the minimum chunk size k for which $S_p > 1$, or equivalently,

$$S_p = \frac{NB}{\frac{N/k}{p}(kB + \sigma)} > 1.$$

After simplification we get

$$k > \frac{\sigma}{B(p - 1)}.$$

As one would expect, the chunk size is inversely proportional to the number of processors executing the loop. For example, if σ = B and p = 2 then at least k = 2 iterations should be allocated each time. The CPS is useful not only for chunk-scheduling but also for the other schemes discussed in this section.

3.2.4.3. Guided Self–Scheduling

Self–scheduling achieves a perfect load balancing but it also incurs maximum overhead. On the other hand chunk–scheduling is an (unsuccessful) attempt to reach a compromise between load balancing and overhead, and the result maybe quite unexpectable. The third scheme, *guided self–scheduling* (or GSS) [PoKu87], is in general, a much better and more stable approach to reach this compromise. The idea is to start the execution of a loop by allocating chunks of iterations whose size starts from $\lceil N/p \rceil$ and keeps decreasing until all the iterations are exhausted. The last p-1 chunks of iterations are of size one. Thus, chunk sizes vary between the two extremes. The guided self–scheduling algorithm is discussed analytically in the following chapter.

The advantages of GSS are many. First, as indicated in Chapter 4, the property of decreasing chunk size is buit–in and no extra computation is required to enforce this policy. This simplicity allows for easy and efficient implementation. Secondly, the two main objectives of perfectly balanced load and small overhead are achieved simultaneously. By allocating large chunks at the beginning of the loop we keep the frequent dispatching and thus the overhead low. At the same time, the small chunks at the end of the loop serve to "patch holes" and balance the load across all processors. For some ideal cases, GSS is provably optimal. This cannot be said for either self or chunk–scheduling. A large number of simulations that we have performed recently show a very significant performance gain due to GSS. Some of our (realistic) test loops were sped up by a factor of three or more using rather optimistic assumptions about run–time overhead.

For a parallel loop with N iterations the average number of dispatch operations per processor for self, chunk, and guided self–scheduling is N/p, N/kp, and $\log_e(N/p)$ respectively.

Another point of interest here is the difference in scheduling flexibility between DOALL and DOACR loops [Cytr86], [PoBa87]. By definition, the iterations of a DOALL loop can be scheduled and executed in any order. For example a DOALL may be scheduled vertically (in which case blocks of consecutive iterations are assigned to the same processor), or horizontally (where consecutive iterations are assigned to different processors). Any permutation of the index space is legal in the case of DOALLs. By contrast, a DOACR loop can be scheduled only horizontally. In a DOACR loop there are cross–iteration dependences between any pair of consecutive iterations. Thus vertical scheduling of a DOACR amounts to essentially executing that loop serially. This fundamental difference between DOALLs and DOACRs should be taken carefully into consideration during implementation of scheduling on parallel machines that support both types of loops.

3.2.5. Beyond Loops: Scalar, Vector, and VLIW Processors

More parallelism can be exploited within a processor, that is, within a process. The granularity of a process may range from medium to fine grain. Processes may be for example, one or more iterations of a scalar or even a vector loop, basic blocks or larger blocks of scalar code. A substantial amount of work has been done on the subject of low level parallelism [Nico84], [Vied85]. Traditional code optimizations aim at improving performance at this level [AhUS86]. Vector optimizations can also be applied at this point if necessary. Long instruction words can be packed within a process to accommodate for VLIW type of processors [Nico84].

One could argue that VLIW parallelism should be exploited starting at higher granularity levels. For example, instead of exploiting the structured parallelism of a loop as we discussed above, one could unroll loops and compile VLIWs by viewing an entire loop as a sequence of scalar instructions [Nico84]. However, so far there has not been a convincing study that either way is better than the other for VLIW or non-VLIW architectures.

As mentioned earlier, by parallel we imply a system that consists of several processors which can operate independently and which can be applied to the same program. In our view, scalar, vector and VLIW should refer to processor architecture rather than to system architecture. In other words, a machine with a single scalar, vector, or VLIW processor is not considered to be parallel even though it is capable of operating in SIMD or MIMD mode. In general, neither vector nor VLIW (probably) processors can utilize the parallelism of a program to the maximum possible degree. However, in principle, an ideal parallel machine can achieve the aforementioned goal (irrespectively of the architecture of the processor–components). Put in other words, if one could conceive the ideal machine which could exploit all the parallelism in any program, our conjecture is that this machine would be "parallel". This is certainly true for vector machines (with infinite number of vector units) and it is probably true for VLIW machines (with infinitely long instruction words). One could view parallel architectures as orthogonal to scalar, vector, or VLIW architectures. In a sense, when it comes to maximum performance parallel architectures seem to be irreplaceable. If we filter out technology and cost considerations and focus on comparable ideal architectures, then a question of interest is which system is more powerful on the average: a parallel/vector or a parallel/VLIW with the same number of processors?

In what follows we focus on large to medium granularity tasks and ignore fine granularity parallelism which is highly processor architecture dependent.

3.3. AUTO–SCHEDULING COMPILERS

One of the motivations behind auto–scheduling compilers (ASC) is to eliminate or greatly reduce the overhead associated with system calls during program execution. Invoking the operating system to perform scheduling at the task level severly limits our ability to exploit parallelism at medium granularity levels.

An auto–scheduling compiler would eliminate most (if not all) of the functions of the operating system pertaining to task creation, scheduling, execution, and deletion. At the same time an auto–scheduling compiler will generate *drive code* as part of the object code. Thus, a program will not only perform its intended calculations but it will distribute and drive itself during execution.

At this point we should underline the experimental nature of this project. Even though the idea of auto–scheduling compilers seems both attractive and feasible, the lack of experimental data and a real system to support our position does not allow us to make any performance claims. With this in mind let us try to analyze the advantages and disadvantages of a hypothetical auto–scheduling compiler.

3.3.1. Possible Advantages & Disadvantages

As mentioned earlier an ASC will bring about "some" reduction in the overhead associated with the parallel execution of tasks. Qualifying the term "some" is impossible at present but we expect it to be quite significant. This overhead reduction can be interpreted in many ways. First, it means that finer granularity tasks can be created and executed efficiently. This will allow us to execute faster existing parallel programs, or equivalently, to build machines with more processors and use them to execute parallel programs more efficiently. Secondly, a higher utilization could be achieved on existing parallel systems. Another benefit would be our ability to execute in parallel certain programs that otherwise would execute serially (due to the high overhead incurred in traditional systems).

Another advantage of an auto–scheduling compiler would be its ability to optimize the drive–code itself. As it is demonstrated below, the drive code depends on the type of tasks involved as well as the topology of the task graph. An operating system does not have knowledge of program characteristics, and hence it performs the most general function whenever invoked. In an ASC the generation of drive code will be done in a customized way and thus it would be more efficient. Finally, debugging for parallel programs may become easier through an ASC. This is true because it becomes easier to keep track of resource allocation and order of execution in such a system.

Potential disadvantages include protection and multiprogramming. Our initial assumption disallows time sharing. However, different programs can still run on physically different processor partitions. In such a case the lack of a supervisory system makes it difficult to detect user space violations.

3.3.2. A General Framework

Our concept of an auto–scheduling compiler was shown in Figure 3.1. The partitioner decomposes a program into tasks as it was explained in Section 3.2.1. The next phase is pre–scheduling where the task graph is reorganized to reduce the possibility of bottlenecks (Section 3.2.2). The function of the drive–code generator and optimizer (DCGO) module is to generate custom drive code for each task based on the type of the task and its position in the task graph. All program information necessary to perform this is readily available to the DCGO module. Optimization of the drive code is also based on available program information. We assume that the hardware supports synchronization primitives such as FETCH_&_ADD or FETCH_&_DECR [ZhYe84], [GGKM83]. Hardware support of powerful

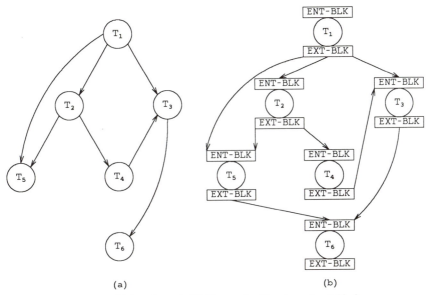

(a) (b)

Figure 3.6. (a) A task graph. (b) The graph with entry and exit blocks.

synchronization primitives can make the task of enforcing order of execution easier and more efficient.

Two blocks of code are generated by the DCGO for each task, an *entry-block* (ENT-BLK) and an *exit-block* (EXT-BLK) (Figure 3.6). The entry block allocates local and shared task variables (in the case of parallel tasks), and performs other implementation–specific functions such as the binding of user to virtual tasks. The entry–block of a parallel task is executed only by the first processor to work on that task.

A task exit–block performs the following three functions, *task deallocation, dependence elimination,* and *new task creation.* Task deallocation involves the elimination of the corresponding entry from the queue (and depending on the implementation, the deallocation of virtual tasks). Dependence elimination updates precedence relations of depending tasks. Finally, new task creation activates new tasks by queueing them to the ready–task queue.

Besides generating the object code, an auto–scheduling compiler also generates another representation of a program consisting of a set of templates called *images,* each corresponding to a specific task. Part of each image is a pointer to the starting address of the actual task code. Only images are queued in the ready–task queue. To facilitate easy manipulation of the queue, images are of fixed size.

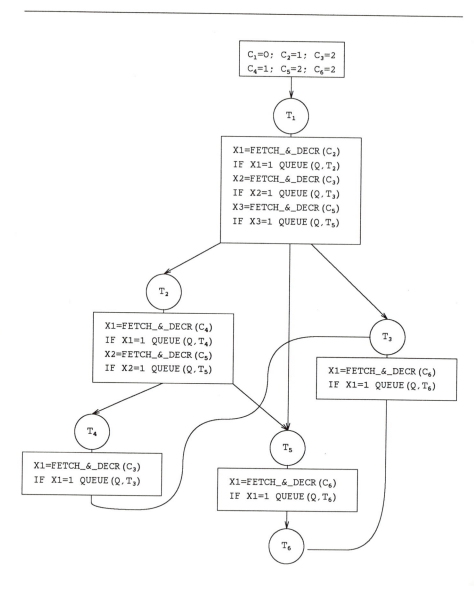

Figure 3.7. The graph of Figure 3.6b with exit–blocks.

In a simplified scenario each physical processor executes the following loop.

```
LOOP FOREVER
     - pick front queue image;
     - load program counter;
     - execute;
END LOOP
```

Recall that part of task execution involves the execution of the drive–code in the task exit–block which updates other tasks and queues their corresponding images. A typical task exit–block which is shown below

---

EXIT–BLOCK:

Task–dependent module:

```
-Barrier synchronization;
-Select processor to dequeue current task;
-Select processor to execute the following;
```

Task–independent module:

```
FOR (all successors of current task) DO
     -Update (dependences of) successors;
     -Queue freed successors;
ENDFOR
```

---

consists of two modules, the task–dependent and task–independent modules. The former is code that the compiler generates to perform barrier synchronization (in the case of parallel tasks), select the processor to dequeue the corresponding task from the queue (e.g., the processor to dispatch the last iteration of a loop), and select the processor to execute the second module of the exit–block (in a parallel task that processor will be the one to clear the barrier). The latter module is independent of the type of the task. Only a specific processor (selected by the first module) executes this part. The code in this module updates the precedence relations and queues those successors that have no pending predecessors.

Similarly, entry–blocks are organized in two modules, a task–independent and a task–dependent module as shown below.

ENTRY–BLOCK:

Task–independent module:

```
-Allocate private variables and/or stack space;
-Copy parent stack (optional);
```

Task–dependent module:

```
-Execute initialization code (if any);
-Compute number of iterations for this processor;
-Update loop indices;
```

If all variables and structures are allocated statically, then stack allocation for each task is unnecessary. Depending on the implementation, copying part of the parent's stack may also be avoided by, for example, passing a pointer to a child's stack that points to the appropriate location in the parent's stack. Similarly, the initialization code phase can be eliminated if a separate image (task) is associated with the serial initialization code. Initialization code is common in parallel loops. Consider for example a double nonperfectly nested loop with a serial outer and a parallel inner loop. The code between the outer and the inner loop is to be executed only by the first processor that starts on the loop. This code can be considered as a separate serial task. The processor that enqueues this in SQ is the same one to queue the image corresponding to the innerloop in PQ. Therefore, by definition, no processor can start on the innerloop before the initialization code is executed.

Another activity of the task–dependent module is to compute the number of iterations which must be allocated to the next processor, and update accordingly the loop index(es). Consider for example a DOALL with N iterations. If it is to be executed under self–scheduling, then the compiler will generate the following code

```
X = FETCH_&_ADD(loop_index, 1);
IF (X+1 > N) THEN EXIT;
        . . . .
        loop body
        . . . .
```

where FETCH_&_ADD is assumed to update the shared variable after it is read. If the same loop is to be executed under chunk–scheduling, then the corresponding piece of code would be

```
X = FETCH_&_ADD(loop_index, k);
IF (X > N) THEN EXIT;
        . . . .
        DO I = X, min(N, X+k)
            loop body
        ENDO
        . . . .
```

Finally, if the same loop was scheduled using guided self–scheduling, one possible way of computing the number of iterations allocated to each processor is shown below. Initially, R = N and J = 1.

```
Lock (R)
     temp = ⌈R/p⌉;
     R = R - temp;
Unlock (R)
X = FETCH_&_ADD(J, temp);
DO I = X, X+temp
     loop body
ENDO
    . . . .
```

When GSS is used, there are many different ways of generating the second module of the corresponding ENT-BLK. In the case above, R is locked until the computation of the number of iterations and the update are complete. This is not necessary as shown in the following alternative implementation.

```
old = R;
temp = ⌈old/p⌉;
new = FETCH_&_DECR(R, temp);
IF (old <> new) THEN FETCH_&_ADD(R, temp) EXIT;
X = FETCH_&_ADD(J, temp);
DO I = X, X+temp
     loop body
ENDO
    . . . .
```

Notice that when several processors make a simultaneous read of R in the above implementation, at least one processor will go through with the dispatch. There are more alternatives, but the best one depends on the type of synchronization mechanisms supported by the hardware.

In the next section we show how the compiler can generate code to enforce precedence relations during execution.

3.3.3. Enforcing Task Execution Order

In this section we show how precedence relations (dependences) can be enforced between tasks through an auto–scheduling compiler. Figure 3.6 shows how a task graph would be transformed to an abstract self–driven program by having the DCGO module add entry–blocks (ENT-BLK) and exit–blocks (EXT-BLK) in each task (Figure 3.6b). Part of the exit–blocks will be the code which is responsible for enforcing order of execution.

Recall that each task is formed at compile–time. The compiler also allocates a *counter* for each task in the program. All counters are allocated and initialized by the compiler. In order to better illustrate the process we assume that the compiler generates initialization code for the counters and inserts it at the beginning of the program (in a real case this code will not appear in the object code). Figure 3.7 shows how the graph of Figure 3.6 will be augmented with the precedence enforcing code. The counter initialization code is shown in the first box. Each counter is initialized to a value which is equal to the number of predecessors of the corresponding node.

Precedence enforcing code is generated as follows. For each task T_i in the program the compiler generates exit–block code which decrements the value of the counter for each task T_j which is dependent on T_i. This decrement operation is performed in a synchronized way. After each decrement operation in an exit–block, code is generated to check whether that counter has become zero. If so, the corresponding task is queued in the ready–task queue. More specifically, for each precedence arc $e = (T_i, T_j)$ in the task graph, the following code is generated for the exit–block of T_j.

```
temp = FETCH_&_DECR(C_j);
IF (temp=1) QUEUE(Q, T_j);
```

Figure 3.7 shows the precedence enforcing code for each task in the graph of Figure 3.6b.

Thus order of execution is enforced through explicit synchronization generated by the compiler as part of the exit–blocks. It is clear that all information required to initialize counters and generate the appropriate instructions is available to the compiler. As a matter of comparison, the Cray machines achieve the same result through the explicit use of run–time routines such as *ctswait()*. One such function call is required for each arc in the abstract task graph.

3.3.4. Optimizing the Drive Code

Of course, initialization of counters and generation of drive code cannot be done correctly based on data dependence information alone. Control flow information must be used to avoid possible deadlocks. Deadlocks may occur depending on whether or not conditional statements are represented as autonomous tasks or are embedded inside other tasks. Consider for example three tasks T_1, T_2 and T_3 such that T_3 is data dependent on the other two neither of which dominates the other. Then if $C_3 = 2$ and since T_1 and T_3 are exclusive we have a deadlock. Such cases can be detected and corrected easily by consulting the flow graph or the dominance tree [AhSU86].

Let us consider now what types of optimizations can be applied on the precedence enforcing code of the exit–blocks. There are three simple optimizations that can decrease the number of instructions in exit–blocks significantly: *elimination of redundant decrements, synchronization,* and *queueing operations.* We discuss each of them by using the task graph of Figure 3.7 as a running example. Although most of the optimizations discussed below can be performed during the generation of exit–blocks we discuss each of them separately starting from exit–blocks which are generated in a "brute–force" manner. In reality however one pass through the task graph will suffice to perform all these optimizations.

3.3.4.1. Eliminating Redundant Decrements

Elimination of redundant decrements from the exit–blocks is equivalent to elimination of precedence arcs. It is clear that all transitive precedence arcs can be eliminated from the task graph without compromising the correct order of execution. A path in the task graph is defined as a sequence of tasks T_i, T_{i+1}, ..., T_{i+n} such that there is a precedence arc from T_{i+j} to T_{i+j+1} for all $(j = 0, 1, ..., n)$.

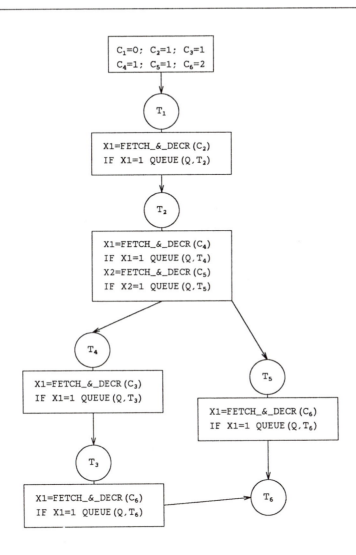

Figure 3.8. The graph of Figure 3.7 after elimination of redundant precedence arcs.

The length of the path is defined to be one less than the number of nodes (n above). A precedence arc e from task T_i to task T_j is said to be *transitive* if there is a path from T_i to T_j of length two or more. Transitive precedence constraints do not have to be explicitly enforced. They are always satisfied by definition. Hence, all transitive precedence arcs can be eliminated without affecting the correct order of execution.

An algorithm similar to the MBFS shown in Figure 3.3 can be used to eliminate transitive dependence arcs. The elimination of transitive arcs must be followed by a corresponding update of the counter variables as well as by the elimination of decrement instructions in the exit–blocks. More specifically, for each eliminated arc $e = (T_i, T_j)$ the following must also be done. The initial value of counter C_j (corresponding to T_j) is decremented by one. The conditional synchronized decrement of C_j instruction from the exit–block of task T_i is eliminated. Together is eliminated the conditional queue (Q, T_j) instruction from the same exit–block.

Using the above in the example of Figure 3.7 results in the elimination of arcs (T_1, T_5) and (T_1, T_3) and the corresponding code from their exit–blocks. The resulting graph is shown in Figure 3.8.

3.3.4.2. Eliminating Redundant Synchronization

The decrement operations on the counters must be synchronized only if the corresponding task has more than one predecessor tasks. However, if a task has only one predecessor the decrement operation in its predecessor exit–block does not need to be synchronized; as a matter of fact the entire decrement operation is superfluous. Thus for all nodes with a single predecessor (indegree of 1) we eliminate the FETCH_&_DECR instruction from the exit–block of their predecessor task. At the same time we decrement their corresponding counter variable. Nodes with indegree of one can also result from the removal of transitive arcs as discussed above. The resulting task graph of Figure 3.8 after eliminating redundant FETCH_&_DECRs is shown in Figure 3.9.

3.3.4.3. Eliminating Unnecessary Queueing Operations

Since parallel tasks are usually executed by more than one physical processor, their corresponding image must be queued. Serial tasks however need not be queued. The first processor to find the counter (of a serial task) to be equal to zero, can proceed with the actual execution of that task. By the definition of our framework, that physical processor would be the same one to otherwise queue the task. Bypassing the queue in such a case is an easy implementation detail. In general this is not possible since a particular task may have several successor serial tasks. Nevertheless there are the following two cases where elimination of the QUEUE operation is always beneficial.

The first case is a pair of adjacent tasks T_i and T_j, such that T_j is serial and depends on T_i, and the outdegree of T_i and indegree of T_j are both one. In this case the processor which would otherwise queue T_j can proceed with its execution. Notice that this will be (one of) the processor(s) that executed (part of) T_i. The second case where the queue can be bypassed without performance loss is as above but with any number of successors for T_i. That is, T_i can have any number of successors but one of them (T_j) is a serial task with a single predecessor. In this case however, *all*

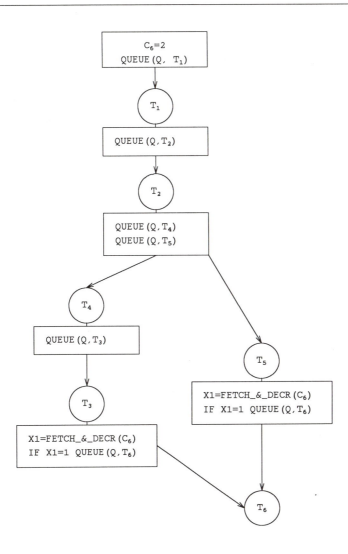

Figure 3.9. The graph of Figure 3.8 after elimination of redundant decrements and queueings.

successor tasks of T_i must be updated/queued before continuing execution with T_j. This is easily done by generating all the update/queue instructions in the exit–block of T_i before control is transferred to T_j. If T_i has a number of successors that fulfil the above condition, the compiler can choose any one of them. Notice that the elimination of queueing operations in these cases is in line with our policy of giving priority to serial tasks.

Finally, for each task T_i whose corresponding counter value is zero, the compiler inserts a QUEUE (Q, T_i) in the initial–block. This queues all tasks without predecessors at the beginning of program execution. All assignments of 0 or 1 values to counter variables in the initial–block are also eliminated and the variables deallocated.

CHAPTER 4

STATIC AND DYNAMIC LOOP SCHEDULING

4.1. INTRODUCTION

Loops are the largest potential source of program parallelism and the problem of using several processors for the fast execution of complex parallel loops has attracted considerable attention in the last few years [PoKu87], [PoKP86], [TaPe86], [KrWe85], [PaKL80], [Cytr84]. A key problem in designing and using large parallel processor systems is determining how to schedule independent processors to execute a parallel program as fast as possible. In this chapter we present a practical method that can be used to obtain very efficient schedules of parallel loops on shared memory parallel machines. The problem of mapping or assigning different tasks of the same program to different processors (otherwise known as "scheduling") has become more pressing than ever before with the recent introduction of many parallel machines in the market.

As we discussed in the previous chapter, existing methods are not adequate because they consider an idealized form of the problem where task execution times are fixed and known in advance, and they ignore "side–effects" (interprocessor communication and synchronization). In reality, however, branching statements in programs, memory access interference, random processor latencies and other "random events" make task execution times impossible to predict accurately in general. Furthermore, side–effects have a very important impact on scheduling. The complexity of the scheduling problem has lead the computing community to adopt heuristic approaches for each new machine. In many cases [Cray85] the problem is entirely left to the user, and it is well known that hand–coding and manually inserting system calls in a program are necessary to achieve high performance.

On the other hand it is difficult or impossible to find a universal solution for problems such as scheduling, minimization of interprocessor communication, and synchronization. This is so because these problems are often architecture dependent. Thus a solution which is efficient for one machine organization may be inefficient for another. We believe however that more general solutions can be found for large classes of machine architectures. It is also clear that the complexity of these problems necessitates an automatic solution by the compiler, the operating system, or by the hardware.

Here we discuss guided self–scheduling (GSS), a method for executing parallel loops on parallel processor systems. The GSS method not only generates efficient (load balanced) schedules, but it also reduces substantially (and often minimizes) the number of synchronized accesses to loop indices, an expensive operation on many shared memory parallel machines [ZhPL83]. As shown later GSS can be easily automated and should be efficient for most shared memory parallel processor systems.

In this chapter we are primarily concerned with DOALL and FORALL loops (i.e., DOALLs with cross–iteration forward dependences). Since synchronization makes FORALLs appear as DOALLs we consider both types of loops to be DOALLs. A *one–way* nested loop with nest depth k, denoted by $L = (N_1, \ldots, N_k)$, has exactly one loop at each nest level, where N_i, ($i = 1, \ldots, k$) is the number of iterations of the loop at the i-th level. A *multi–way* nested loop has at least two loops at some nest level. Nested loops that contain combinations of DOALL, DOACR, and DOSERIAL loops are called *hybrid*.

Loop coalescing can be used to transform multiple one–way nested loops into singly nested loops, as shown in the previous chapter. This transformation is useful for self–scheduling of parallel loops. The overhead associated with the access of loop indices is reduced sharply in many cases when loop coalescing is applied. Another transformation that can be useful in our case is loop distribution. It is useful for transforming multi–way nested loops to one–way nested. Thus when coalescing is applied in conjunction with loop distribution multi–way nested loops can also be transformed into single loops. Another transformation which can also be useful here is loop interchange.

4.1.1. Parallel Loops

Because of the well–defined structure of loop tasks, scheduling of such constructs is less complicated. Furthermore it has been shown that parallel loops account for the greatest percentage of program parallelism [Kuck84]. Therefore designing low–overhead methods for the efficient allocation of parallel loops is crucial to machine performance.

Due to high run–time overhead, the first parallel processor machines (e.g., Cray X–MP with multitasking) looked for parallelism at the subroutine level; parallelism at the loop level was too expensive to exploit. Soon thereafter Cray systems employed microtasking [Rein85] that now can be used to utilize parallelism at the loop level. The microtasking library is a tool supplied to the user, but how to use it effectively is again the user's responsibility. One of the few commercial systems that can schedule parallel loops automatically is the Alliant FX/8 multiprocessor. The machine consists of a set of computational processors each with pipelined arithmetic units. Thus parallel loops with vector statements can fully utilize the concurrency features of this system. Different iterations of parallel loops are assigned to different processors. Below we show why this scheme is inefficient. Again up to two levels of parallelism can be utilized by the Alliant FX/8. On future systems with large numbers of processors it will be necessary to exploit multidimensional parallelism, i.e., execute several nested loops concurrently.

A straightforward practice that has been widely discussed by users and system designers, is exploiting the parallelism in DOALL loops by allocating successive iterations to successive processors. Depending on the implementation, this scheme can be anywhere from suboptimal to very inefficient. Thus, in a system with p processors it is common to execute a DOALL loop with $N > p$ iterations in the following way: Iteration 1 is assigned to processor 1, iteration 2 to processor 2, ..., iteration p to processor p, iteration $p + 1$ to processor 1 and so on. Therefore processor i will execute iterations i, $i + p$, $i + 2p$, ... However it is more efficient to make the assignment so that a block of successive iterations is allocated to the same processor. For example in the above case it would be more wise to assign iterations $1, 2, \ldots, \lceil N/p \rceil$ to the first processor, iterations $\lceil N/p \rceil + 1$, $\lceil N/p \rceil + 2$, $\ldots, 2 \lceil N/p \rceil$ to the second processor and so on. Memory interleaving can not be brought up as an argument against the latter approach since memory allocation can be done to best facilitate scheduling in either case.

There are several advantages that favor the second approach of assigning iterations to processors. When iterations of a parallel loop are assigned to processors by blocks of successive iterations, each processor does not have to check the value of the loop index each time it executes an iteration. Recall that the loop index is a shared variable and each processor must lock and unlock a semaphore in order to be granted access to it and get the next iteration. In case all processors finish simultaneously they will all access the loop index serially going through a time consuming process. In the worst case a time delay equivalent to the time required for N accesses to a shared variable will be added to at least one processor. If the assignment of blocks of iterations is performed instead, this worst case delay will be equivalent to only p accesses to the shared loop index. For a large N and a small p this will result in a substantial savings, considering the fact that each access to the loop index will have to go through the processor–to–memory network. Note that the number of accesses to the loop index is independent of N in our case. Another advantage of this scheme is that when we execute FORALL loops in parallel, the block assignment can be done so that the cross–iteration dependences are contained within one block and the dependences are therefore satisfied by virtue of the assignment. Thus synchronization needs to be used only selectively which, in certain cases, may result in shorter execution times. In what follows the second method is used, that is, whenever a parallel loop (excluding DOACRs) is executed on several processors, the allocation will be done so that each processor is assigned a block of successive iterations.

4.1.2. Self–Scheduling Through Implicit Coalescing

Most of the schemes that have been proposed so far [KrWe85], [TaPe86], implement self–scheduling by making extensive use of synchronization instructions. For example in [TaPe86] a barrier synchronization is associated with each loop in the construct. In addition all accesses to loop indices are, by necessity, synchronized. Another common characteristic of these schemes is that they assign only one loop iteration to each incoming idle processor. Our scheme differs in all aspects discussed above. Only one barrier per serial loop is used. Furthermore, independently of the nest pattern and the number of loops involved we need synchronized access to only a single loop index. In contrast the above schemes need synchronized access to a number of indices which is equal to the number of loops in the construct.

Self–scheduling can become more effective by using loop coalescing (Chapter 2). The key characteristic of this transformation which is useful here, is its ability to express all indices in a loop nest as a function of a single index. This makes it clear why synchronized access to each loop index is wasteful. We can always use a single index. If the loop bounds are known at run–time just before we enter the loop, we may decide exactly how many iterations each processor will receive. Thus when a processor accesses the single loop index to dispatch a range of consecutive iterations, it goes through a single synchronization point. Since the range of iterations is determined before–hand, each processor will dispatch all the work it is responsible for, the very first time it accesses the corresponding loop index. Therefore only a total of p synchronization instructions will be executed. As a matter of comparison, in the schemes mentioned above each processor executes a synchronization instruction for each loop in the nest, and each time it dispatches a new iteration. In a nested loop that consists of m separate loops we would then have a total of $m \prod_{i=1}^{m} N_i$ synchronization instructions that will execute before the loop completes. The difference between p and $m \prod_{i=1}^{m} N_i$ can obviously be tremendous. The schemes in [TaPe86] and [KrWe85] for example, involve an overhead which is unbounded on p. In the general case however where loops contain conditional statements the assignment of $\lceil N/p \rceil$ iterations to each processor will compromise load balancing. Therefore we need something in between which will involve less overhead than self–scheduling, but it will also achieve load balancing.

4.2. THE GUIDED SELF–SCHEDULING (GSS(k)) ALGORITHM

This scheme is simple, yet powerful for dynamic scheduling. The idea is to implement *Guided Self–Scheduling* with bound k (GSS(k)), by "guiding" the processors on the amount of work they choose. The *bound* is defined to be the minimum number of loop iterations assigned to a given processor by GSS. The algorithm is discussed below in great detail and is summarized for k=1 in Figure 4.3. First we present the case of k=1, GSS(1) or GSS for short, and later we discuss the general case for k > 1. The GSS algorithm achieves optimal execution times in many cases. Actually optimality is achieved in two dimensions. First, assuming that synchronization overhead is counted as part of a loop's execution time, GSS obtains optimal load

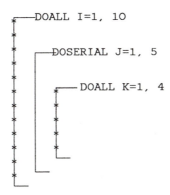

```
┌──DOALL  I=1,  10
│
│   ┌──DOSERIAL  J=1,  5
│   │
│   │   ┌── DOALL  K=1,  4
│   │   │
│   │   │
│   │   │
│   │   │
│   │   └─
│   │
│   └─
│
└─
```

Figure 4.1. Example loop for the application of GSS.

balancing between processors and thus optimal execution time. At the same time GSS uses the minimum number of synchronization instructions that are needed to guarantee optimal load balancing.

4.2.1. Implicit Loop Coalescing and Interchange

Let us describe in more detail how self–scheduling through implicit loop coalescing works. First, assume that we have a perfectly (one–way) nested loop $L = (N_1, \ldots, N_m)$. Loop coalescing coalesces all m loops into a single loop $L' = (N = \prod_{i=1}^{m} N_i)$ through a set of transformations f that map the index I of the coalesced loop L' to the indices I_i, (i=1, 2, ..., m) of the original loop L such that $I_i = f_i(I)$, (i=1, 2, ..., m). This transformation is needed to express indices of array subscripts, (that occur in the original loop body) as functions of the index I of the coalesced loop. Thus, a reference to an array element of the form $A(I_1, I_2, \ldots, I_m)$ in L can be uniquely expressed as $A(f_1(I), f_2(I), \ldots, f_m(I))$ in L' using the above transformation. Therefore each processor can compute locally f_i for a given I. Better yet, each processor can compute locally a range of values $f(x:y)$ for a range of $x \leq I \leq y$. The global index I is then kept in the shared memory as a shared variable. Each processor accesses I in a synchronized way and dispatches the next set of consecutive iterations of L along with a pointer to its code. Then inside each processor, mappings f_i as defined by (2.11) are used to compute the corresponding range for each index I_i of the original loop. After the index ranges are computed for each processor, execution proceeds in the normal mode. In case all loops in L are parallel and in the absence of conditional statements, no processor will ever go back to dispatch another range of iterations of

I. This is obviously the minimum possible amount of synchronization that is needed with any self–scheduling scheme.

The process is more complicated with self–scheduling of hybrid loops. Let us look at the case of hybrid loops that consist of DOALLs and DOSERIAL loops, and in particular consider the example of Figure 4.1. In this example the innermost and outermost loops are DOALLs and the second is a serial loop. Let us denote this loop with $L = (N_1, N_2, N_3) = (10, 5, 4)$. We have a total of $N=200$ iterations. On a machine with an unlimited number of processors (200 in this case) each processor would execute 5 iterations of L, and this is the best possible that we can achieve. On a system with p processors self–scheduling should be done such that iterations of L are evenly distributed among the p processors (assuming an equal execution time for all iterations). The presence of the serial loop in L however limits our ability to do this. It is noteworthy that the approach of assigning consecutive iterations of I to each processor would fail here. (This is true because after coalescing we have a single iteration space and assignments are done in blocks of consecutive iterations.) At most 4 successive iterations may be assigned at once. If all 4 are given to the same processor, the loop is executed serially. If each processor receives one iteration on the other hand, we can use only up to 4 processors.

This problem can be eliminated by permuting the indices of the original loop, or equivalently, by applying implicit loop interchange [Wolf82]. Our goal is to permute the indices so that the longest possible set of parallel iterations corresponds to successive values of the index I of L. This can be done by permuting the indices I and J so that the serial loop becomes the outermost loop or by permuting J and K so that the serial becomes the innermost loop — which would violate dependences in this case. In general a serial loop can be interchanged with any DOALL that surrounds it, but it cannot be interchanged with a loop surrounded by it. Therefore in the case of our example we implicitly interchange loops I and J.

The interchange can be implemented trivially using implicit coalescing as follows. The mappings of I and J are permuted such that I is defined by the mapping of J and vice versa. No physical loop interchange takes place (neither physical coalescing). More specifically, if I_c is the global index of the coalesced loop for the example loop of Figure 4.1, then the original indices I, J and K are mapped to I_c by (1) as follows

$$I = \left\lceil \frac{I_c}{20} \right\rceil - 10 \left\lfloor \frac{I_c - 1}{200} \right\rfloor$$

$$J = \left\lceil \frac{I_c}{4} \right\rceil - 5 \left\lfloor \frac{I_c - 1}{20} \right\rfloor$$

$$K = I_c - 4 \left\lfloor \frac{I_c - 1}{4} \right\rfloor.$$

After implicit loop interchange the mappings become:

$$I = \left\lceil \frac{I_c}{4} \right\rceil - 10 \left\lfloor \frac{I_c - 1}{40} \right\rfloor$$

$$J = \left\lceil \frac{I_c}{40} \right\rceil - 5 \left\lfloor \frac{I_c - 1}{200} \right\rfloor$$

$$K = I_c - \left\lfloor \frac{I_c - 1}{4} \right\rfloor .$$

The result is that the first 40 successive values of I_c correspond now to 40 parallel iterations (instead of 4 iterations previously). Therefore up to 40 processors can be used in parallel. Extra synchronization is still needed however. Each serial loop in L needs a barrier synchronization to enforce its seriality. The following proposition tells us when it is legal to apply loop interchange in order to maximize the number of consecutive parallel iterations.

Proposition 4.1. In a hybrid perfectly nested loop, any DOALL can be interchanged with any serial or DOACR loop that is in a deeper nest level. This loop interchange can be applied repeatedly and independently for any pair of (DOALL, DOSERIAL/DOACR) loops.

Proof: The proof is clear for the case of two loops. The general case follows by induction on the number of loops interchanged. ∎

The only case that remains to be discussed is nonperfectly (multi–way) nested loops. This is identical to the one–way nested loop case, unless one of the following two conditions is met. 1) Loops at the same nest level have different loop bounds. 2) High level spreading is to be applied to loops at the same nest level (i.e., loops at the same nest level are executed in parallel). In the first case, if k loops N_{i+1}, N_{i+2}, . . . , N_{i+k} happen to be at the i–th nest level, the global index I_c is computed with N_i iterations for the i–th level, which is given by

$$N_i = \max_{1 \le j \le k} \{N_{i+j}\} .$$

Then during execution, loop N_{i+j} at the i–th level will have $N_i - N_{i+j}$ null iterations (which are not actually computed). Therefore some of the processors execute only part of the code at level i. This corresponds to computing slices of each loop on the same processor. Thus slices of the two loops corresponding to the same index values will be assigned to each idle processor. In general if loops at the same nest level are independent or involve dependences in only one direction, outer loops can be distributed [KKPL81] around them and each loop is considered separately (i.e., we coalesce each of them and consider them as separate tasks). When there are bidirectional dependences across loops at the same nest level, barrier synchronization can be used as mentioned above. If high level spreading is to be applied, then implicit loop coalescing and a global index I_c will be computed for each loop that is spread.

4.2.2. The Scheduling Algorithm

So far we have seen how GSS coalesces the loops and assigns blocks of iterations to incoming (idle) processors. We have not mentioned however how the algorithm decides the number of iterations to be assigned to each idle processor. The schemes that have been proposed so far [Allia85], [KrWe85], [Smith81], [TaPe86] assign a single iteration at a time. For nested loops with many iterations this approach involves a tremendous amount of overhead since several critical regions must be accessed each time a single iteration is dispatched. The GSS algorithm follows another approach by assigning several iterations (or an *iteration block*) to each processor. The size of each block varies and is determined by using a simple but powerful rule that is described below. Before we describe how block sizes are computed let us state our constraints.

Suppose that a parallel loop L (e.g., a DOALL) is to be executed on p processors. We assume that each of the p processors starts executing some iteration(s) of L at different times (i.e., not all p processors start computing L simultaneously). This is clearly a valid and practical assumption. If L for example is not the first loop in the program, the processors will be busy executing other parts of the program before they start on L. Therefore, in general, they will start executing L at different times which may vary significantly. (Of course one could force all p processors to start on L at the same time by enforcing a join (or barrier) operation before L; this would clearly be very inefficient.) Given now the assumption that the p processors will start executing L at arbitrary times, our goal is to dispatch a block of consecutive iterations of L to each incoming processor such that all processors terminate at approximately the same time. This is a very desirable property. If L_d for example is nested inside a serial loop L_s, then a barrier synchronization must be performed each time L_d completes (i.e., for each iteration of L_s). If the processors working on L_d do not terminate at the same time, a very significant amount of idle processor time (overhead) may be accumulated by the time L_s completes.

In general the best possible solution is that which guarantees that all p processors will terminate with at most B units of time difference from each other; where B is the execution time of the loop body of L. This goal can be achieved if blocks of iterations are assigned to idle processors following the next principle. An incoming processor p_i^x will dispatch a number of iterations x_i considering that the remaining p-1 processors will also be scheduled at this (same) time. In other words p_i^x should leave enough iterations to keep the remaining p-1 processors busy (in case they all decide to start simultaneously) while it will be executing its x_i iterations. If N is the total number of iterations, this can be easily done as follows. Since GSS coalesces loops, there will be a single index $I_c = 1 \ldots N$, from which idle processors will dispatch blocks of iterations. Therefore the assignment of iteration blocks is done by having each idle processor p_i perform the following operations:

$$x_i = \left\lceil \frac{R_i}{p} \right\rceil \; ; \qquad R_{i+1} \leftarrow R_i - x_i, \qquad (4.1)$$

and the range of iterations assigned to the i-th processor is given by $[N - R_i + 1, \ldots, N - R_i + x_i]$, where $R_1 = N$. The detailed algorithm is described in Figure 4.3.

As an example consider the case of a DOALL L with N=100 iterations that executes on five processors. All five processors start on L at different times. Each idle processor is assigned a block of consecutive iterations using the rule described above. The resulting execution profile is shown in Figure 4.2. Even though the results presented in this section hold for the general case where different iterations of the same loop have different execution times, for this example we assume that all 100 iterations have equal execution times. Each vertical line–segment in Figure 4.2

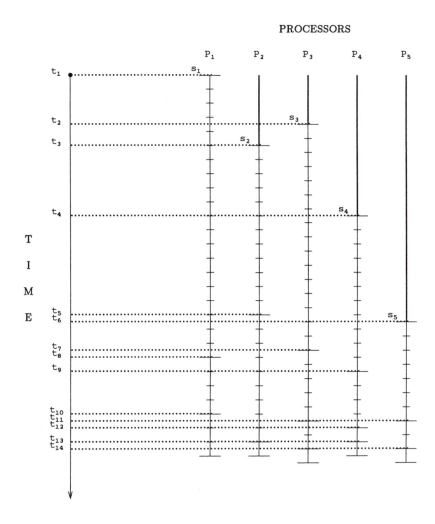

Figure 4.2. An example of the application of the GSS algorithm for N=100, p=5.

Time	No. of unused iterations (I)	Next processor to be scheduled	No. of iterations assigned to this processor
t_1	100	P_1	20
t_2	80	P_3	16
t_3	64	P_2	13
t_4	51	P_4	11
t_5	40	P_2	8
t_6	32	P_5	7
t_7	25	P_3	5
t_8	20	P_1	4
t_9	16	P_4	4
t_{10}	12	P_1	3
t_{11}	9	P_3	2
t_{12}	7	P_5	2
t_{13}	5	P_4	1
t_{14}	4	P_4	1
t_{15}	3	P_2	1
t_{16}	2	P_3	1
t_{17}	1	P_5	1
			TOTAL= 100

Table 4.1. The detailed scheduling events of the example of Figure 4.2 ordered by time.

represents the execution time of a loop iteration. The thick lines represent the execution of previous (unrelated to L) tasks on processors P_2, P_3, P_4, and P_5. The wider horizontal line–segments mark the time when iteration blocks are actually dispatched by idle processors. For example, at time t_1 processor P_1 dispatches $\lceil 100/5 \rceil = 20$ iterations. The next processor to become available is P_3 which at time t_2 dispatches $\lceil (100-20)/5 \rceil = 16$ iterations. Processor P_1 will receive its next assignment at time t_8. The detailed assignment of iterations to processors for this example is shown in Table 1. The events in the table are ordered by virtual time. From Figure 4.2 we observe that although the five processors start executing L at different times, they all terminate within B units of time difference from each other. In general if p processors are assigned to a DOALL with N iterations using the above scheme, we have the following.

Lemma 4.1. Each of the *last* p-1 processors to be scheduled under the GSS algorithm is assigned exactly one iteration of L. These p-1 processors are not necessarily physically different.

Proof: First we will show that there exists an i such that R_i (as defined by (4.1)) is

The GSS Algorithm

Input An arbitrarily nested loop L, and p processors.

Output The optimal dynamic schedule of L on the p processors. The schedule
is reproducible if the execution time of the loop bodies and the
initial processor configuration (of the p processors) are known.

• Distribute the loops in L wherever possible.

• For each ordered pair of (DOALL, DOSERIAL/DOACR) loops, (DOALL is the outer loop)
perform loop interchange.

• Apply implicit loop coalescing, and let I_c be the index of the coalesced iteration space.

• For each index i_k of the original loop define the index mapping as in (1),

$$i_k = f_{i_k}(I_c)$$

• If R_i is the number of remaining iterations at step i, then set $R_1 = N$, i=1,
and for each idle processor do.

REPEAT

• Each idle processor (scheduled at step i) receives
$$x_i = \left\lceil \frac{R_i}{p} \right\rceil$$
iterations.

• $R_{i+1} = R_i - x_i$

• The range of the global index is
$$I_c \in [N-R_i+1, \ldots, N-R_i+x_i] \equiv [l_i, \ldots, u_i]$$

• The range of each original loop index for that processor is given by
$$i_k \in [f_{i_k}(l_i), \ldots, f_{i_k}(u_i)]$$

• i = i + 1

UNTIL $(R_i = 0)$

Figure 4.3. Guided Self–Scheduling

$$R_i = p+1 \quad \text{or} \quad R_i = p \quad\quad (4.2)$$

where p is the number of processors. Suppose that such an i does not exist. Then there exists an i for which

$$R_i \geq p+2 \quad \text{and} \quad R_{i+1} \leq p-1.$$

But $R_{i+1}=R_i-\lceil R_i/p \rceil$ by definition. Thus $\lceil R_i/p \rceil=R_i-R_{i+1}\geq p+2 - (p-1)=3$, hence $R_i>2p$.

Let $R_i=kp+r$ where $k\geq 2$ and $r>1$. But $R_{i+1}=R_i-\lceil R_i/p \rceil<p$, or $kp+r- (k+1) <p$, and since $r>1$, $(k-1)p-k<0$ or finally $p<k/(k-1)$. But since $k\geq 2$ it follows that $p<2$ which contradicts the initial hypothesis that $p>1$. Hence (4.2) is true.

From (4.1) and (4.2) it follows directly that at least the last $p-1$ and at most the last p assignments will involve iteration blocks of size 1. ∎

Theorem 4.1. Independently of the initial configuration (start–up time) of the p processors that are scheduled under GSS, all processors finish executing L within B units of time difference from each other.

Proof: We will prove the theorem for the case where all p processors start executing L simultaneously. The proof for the general case is similar. By Lemma 4.1, at least the last $p-1$, and at most the last p assignments will involve single iterations. Let us consider the latter case. The are two possible scenarios during the scheduling of L under GSS. In the first case each of the last p iterations is assigned to a different processor. Then by virtue of GSS it is easy to see that if t_i, t_j are the termination times for processors p_i, p_j, $i, j \in [1..p]$ respectively, we have $|t_i-t_j| < B$.

The second case is when the last p iterations of L are assigned to at most $p - 1$ different processors. Let p_i^x denote a processor whose last assignment was an iteration block of size x, and p_j^1 a processor that is assigned one or more of the last p iterations. Let t_i^x and t_j^1 be their corresponding completion times. Using the same argument as above we can show that all processors that received one of the last p iterations, finish within B units of time apart from each other. It remains to show that any p_i^x and any p_j^1 terminate within B units of time from each other. We consider the case for x=2. The general case is similar. We will prove that for any p_i^x and any p_j^1, $|t_i^x - t_j^1| \leq B$.
Case 1: $t_i^x > t_j^1$, and suppose that $t_i^x - t_j^1 > B$ or equivalently, $t_i^x - 2B > t_j^1 - B$. The last inequality implies that p_j^1 was assigned a single iteration before the iteration block of size x=2 was assigned to p_i^x. Clearly this contradicts the basic steps of the GSS algorithm. Therefore $t_i^x - t_j^1 \leq B$.
Case 2: $t_i^x < t_j^1$ and suppose $t_j^1 - t_i^x < B$ or, $t_j^1 - B > t_i^x$. But the last inequality can never be true since p_i^x would have been assigned the last iteration instead of p_j^1. Therefore $t_j^1 - t_i^x \leq B$ and thus the statement of the theorem is true.

Note that if the p processors start executing L at different times $s_1 \leq s_2 \leq \ldots \leq s_p$, the theorem still holds true under the following condition:

$$N > \frac{1}{B} \sum_{i=1}^{P} (s_p - s_i) . \qquad \blacksquare$$

In reality B varies for different iterations (due to the presense of conditional statements) and $B \in \{b_1, b_2, \ldots, b_k\}$, where b_i, $(i=1, \ldots, k)$ are all possible values of B. Suppose that B can assume any of its possible values with the same probability, i.e., $P[B=b_i]=1/k$, $(i=1, 2, \ldots, k)$. Then Lemma 4.1 and Theorem 4.1 are still valid. Of course a uniform distribution is not always a valid assumption. For example, in numerical software we often have the exit-IFs inside loops that test for some error condition. The loop is exited if the error condition arises. In such cases we can safely ignore the conditional statements. If the user or the compiler cannot make any assertion about the distribution of true/false branches other heuristic tunnings can be used in GSS. For example if we know that the probability of clustered true (false) branches (of a conditional statement inside a loop) is high, then we can make p artificially large to decrease the size of the iteration blocks assigned to each processor by GSS. Even though simulation results show that even in such cases GSS is still superior to self–scheduling, we can no longer prove that GSS is optimal. Under the above assumptions we also have the following.

Theorem 4.2. If iterations have constant execution time the GSS algorithm obtains the optimal schedule under any initial processor configuration. GSS also uses the minimum possible number of synchronization points necessary to achieve optimal load balancing.

By synchronization points we mean the number of times processors enter critical regions (i.e., loop indexing). An implementation of GSS can be done so that when q (out of the p) processors become simultaneously available at step i, the first $q-1$ receive $\lceil R_i/p \rceil$ iterations and the q-th processor receives $\min(\lceil (R_i - (q-1) \lceil R_i/p \rceil)/p \rceil, \lceil R_i/p \rceil)$ iterations, where R_i is the number of unassinged iterations at the i-th step of GSS. In general when GSS is applied using (4.1) the number of synchronized accesses to loop indices is given by the following theorem.

Theorem 4.3. The number of synchronization points required by GSS is p in the best case, and $O(pH_{\lceil N/p \rceil})$ in the worst case, where H_n denotes the n-th harmonic number and $H_n \approx \ln(n) + \gamma + 1/2n$ (γ is Euler's constant).

Proof: The best case is obvious from the above discussion. In general it is clear that the number of iterations assigned to each processor will be (possibly multiple) occurrences of (some of) the integers

$$\left\lceil \frac{N}{p} \right\rceil, \quad \left\lceil \frac{N}{p} \right\rceil - 1, \quad \left\lceil \frac{N}{p} \right\rceil - 2, \ldots, 1$$

in this order. Obviously there will be at least $p-1$ and at most p assignments of exactly one iteration. It can be also observed that the number of different assignments of iteration blocks of size $\lceil N/p \rceil - k$, $(k=1, 2, \ldots, \lceil N/p \rceil - 2)$ depends on the relative values of p and $\lceil N/p \rceil - k$. More precisely, we can have at most

$$\left[\frac{p}{\lceil N/p \rceil - k} \right], \quad (k = 1, 2, \ldots, \lceil N/p \rceil - 2)$$

different assignments of iteration blocks of size $\lceil N/p \rceil$ - k. Therefore the total number of different assignments and thus the total number σ of synchronization points in the worst case is given by

$$\sigma \leq p + \sum_{i=2}^{\lceil N/p \rceil} \left\lceil \frac{p}{i} \right\rceil = \sum_{i=1}^{\lceil N/p \rceil} \left\lceil \frac{p}{i} \right\rceil.$$

For computing the order of magnitude we can ignore the ceiling and finally have

$$\sigma \approx \sum_{i=1}^{\lceil N/p \rceil} \frac{p}{i} = p \sum_{i=1}^{\lceil N/p \rceil} \frac{1}{i} = pH_{\lceil N/p \rceil}.$$

Therefore the number of synchronization points in the worst case is $\sigma = O(pH_{\lceil N/p \rceil})$.
∎

Thus GSS goes through $O(p \ln(N/p))$ synchronization points in the worst case compared to $O(mN)$ synchronization points used by the schemes in [KrWe85] and [TaPe86]. Note that if barriers are used, GSS can coalesce all loops, serial and parallel. Consider for example a DOALL loop with $\prod_{i=1}^{m} N_i$ iterations which is the result of coalescing m DOALLs. Suppose now that this DOALL is nested inside a serial loop with M iterations. GSS works fine on this doubly nested loop but it still must access two shared variables (loop indices) for each assignment. The other alternative is to implicitly coalesce the serial and parallel loops into a single *block–parallel* loop or BDOALL with MN iterations. To do this a barrier synchronization must be executed every N iterations. If $I_c = 1 \ldots MN$, the number of remaining iterations R_i (in 2) still assumes an initial value N. The difference here is that each time $(I_c \mod N = 0)$ a barrier synchronization is executed and R is reinitialized to N. This happens M times before the entire loop completes execution.

It should be noted that since GSS is a dynamic scheme the assumption that loop bounds are known is a realistic one. By the Fortran semantics the index bounds of DO loops must be known just before we enter the loop.

4.2.3. Further Reduction of Synchronization Operations

Another interesting feature of the GSS algorithm is that it can be tuned to further reduce the number of synchronization operations that are required during scheduling. As mentioned above, the last p - 1 allocations performed by GSS assigned exactly one iteration to each processor. The synchronization overhead involved in these p - 1 allocations may still be very high, especially when p is very large and the loop body is small.

We shall see now how to eliminate the last p - 1 assignments of single iterations of GSS. In fact we can eliminate all assignments of iteration blocks of size k ($< \lceil N/p \rceil$) or less. Let us discuss first the problem of eliminating assignments of single iterations from GSS. We show how this can be done by means of an example. Consider the application of GSS to a DOALL with N=14 iterations on p=4 processors. The assignment of iterations to processors (using (4.1)) is shown below in detail:

$$\lceil 14/4 \rceil = 4, \ \lceil 10/4 \rceil = 3, \ \lceil 7/4 \rceil = 2, \ \lceil 5/4 \rceil = 2, \ \lceil 3/4 \rceil = 1, \ \lceil 2/4 \rceil = 1, \ \lceil 1/4 \rceil = 1.$$

The seven successive assignments were done with iteration blocks of size 4, 3, 2, 2, 1, 1, 1. In this case the single iteration assignments account for almost half of the total assignments. We can eliminate the single iteration assignments by increasing the block size of the first $p - 1$ assignments by 1. The successive assignments in that case would be 5, 4, 3, and 2. Therefore the total number of scheduling decisions (and thus synchronization operations) is reduced by $p - 1$. This reduction can be performed automatically by setting $R_1 = N + p$ in (4.1). Thus the first assignment will dispatch $x_1 = \lceil (N+p)/p \rceil$ iterations. Otherwise GSS is applied in precisely the same way. However now it terminates not when the iterations are exhausted, but when for some i, $x_i < 2$. For the above example the application of GSS will generate the following assignments ($R_1 = \lceil (N+p)/p \rceil$).

$$\lceil 18/4 \rceil = 5, \quad \lceil 13/4 \rceil = 4, \quad \lceil 9/4 \rceil = 3, \quad \lceil 6/4 \rceil = 2.$$

When the ratio N/p is rather small, GSS(k) for k=2 may result in considerable savings. There is still a drawback however, since the rule of making all the assignments of iteration blocks of size two or more is not always accurate. Consider again the previous example but now let N=15. The assignments generated by GSS(2) will now be:

$$\lceil 19/4 \rceil = 5, \quad \lceil 14/4 \rceil = 4, \quad \lceil 10/4 \rceil = 3, \quad \lceil 7/4 \rceil = 2, \quad \lceil 5/4 \rceil = 2.$$

But $5 + 4 + 3 + 2 + 2 = 16 > N = 15$, i.e., the number of iterations assigned by GSS(2) is more than the iterations of the loop. Fortunately the number of superfluous iterations in such cases cannot be more than one, and the termination problem can be easily corrected. The solution is given by the following theorem.

Theorem 4.4. Let k be the step in (4.1) such that $x_k = 2$ and $x_{k+1} = 1$. If $R_{k+1} = p$ then

$$\sum_{i=1}^{k} x_i = N$$

else, if $R_{k+1} = p - 1$ then

$$1 + \sum_{i=1}^{k-1} x_i = N.$$

Proof: The algorithm starts with a total of $N + p$ iterations, and it must assign a total of N iterations in blocks of size ranging from $\lceil (N+p)/p \rceil$ to 2. Since (for $p \geq 2$) at least one iteration block will be of size 2, and all assignments of iteration blocks of size 2 must be performed, it follows that the last assignment of GSS(2) will involve $R_k = p + 1$ or $R_k = p + 2$. In the latter case the last assignment will dispatch 2 iterations and the algorithm will terminate assigning therefore a total of $N + p - R_{k+1} = N$ iterations. If $R_k = p + 1$, the last assignment will also dispatch 2 iterations. In that case however the total number of iterations assigned will be $N + p - (p - 1) = N + 1$. Thus $1 + \sum_{i=1}^{k-1} x_i = N$. ∎

Theorem 4.4 supplies the test for detecting and correcting superfluous assignments. The assignment and termination condition for GSS(2) is now given by

$$x_i = \left\lceil \frac{R_i}{p} \right\rceil \; ; \qquad R_{i+1} \; \longleftarrow \; R_i - x_i \qquad (4.3)$$

```
if (R_{i+1} ≤ p) then
    { stop;
      if (R_{i+1} < p) then x_i = 1 }
```

Using (4.3) now, the last assignment of GSS(2) for the last example will dispatch a single iteration. The same process can be applied to derive GSS(k) for any $2 < k < \lceil N/p \rceil$. The best value of k is machine and application dependent.

It should be emphasized that the GSS scheme can be implemented in hardware, it can be incorporated in the compiler, or it can be explicitly coded by the programmer. In the latter case the programmer may compute the iteration block size for each assignment, and force the assignment of such blocks by coding the corresponding loop appropriately. Consider for example the loop of Figure 4.4a. If array B holds the block size and S holds the starting iteration for each assignment, the loop of Figure 4.4a can be coded as in Figure 4.4b. Assuming that self–scheduling (SS) is implemented in the target machine, the above loop will be executed as if GSS was supported by the machine (with some additional overhead involved with the manipulation of the bookkeeping arrays).

4.3. SIMULATION RESULTS

A simulator was implemented to study the performance of self–scheduling (SS) and GSS (GSS(1)). In the SS scheme loop scheduling was done by assinging a single iteration to each idle processor [Alli85], [Cray85], [TaPe86]. Idle processors access

```
           DOALL 1 I = 1, N
                  . . .
                  . . .
                  . . .
           ENDOALL

                   (a)

           DOALL 1 I = 1, K
               DOSERIAL 2 J = S(I), S(I)+B(I)
                      . . .
                      . . .
                      . . .
               ENDOSERIAL
           ENDOALL

                   (b)
```

Figure 4.4. Example of the application of GSS at the program level.

each loop index in a loop nest by using appropriate synchronization instructions. The simulator was designed to accept program traces generated by Parafrase, and it can be extended easily to implement other scheduling strategies. The experiments conducted for this work however used four representative loops which are shown in Figure 4.5.

4.3.1. The Simulator

The simulator input consists of a set of tuples, where each tuple represents a single loop or a block of straight–line code [AhSU86]. Each tuple includes information such as number of iterations, execution time of basic blocks inside the loop, branching frequencies for the branches of each conditional statement inside a loop, dependence information, type of loop etc. In the presence of conditional statements the conditions are "evaluated" separately for each iteration of the loop and the appropriate branch is selected. The user supplies the expected frequency with which each branch is selected. Otherwise the simulator considers each branch equally probable. For this purpose a random number generator is used with a period of $2^{31} - 1$ [Koba81]. Random numbers are generated using a uniform distribution and are normalized (in $[0..1]$). For each conditional statement in the loop, the interval $[0..1]$ is partitioned into a number of subintervals equal to the number of counted paths in that statement. The size of each subinterval is proportional to the expected frequency of that branch. For each iteration of the loop, a random number is generated and the subinterval to which it belongs is determined. Then the branch corresponding to that subinterval is taken.

The execution of arbitrary loops on multiprocessor systems with 2 to 4096 processors can be simulated. Processors can start on a loop at random times. The simulator also takes into account overhead incurred with operations on shared variables. For our purposes shared variables are considered to be only loop indices. Although the current version of the simulator assumes a fixed memory access time, it can be easily extended to take into account random delays (due to network contention in shared memory systems). For each memory access, a random delay may be computed to fall within given upper and lower bounds. These bounds may be readjusted each time the number of processors (and thus the number of stages of the network) grows.

4.3.2. Experiments

The four loops L1, L2, L3, and L4 of Figure 4.5 were used to conduct the experiments for this work. These loops are representative of those found in production numerical software. Serial and parallel loops are specified by the programmer, or are created by a restructuring compiler (e.g., Parafrase). The loops of Figure 4.5 cover most cases since they include loops that are i) all parallel and perfectly nested (L1), ii) hybrid and perfectly nested (L3), iii) all parallel and nonperfectly nested (L2), iv) hybrid nonperfectly nested (L4), v) and finally one–way (L2), and multi–way nested (L4). The arrows in L4 indicate flow dependences between adjacent loops. The numbers enclosed in brackets give the execution times of straightline code in the corresponding positions.

Two sets of experiments were conducted, E_1 and E_2. The first set used the four loops of Figure 4.5 ignoring the conditional statements which are enclosed in square brackets. Therefore for E_1 all iterations of a particular loop had equal execution

```
              DOALL 1 I1 = 1, 100
                DOALL 2 I2 = 1, 50
                  DOALL 3 I3 = 1, 4
L1:                     {20}
                        [if C then {10}]
                  ENDOALL
                ENDOALL
              ENDOALL
```

(a)

```
              DOALL 1 I1 = 1, 50
                 {5}
                 [if C then {10}]
                 DOALL 2 I2 = 1, 40
                    {5}
                    DOALL 3 I3 = 1, 4
L2:                    {10}
                       [if C then {20}]
                 ENDOALL
                 ENDOALL
              ENDOALL
```

(b)

```
              DOSERIAL 1 I1 = 1, 40
                DOALL 2 I2 = 1, 500
L3:                  {100}
                     [if C then {50}]
                ENDOALL
              ENDOSERIAL
```

(c)

CONTINUED (Figure 4.5)

times. For E_2 the conditional statements were taken into account as well. Thus in E_2 different iterations of a given loop had different execution times. The next step will be to consider loops with multiple and nested conditionals which were not included in these experiments.

In the previous chapter we discussed the various types of overhead that are incurred during dynamic scheduling. One type of overhead is the time spent accessing and operating on a shared variable; in our case loop indices. This time is not constant in practice and it depends on several factors such as network traffic, number of simultaneous requests for a particular index and so on. For our experiments we chose this overhead to be constant and independent of the loop size or the number of processors. Since the purpose of our experiments is to study the relative (rather than the absolute) performance of GSS(1) and SS, the above assumption is not very restricting. For each scheduling decision the overhead is assumed to be a constant which represents, for instance, the number of clock cycles spent operating on a shared variable. Let o denote the overhead constant. We conducted the simulations for a best case (o_b), and a "worst" case (o_w) overhead. For the best case $o_b=2$ since at least two clock cycles are needed to operate on a shared variable. For the worst case we chose $o_w=10$. The value of 10 was chosen arbitrarily. In real parallel processor machines o_b and o_w can be much greater, but we are more interested in the difference $o_b - o_w$ rather than in their absolute values. E_1^b and E_1^w denote the set of experiments that ignored if statements for $o_b=2$ and $o_w=10$ respectively. Similarly, E_2^b and E_2^w denote the set of experiments using L1, L2, L3, and L4 with if statements, for $o_b=2$ and $o_w=10$ respectively.

The plots of Figures 4.6 and 4.7 show the speedup of the four loops L1 - L4 of Figure 4.5, for different numbers of processors, for the experiment E_1 (E_1^b and E_1^w). There are four curves in each plot. Solid lines plot the speedup curves for GSS(1), and dashed lines the speedup curves for SS. More specifically the plot of Figure 4.6a corresponds to loop L1. The upper and lower solid lines are the speedup curves resulting from the schedule of L1 under GSS(1) and for $o_b=2$, $o_w=10$ respectively. The upper and lower dashed lines are the speedup curves of L1 under SS for $o_b=2$, and $o_w=10$. The plot of Figure 4.6b shows the performance of GSS(1) and SS for L2 in E_1. Similarly Figures 4.7a and 4.7b correspond to L3 and L4 for E_1. In all plots the upper solid and dashed lines correspond to GSS(1) and SS for $o_b=2$ respectively. The lower solid and dashed lines correspond to GSS(1) and SS for $o_w=10$.

In the same way Figures 4.8 and 4.9 correspond to L1, L2, and L3, L4 respectively, for the E_2 experiments, i.e., with the if statements taken into account. Therefore in each plot we can see the relative performance of GSS(1), $o_b=2$ versus GSS(1), $o_w=10$; SS, $o_b=2$ versus SS, $o_w=10$; GSS(1), $o_b=2$ versus SS, $o_b=2$; and GSS(1) $o_w=10$ versus SS, $o_w=10$, for E_1 and E_2.

Except in the case of L3 where both GSS(1) and SS perform almost identically, we observe that in all other cases GSS(1) is better than SS by almost a factor of two in E_1 and E_2. In L3 for $p \geq 500$ we have the case of unlimited processors where each processor is assigned one iteration by both schemes. It is also clear from the plots that the difference in performance between GSS(1) and SS grows as the overhead grows. As it should be expected GSS(1) is less sensitive to scheduling overhead

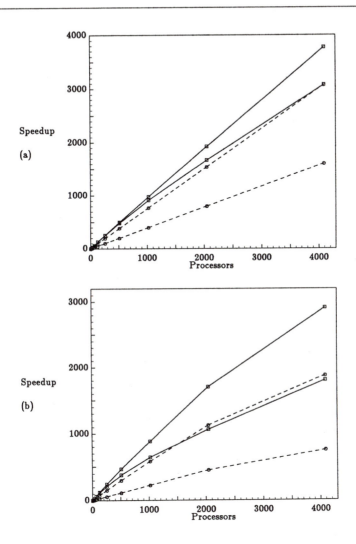

Figure 4.6. GSS and SS speedups for (a) L1, and (b) L2 without ifs.

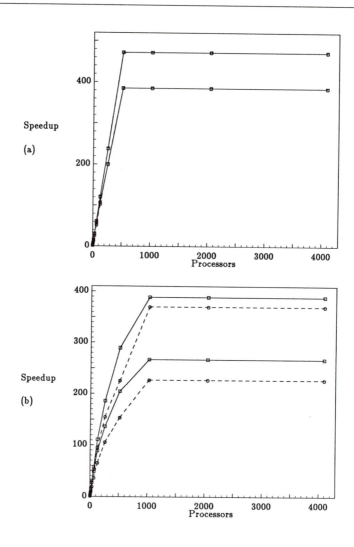

Figure 4.7. GSS and SS speedups for (a) L3, and (b) L4 without i fs.

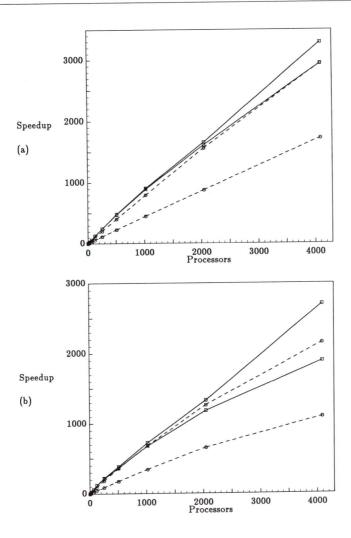

Figure 4.8. GSS and SS speedups for (a) L1, and (b) L2 with ifs.

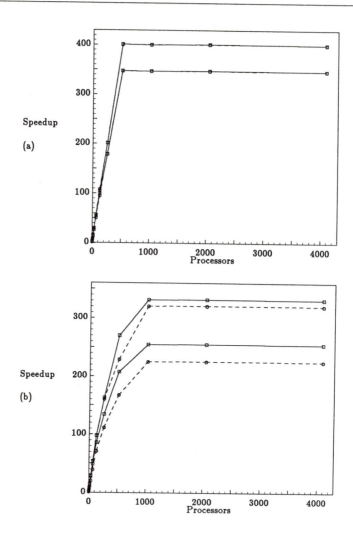

Figure 4.9. GSS and SS speedups for (a) L3, and (b) L4 with i fs.

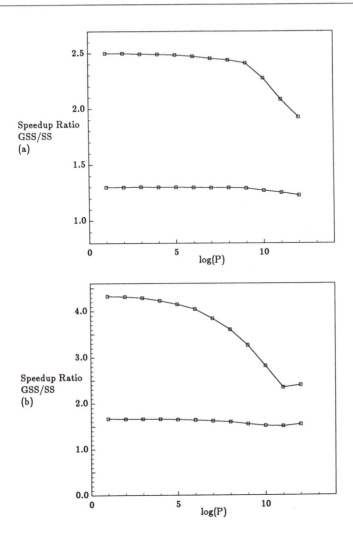

Figure 4.10. Speedup ratio of GSS/SS for (a) L1, and (b) L2 without i fs.

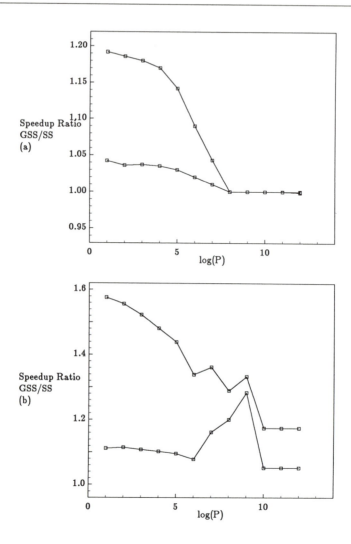

Figure 4.11. Speedup ratio of GSS/SS for (a) L3, and (b) L4 without i fs.

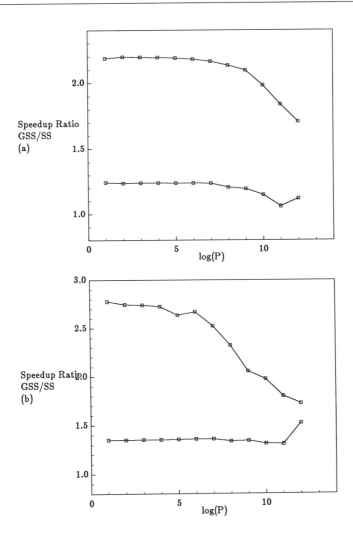

Figure 4.12. Speedup ratio of GSS/SS for (a) L1, and (b) L2 with i fs.

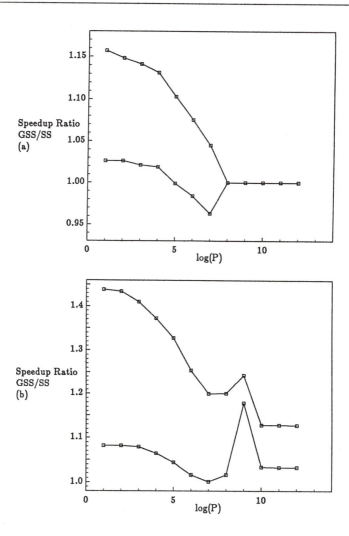

Figure 4.13. Speedup ratio of GSS/SS for (a) L3, and (b) L4 with ifs.

than SS.

The plots in Figures 4.10, 4.11, 4.12, and 4.13 correspond to Figures 4.6, 4.7, 4.8, and 4.9 respectively, and illustrate the speedup ratio GSS(1)/SS for each case for E_1 and E_2. The horizontal axis shows the log of the number of processors. In each plot there are two curves. The upper curve plots the speedup ratio GSS/SS for $o_b=10$. The lower curve plots the same ratio for $o_w=2$. The common characteristic of all ratio plots is that as the number of processors grows very large, the performance difference between GSS and SS becomes less significant. The large perturbations in the ratio curves can be explained by the fact that GSS is "logarithmically sensitive" while SS is "linearly sensitive" to scheduling overhead. Thus the performance of SS tends to saturate much earlier (as the number of processors grows) than that of GSS. As the overhead grows the improvement offered by GSS becomes more significant. This is apparent in the plots of Figures 4.10–4.13 where the ratio GSS(1)/SS is significantly larger for $o_w=10$.

4.4. STATIC LOOP SCHEDULING

An alternative to dynamic scheduling is static processor allocation for parallel loops. While static allocation minimizes run–time overhead associated with scheduling, dynamic approaches may involve considerable overhead that may make the parallel execution of small loops impractical. On the other hand dynamic scheduling offers more flexibility and it may actually be more practical on the average. If the execution time of loop bodies is not constant, or if the loop bounds are unknown at compile–time, then dynamic loop scheduling seems to be a more attractive approach. This is also the case when the exact number of processors allocated to a loop is decided at run–time.

Static scheduling may be more efficient, however, in the absence of branches and when the loop iterations and the number of processors are known. In the remaining of this section we concentrate only on static processor allocation schemes. An interesting extension of this work would involve the comparison of the performance of dynamic and static scheduling algorithms on realistic loops.

A dynamic programming approach can be used by the compiler to decide the number of processors that need to be allocated to each individual loop, such that the parallel execution time of the entire loop construct is minimized. The terms processor allocation and assignment are used interchangeably in this section. A compile–time algorithm was implemented in Parafrase and experiments were conducted using subroutines from the EISPACK and the IEEE/DSP packages [IEEE79].

4.4.1. Definitions and Basic Concepts

We assume that any (serial or parallel) DO loop has the following form:

```
DO I = 1, N
    {B}
ENDO
```

where N is the upper bound of the loop index, and B is a set of assignment statements or another loop. In a nested loop the *nest–depth* is the maximum number of loops nested in each other. A *perfectly nested* or one–way nested loop is a loop of the form

$$DO \ I_1 = 1, \ N_1$$
$$DO \ I_2 = 1, \ N_2$$
$$\cdot \ \cdot \ \cdot$$
$$\cdot \ \cdot \ \cdot$$
$$DO \ I_m = 1, \ N_m$$
$$\{B\}$$
$$ENDO$$
$$\cdot \ \cdot \ \cdot$$
$$\cdot \ \cdot \ \cdot$$
$$ENDO$$
$$ENDO$$

where m is the nest–depth and B is as defined above. To simplify our notation, each loop is assumed to be normalized (i.e., its iteration space is of the form $[1, \ldots, N]$, $N \in Z^+$), and is denoted by the upper bound of its iteration space. Thus, N_i denotes a DO loop whose body is executed N_i times. In a perfectly (or one–way) nested loop there is exactly one loop at nest level i, $(i = 1, 2, \ldots, m)$. A loop is k–way nested if there exist k disjoint loops at the same nest level. A perfectly nested loop of nest–depth m is denoted by $L_{1,m} = (N_1, N_2, \ldots, N_m)$. For $1 \leq i \leq j \leq m$, $L_{i,j} = (N_i, N_{i+1}, \ldots, N_j)$ is a subset of $L_{1,m}$ that includes loops i through j. A number of processors P is said to be *useful* with respect to a parallel loop $L_{1,m}$, if there exists an assignment which can allocate exactly P processors to the components (loops) of $L_{1,m}$. Let T_P be the parallel execution time of a loop $L_{1,m}$ on P processors. Then P is the *maximum* number of useful processors for $L_{1,m}$ iff it is the smallest integer such that for any $q > P$ and any processor allocation scheme $T_q = T_P$.

4.4.2. Optimal Processor Assignment to Parallel Loops

The processor assignment problem becomes especially important when we deal with nested parallel loops where inefficient assignment algorithms may result in an execution time far worse than the optimal. In programs with several nested parallel loops the efficiency may then drop down to unacceptable levels. We can informally define the limited processor assignment problem as follows: Given an arbitrary multiply nested loop which contains serial and parallel (DOACROSS, DOALL) loops and a number of processors P, find the (optimal) way of assigning the P processors to the loops so that the parallel execution time of the entire module is minimized. For loops with very few nest levels and systems with a small number of processors, exhaustive search might be affordable at compile time. But as the number of processors increases, the number of processor–loop combinations grows exponentially. Moreover, loops with large nest levels are not very uncommon in scientific computations. As an example, 10 to 17 deeply nested parallel loops were observed in several subroutines of the restructured (by Parafrase) IEEE Digital Signal Processing Package.

In the case of a perfectly nested (one–way) loop where all loops are DOALLs, processor assignment becomes an easy problem to solve: If N is the product of the loop bounds, then each processor (but possibly the last) is assigned $\lceil N/P \rceil$ iterations of the loop. Then for each loop the range of its index values corresponding to each processor is computed directly. However, in the general case of arbitrarily nested loops that contain combinations of DO, DOALL, and DOACROSS loops, the above method would not work. The algorithm described in this section solves the general problem optimaly in the context of static scheduling. This means that optimality is obtained assuming that the structure of the target loop is to be preserved. The solutions obtained are not necessarily optimal when compared with loops containing branches and which are scheduled dynamically (even though they may still be more efficient in certain cases).

4.4.2.1. Optimal Simple Processor Assignment to DOALLs

In what follows the number of available processors P is always assumed to be "useful", that is, less than or equal to the maximum number of processors that a loop L can fully utilize. First we discuss the case of allocating factors of P to the individual loops of a nested loop. Thus, all P processors are involved in such an assignment. We then compute the "optimal" assignment of P by determining the optimal factorization of P and then the optimal assignment of these factors to the individual loops. These solutions are optimal assuming that all P processors must be used. However, as it will be shown later, a better solution may exist for the same loop and for a number of processors q < P.

A metric called the *efficiency index* is used throughout this section. The usefulness of this metric is twofold. First it makes it easier to formulate the processor assignment problem, and secondly it allows us to observe several interesting properties of the problem that are otherwise hidden in modular arithmetic. The optimal processor assignment is guided by the use of a function called the *assignment function*. The assignment function can be easily defined to measure parallel execution time. Processor assignment in an arbitrarily nested parallel loop is performed by allocating (possibly) different numbers of processors to different loops in the nest. The techniques described below partition a P–processor machine hierarchically into sets of processors, and assign different sets of processors to different loops in the nest. To simplify our terminology we invariably refer to partitions of any size as "processors". Consider for example two nested DOALL loops $L_{1,2} = (N_1, N_2)$ and a 6–processor machine. One possible allocation of the six processors to these loops would be one that assigns 2 (clusters of) processors to the outer loop and 3 processors to the inner loop. More precisely, this means that the machine is partitioned into two halfs, each half consisting of 3 physical processors. Then, each iteration of the outer loop N_1 is assigned a one half partition and the corresponding iterations of the inner loop are allocated 3 physical processors. Therefore, the term "processor" is used generically in this section and refers to clusters of physical processors of (possibly) different sizes.

For a DOALL with N_i iterations that has been assigned p_i processors we define ϵ_i, the *efficiency index* or *EI* of N_i as follows:

$$\epsilon_i^{p_i} = \frac{N_i/p_i}{\left\lceil N_i/p_i \right\rceil}. \tag{4.4}$$

The efficiency index is an indicator of how efficiently a loop is statically scheduled on a given number of processors. The higher the EI the higher the efficiency (as defined in Chapter 1). Some other properties of the efficiency index that will be used directly or indirectly in the following sections are the following. For any DOALL N_i and any number of processors p we have: $0 < \epsilon_i^p \leq 1$. For any N_i, $\epsilon_i^1 = 1$. For

$N_i \geq p$, $\epsilon_i^p > 1/2$. It should also be noted that $p \neq q$ does not necessarily imply $\epsilon_i^p \neq \epsilon_i^q$. It is clear that always $p_i \geq 1$. If during allocation a loop N_i is not assigned processors explicitly, it is implied that $p_i = 1$ and thus its corresponding $\epsilon_i = 1$.

For a nested DOALL $L_{1,m} = (N_1, N_2, \ldots, N_m)$, a number of processors $P = p_1 p_2 \cdots p_m$ and a particular assignment of P to L we define the *efficiency index vector* $\omega = (\epsilon_1^{p_1}, \epsilon_2^{p_2}, \ldots, \epsilon_m^{p_m})$, of L, where $\epsilon_i^{p_i}$ is the EI for loop N_i when it is allocated p_i processors.

In what follows the terms "assignment of P" and "decomposition of P" are used interchangeably. For the moment we can assume that any assignment of P to L defines implicitly a decomposition of P into factors $P = p_1 p_2 \cdots p_m$ where each of the m different loops receives p_i, $(i=1, 2, \ldots, m)$ processors. A processor assignment profile $(p_1, p_2, \ldots, p_m)$ (where loop N_i receives p_i processors) can also be described by its efficiency index vector as defined above.

For an assignment of $P = p_1 p_2 \cdots p_m$ processors to L described by $\omega = (\epsilon_1^{p_1}, \ldots, \epsilon_m^{p_m})$, we define E_L, the *compound efficiency index* (*CEI*) of L as

$$E_L = \prod_{i=1}^{m} \epsilon_i^{p_i}. \tag{4.5}$$

For any L and P, we also have $0 < E_L \leq 1$. Let T_1 be the serial execution time of a perfectly nested DOALL L. Next, suppose that L is executed on P processors and let T_P and T_P' denote the parallel execution times for two different assignments $\omega = (\epsilon_1, \epsilon_2, \ldots, \epsilon_m)$ and $\omega' = (\epsilon_1', \epsilon_2', \ldots, \epsilon_m')$ of P to L, where $P = p_1 \cdots p_m = p_1' \cdots p_m'$. We can express the parallel execution time T_P of L in terms of its CEI as shown in the following lemma.

Lemma 4.2. If B is the execution time of one iteration of the loop, and $N = \prod_{i=1}^{m} N_i$ is the total number of iterations, then $\quad T_P = \dfrac{NB}{E_L P}$.

Proof: By definition we have that T_P is given by

$$T_P = \prod_{i=1}^{m} \lceil N_i/p_i \rceil \, B \quad , \text{or} \quad \frac{1}{T_P} = (1/B) \, \frac{\displaystyle\prod_{i=1}^{m} N_i/p_i}{\displaystyle\prod_{i=1}^{m} \lceil N_i/p_i \rceil} \, \prod_{i=1}^{m} p_i/N_i =$$

$$(1/B) \left(\prod_{i=1}^{m} \frac{N_i/p_i}{\lceil N_i/p_i \rceil} \right) \frac{\displaystyle\prod_{i=1}^{m} p_i}{\displaystyle\prod_{i=1}^{m} N_i} = \prod_{i=1}^{m} \epsilon_i^{p_i} \, \frac{P}{NB} = \frac{E_L P}{NB}, \quad \text{or}$$

$$T_P = \frac{NB}{E_L P}. \quad \blacksquare \tag{4.6}$$

The following lemma is a direct application of (4.6).

Lemma 4.3. $T_P < T_P'$ iff $E_L > E_L'$.

As it was indicated by the previous lemma the optimality criterion used in this section is based on the assumption that the total number of processors P remains fixed, and that at each time, all P processors are utilized by a particular loop. However, as it will be shown later, in the course of computing the optimal allocation of P processors to the individual loops in a loop nest, we also compute the minimum number of processors $q < P$ for which an equivalent optimal solution is achievable (i.e., one that results in the same execution time). In the next few sections we show how the efficiency index can be used to direct the efficient assignment of processors to perfectly nested parallel loops.

Given a perfectly nested loop L and a number of processors P we call a *simple* processor assignment one that assigns all P processors to a single loop N_i of L. A *complex* processor assignment on the other hand is one that assigns two or more factors of P to two or more loops of L.

Theorem 4.5. The optimal simple processor assignment over all simple assignments of P processors to loop L, is achieved by assigning P to the loop with $\epsilon = \max_{1 \leq i \leq m} \{\epsilon_i^P\}$.

Proof: Without loss of generality assume that $\epsilon = \epsilon_1$. Then $\epsilon_i = 1$ for $(i = 2, 3, \ldots, m)$ and $E_L = \epsilon_1$. For any other simple allocation of P to N_j, $j \neq 1$, with a CEI of E_L' we have $\epsilon_1 = E_L \geq E_L' = \epsilon_j$. The optimality follows from Lemma 4.3. ∎

The following two lemmas are used in subsequent discussion.

Lemma 4.4. $\displaystyle\prod_{i=1}^{m} \left\lceil \frac{N_i}{P_i} \right\rceil \geq \left\lceil \prod_{i=1}^{m} \frac{N_i}{P_i} \right\rceil$

Proof: By definition we have that

$$\prod_{i=1}^{m} \left\lceil \frac{N_i}{P_i} \right\rceil \geq \prod_{i=1}^{m} \frac{N_i}{P_i} \tag{4.7}$$

and since the left hand side of (4.7) is an integer it follows directly that

$$\prod_{i=1}^{m} \left\lceil \frac{N_i}{P_i} \right\rceil \geq \left\lceil \prod_{i=1}^{m} \frac{N_i}{P_i} \right\rceil . \blacksquare$$

The next lemma follows directly from Lemma 4.4.

Lemma 4.5. For any integer n we have $n \left\lceil \dfrac{N}{pn} \right\rceil \geq \left\lceil \dfrac{N}{p} \right\rceil$.

For the next lemma and most of what follows we assume that processors are assigned in units that are equal to products of the prime factors of P unless explicitly stated otherwise. Therefore each loop is assigned a divisor of P including one.

Lemma 4.6. If N is a (single) DOALL loop, $P = p_1 p_2 \cdots p_m$ is the number of available processors and ϵ_i, $(i = 1, 2, \ldots, m)$ are the efficiency indices for assigning $p_1, p_1 p_2, p_1 p_2 p_3, \ldots, p_1 p_2 \cdots p_m$ respectively, then

$$\epsilon_1 \geq \epsilon_2 \geq \epsilon_3 \geq \cdots \geq \epsilon_m.$$

Proof: From Lemma 4.5 we have:

$$p_{i+1} \left\lceil \frac{N}{p_i p_{i+1}} \right\rceil \geq \left\lceil \frac{N}{p_i} \right\rceil \rightarrow \frac{N/p_i}{\lceil N/p_i \rceil} \geq \frac{N/p_i p_{i+1}}{\lceil N/p_i p_{i+1} \rceil} \rightarrow \epsilon_i \geq \epsilon_{i+1} \quad \blacksquare$$

According to Lemma 4.3 the optimal processor assignment of P to L is the one that maximizes E_L. Each assignment defines a decomposition of P into a number of factors less than or equal to the number of loops in L. As P grows the number of different decompositions of P into factors grows very rapidly. From number theory we know that each integer is uniquely represented as a product of prime factors. Theorem 4.6 below can be used to prune (eliminate from consideration) several decompositions of P (i.e., several assignment profiles of P to L that are not close to optimal). From several hand generated tests we observed that the use of Theorem 4.6 in a branch and bound algorithm for determining the optimal assignment of processors, eliminated the majority of all possible assignments. In some instances all but the optimal assignments were pruned by the test of Theorem 4.6.

Again let $L_{1,m} = (N_1, \ldots, N_m)$ be a perfectly nested DOALL that executes on P processors and let $P = p_1 p_2 \cdots p_k$ be any decomposition of P where $k \leq m$. Now let $\epsilon = \max_{1 \leq i \leq m} \{\epsilon_i^P\}$ be the maximum efficiency index over all simple assignments of P to L, and let $\epsilon_i = \max_{1 \leq j \leq m} \{\epsilon_j^{p_i}\}$, $(i=1, 2, \ldots, k)$ be the maximum efficiency indices (over all loops of L) for the factors $p_1, p_2, \ldots, p_k$ of P respectively (i.e., $\epsilon_j^{p_i} = (N_j/p_i)/(\lceil N_j/p_i \rceil)$). Note that here we do not perform any actual assignment of processors to loops but simply compute the maximum efficiency index for each factor p_i of P over all loops of L, excluding the loop that corresponds to ϵ. If T_s and T_c are the parallel execution times for L corresponding to the optimal simple assignment of P and the optimal complex assignment of the factors of P respectively, and S_s and S_c their respective speedups, we have the following theorem (using the notation of this paragraph).

Theorem 4.6. If there exists $i \in \{1, 2, \ldots, k\}$ for which $\epsilon \geq \epsilon_i$ then $T_s \leq T_c$ and thus $S_s \geq S_c$. Equivalently, if one of the factors of P has a maximum efficiency index equal to or less than the maximum efficiency index of P, then we obtain a better assignment by assigning all P processors to a single loop than from any complex assignment of the factors of P (including the optimal).

Proof: Without loss of generality we can assume that the optimal complex allocation assigns more than one processor to the first k loops $(k \leq m)$, and implicitly one processor to the remaining m−k loops. Therefore the corresponding efficiency index vector for the optimal complex allocation is $\omega_c = (\epsilon_1^{p_1}, \ldots, \epsilon_k^{p_k}, 1, \ldots, 1)$, and for the optimal simple allocation of P is $\omega_s = (1, \ldots, 1, \epsilon, 1, \ldots, 1)$, where ϵ corresponds to the j−th position. Then the parallel execution times of the optimal simple and complex allocations are:

$$T_s = N_1 N_2 \ldots N_{j-1} \left\lceil \frac{N_j}{P} \right\rceil N_{j+1} \ldots N_m \quad \text{and} \quad T_c = \left\lceil \frac{N_1}{P_1} \right\rceil \cdots \left\lceil \frac{N_k}{P_k} \right\rceil N_{k+1} \cdots N_m \quad (4.8)$$

Suppose now that for some $i \in \{1, 2, \ldots, k\}$ we have $\epsilon \geq \epsilon_i$ or equivalently,

$$\frac{N_j/P}{\lceil N_j/P \rceil} \geq \frac{N_i/P_i}{\lceil N_i/P_i \rceil} \quad \rightarrow \quad \frac{N_j}{P_1 \cdots P_i \cdots P_k} \left\lceil \frac{N_i}{P_i} \right\rceil \geq \frac{N_i}{P_i} \left\lceil \frac{N_j}{P} \right\rceil \quad (4.9)$$

Again without loss of generality we may assume that $j > i$ and we can multiply both sides of (4.9) by $N_1 \ldots N_{i-1} N_{i+1} \cdots N_{j-1} N_{j+1} \ldots N_m$ resulting in

$$\frac{N_1}{P_1} \cdots \frac{N_{i-1}}{P_{i-1}} \left\lceil \frac{N_i}{P_i} \right\rceil \frac{N_{i+1}}{P_{i+1}} \cdots \frac{N_k}{P_k} \ldots N_m \geq N_1 \ldots N_{j-1} \left\lceil \frac{N_j}{P} \right\rceil N_{j+1} \ldots N_m. \quad (4.10)$$

If we denote the left hand sides of (4.10) by M1 and M2 respectively, we have $T_c \geq M1 \geq M2 = T_s$ or finally,

$$T_c \geq T_s \quad \text{and} \quad S_c \leq S_s. \quad \blacksquare$$

Thus, given any decomposition of P into factors $P = p_1 \ldots p_k$, a necessary (but not sufficient) condition for a complex assignment to be better than the best simple assignment is $\epsilon < \epsilon_i$, for all $(i=1, 2, \ldots, k)$ (where ϵ_i is the maximum efficiency index for factor p_i over all loops of L). Obviously if $\epsilon = 1$ then the optimal simple assignment is the overall optimal as well. The next theorem is a generalization of Theorem 4.6 when only factors of P are considered.

Theorem 4.7. If in Theorem 4.6 $P=p_1 p_2 \cdots p_k$ is the *prime* factor decomposition of P and there exists $i \in \{1, \ldots, k\}$ for which $\epsilon \geq \epsilon_i$, then the simple allocation of P to L (corresponding to ϵ) is the overall optimal.

Proof: Suppose that for some $i \in \{1, \ldots, k\}$ we have $\epsilon \geq \epsilon_i$. Suppose further that ϵ_i corresponds to loop N_i. We therefore have that

$$\epsilon_i \geq \epsilon_j \quad \text{for all} \quad j \neq i \text{ and for the same } p_i. \quad (4.11)$$

Any other complex allocation of P to L defines another decomposition $P=p_1' p_2' \cdots p_r'$, $r \leq k$ and since p_i is a prime factor of P there exists some p_i' that includes p_i, that is, $p_i'=p_i p_i''$, for some integer p_i''. We consider the following two scenarios:

Case 1: Suppose that in this new allocation p_i' is assigned to the same loop N_i as p_i in the prime factor allocation. Then if ϵ_i' is the efficiency index of p_i' and since $p_i'=p_i p_i''$ it follows directly from Lemma 4.6 that $\epsilon_i \geq \epsilon_i'$ and therefore $\epsilon \geq \epsilon_i \geq \epsilon_i'$.

Case 2: Suppose now that p_i' is assigned to a loop different than N_i, say N_j. If ϵ_j is the efficiency index for N_j when p_i is allocated to it and ϵ_j' when p_i' is allocated to it, then from Lemma 4.6, the initial hypothesis and relation (4.11) we have,

$$\epsilon \geq \epsilon_i \geq \epsilon_j \geq \epsilon_j' \quad (4.12)$$

Therefore in any complex allocation of P to L, there is at least one loop of L that has a maximum efficiency index less than or equal to ϵ, the efficiency index of the optimal simple allocation of P to L. Thus the optimal simple allocation is the overall optimal. ■

Corollary 4.1. If $N = \prod_{i=1}^{m} N_i$, ϵ is the efficiency index of the optimal simple assignment, ϵ_i is the efficiency index for the i-th loop in a complex optimal assignment $(i=1, 2, \ldots, m)$, and E_L the corresponding compound efficiency index, then any optimal complex assignment should satisfy,

$$\epsilon < \epsilon_i \leq 1, \quad (i= 1, 2, \ldots, m) \quad \text{and} \quad \epsilon < E_L \leq 1.$$

Let

$$E_O = \frac{N/P}{\lceil N/P \rceil} \quad \text{where} \quad N = \prod_{i=1}^{m} N_i.$$

Then any optimal assignment of P to L satisfies

$$E_L \leq E_O \tag{4.13}$$

where E_L is the CEI of an optimal assignment. Only in special cases there would be an optimal assignment of P to L for which the equality in (4.13) holds. If loop coalescing is applied to certain types of loops it always results in $E_L = E_O$.

Corollary 4.1 can be used to check whether a given complex assignment is better than an optimal simple assignment. It would be useful however to be able to answer the question about the existence of such an assignment. That is, given a loop L and a number of P processors, is there an optimal complex assignment better than the optimal simple assignment? If for a particular loop the answer is negative the optimal simple assignment is chosen and therefore the problem for that loop is solved in linear time. Corollary 4.2 below provides the test for the existence of an optimal complex assignment.

For each loop $N_i \in L$ we define the *critical assignment* g_i, of N_i as the maximum number of processors that can be assigned to N_i with its efficiency index remaining strictly greater than ϵ (the maximum efficiency index of P). In other words, for each N_i, g_i is chosen to satisfy,

$$\epsilon_i^{g_i} > \epsilon \quad \text{and} \quad \epsilon_i^{g_i+r} \leq \epsilon$$

for any $r \geq 1$. Then we have the following corollary.

Corollary 4.2. A necessary condition for the existence of a complex assignment of P to L which is better than the corresponding optimal simple assignment is

$$\prod_{i=1}^{m} g_i \geq P.$$

Proof: If we had $\prod_{i=1}^{m} g_i < P$, then in any complex allocation there would be at least one loop N_i with $\epsilon_i \leq \epsilon$ (assuming that all P processors are useful). From Theorem 4.6 it then follows that the optimal simple allocation is also the overall optimal. ■

The obvious approach for optimally solving the general instance of the static processor assignment problem is exhaustive search. For small nested loops and a very small number of processors exhaustive search would be fast at compile time. For medium size loops and a few tens of processors however, the cost of exhaustive search becomes intolerable even at compile time. For example the number of different assignments of 50 processors to 15 nested loops is of the order of 10^{13}. If it takes a microsecond (on a fast machine) to process each different assignment it would take almost two years of CPU time to find the optimal assignment of 50 processors to 15 loops. In the next section we present a processor assignment algorithm that has a low polynomial complexity and finds the optimal assignment for all types of loops and any number of processors.

4.4.2.2. Optimal Complex Processor Assignment to Parallel Loops

In order to better illustrate the ideas of this section we start by considering perfectly nested DOALLs and $P=2^k$ processors. As we proceed the concepts are generalized to include more complex loop structures such as nonperfectly nested combinations of serial, DOALL, and DOACROSS loops. Let us consider an m–level nested DOALL $L_{1,m}=(N_1, N_2, \ldots, N_m)$ which is to be executed on $P=2^k$ processors. For each such loop we compute the *efficiency table* M as shown in Figure 4.14. Column j of M corresponds to loop N_j of $L_{1,m}$ and row i corresponds to a number of 2^i processors, $(i=0,1,\ldots,k)$. An entry (i,j) of table M contains the efficiency index for assigning 2^i processors to loop N_j. This $(m \times k)$ efficiency table will be used repeatedly by OPTAL (Figure 4.18) to obtain the optimal assignment of P processors to loop $L_{1,m}$.

From Lemma 4.6 we observe that each column of M is ordered in nonincreasing order. If the loops are ordered by size then each row of M is also ordered in nonincreasing order. Therefore if ϵ_{ij} is the element of M in the i–th row and j–th column, then $\epsilon_{ij} \geq \epsilon_{iw}$ for $w \geq j$. It is clear that in any assignment of P processors to $L_{1,m}$ there can be at most one entry of the lower half of M involved in that assignment. Let us give an outline of the basic steps of the algorithm. The process starts by

	N_1	N_2	N_3	.	.	.	N_m
1	ϵ_{11}	ϵ_{12}	ϵ_{13}	.	.	.	ϵ_{1m}
2	ϵ_{21}	ϵ_{22}	ϵ_{23}	.	.	.	ϵ_{2m}
2^2	ϵ_{31}	ϵ_{32}	ϵ_{33}	.	.	.	ϵ_{3m}
.	.	.	.	.	.	.	.
.	.	.	.	.	.	.	.
.	.	.	.	.	.	.	.
2^k	ϵ_{k1}	ϵ_{k2}	ϵ_{k3}	.	.	.	ϵ_{km}

Figure 4.14. The efficiency table for $P=2^k$ and m nested loops.

assigning the P processors to the innermost or outermost loop, and let us always start from the innermost loop. The next step finds the optimal assignment of P to the two innermost loops. During the process, we also need to compute the optimal assignment of 1, 2, 2^2, . . . , 2^k processors respectively to the two innermost loops. These assignments however are computed only once for each loop and stored for later use by the following steps.

In general, after the $(m - i)$-th step the algorithm computes the optimal assignment of 1, 2, 2^2, . . . , P processors to loops $L_{i,m} = (N_i, N_{i+1}, \ldots, N_m)$. The next $(m - i + 1)$-th step considers loop N_{i-1} and finds the optimal assignment of 1, 2, 2^2, . . . , P processors to loop $(N_{i-1}, L_{i,m})$ possibly by reassigning processors from L_i to N_{i-1}. All possible assignments for N_{i-1} are considered. Note that all possible assignments for L_i have already been computed. At the end of the m-th step OPTAL has computed the profile of the optimal assignment of $P = 2^k$ to $L_{1,m} = (N_1, N_2, \ldots, N_m)$. Based on Lemma 4.3 the optimal assignment of P to $L_{1,m}$ would be the one that maximizes E_L. This is precisely what this algorithm does.

We use this as a special case of the general algorithm which is described in the next section. It is followed by a simple example that illustrates the details of computing the optimal assignment. The kernel of OPTAL is a recursive function G, that is defined as follows: Given $P = 2^k$ and $L_{1,m}$, we define $G_i(q)$ as the product of efficiency indices of the optimal assignment of q processors to loops $(N_i, N_{i+1}, \ldots, N_m)$. More specifically a closed form expression of function $G_i(q)$ is given by,

$$G_i(q) = \max_{1 < p_j < q} \left\{ \prod_{j=i}^{m} \epsilon_j^{p_j} \right\}$$

such that $q = \prod_{j=i}^{m} p_j \leq P$. The recursive definition of $G_i(q)$ and the one that will be used from now on is given by (4.14)

$$G_i(P) = \max_{0 \leq r \leq k} \left\{ \epsilon_i^{2^r} G_{i+1}(P/2^r) \right\} \quad \text{or} \quad (4.14)$$

$$G_i(P) = \max \left\{ G_{i+1}(P), \ \epsilon_i^2 G_{i+1}(P/2), \ \epsilon_i^4 G_{i+1}(P/4), \ \epsilon_i^8 G_{i+1}(P/8), \ldots, \epsilon_i^P G_{i+1}(1) \right\}$$

where ϵ_i^q is the efficiency index for assigning q processors to loop N_i (available from table M). Relation (4.14) indicates that the optimal assignment of P processors to loops $(N_i, N_{i+1}, \ldots, N_m)$ can be found by selecting from all assignments of 2^r processors to loop N_i and 2^{k-r} processors to $(N_{i+1}, \ldots, N_m)$, $(r = 0, 1, \ldots, k)$, the one that maximizes $\prod_{j=i}^{m} \epsilon_j$.

The function in (4.14) is computed for $(i = m, m-1, \ldots, 1)$, and for each i we also compute $G_i(1)$, $G_i(2)$, $G_i(2^2)$, . . . , $G_i(P = 2^k)$. The optimal assignment of the P processors to $L_{1,m}$ will be given at the end of the m-th step by $G_1(2^k)$. Initially (first step), for $i = m$ we have $G_m(q) = \epsilon_i^q$. For each $G_i(q)$ the corresponding processor assignment profile is stored and when $G_1(2^k)$ is computed the profile for the optimal assignment is available.

The algorithm completes in m steps. In each of the m steps, $k=\log P$ function evaluations are performed and each of the $(r=1,2,\ldots,k)$ function evaluations involves the computation of the maximum of r values. The overall complexity of the algorithm is therefore $O(m\log^2 P)$. Using the results of the previous sections we can avoid unnecessary computations and further reduce the complexity of the algorithm.

```
DOALL 1 I1=1,15
    DOALL 2 I2=1,17
        DOALL 3 I3=1,17
            DOALL 4 I4=1,25
                .   .   .
                .   .   .
                .   .   .
4           CONTINUE
3       CONTINUE
2   CONTINUE
1 CONTINUE
```

Figure 4.15. The nested loop of Example 4.1.

	1	2	4	8	16	32
$G_4()$	1	$\dfrac{25}{26}$	$\dfrac{25}{28}$	$\dfrac{25}{32}$	$\dfrac{25}{32}$	$\dfrac{25}{32}$
$G_3()$	1	$\dfrac{25}{26}$	$\dfrac{25}{26}*\dfrac{17}{18}$	$\dfrac{25}{28}*\dfrac{17}{18}$	$\dfrac{25}{32}$	$\dfrac{25}{32}$
$G_2()$	1	$\dfrac{25}{26}$	$\dfrac{25}{26}*\dfrac{17}{18}$	$\dfrac{25}{26}*\left(\dfrac{17}{18}\right)^2$	$\dfrac{25}{28}*\left(\dfrac{17}{18}\right)^2$	$\dfrac{25}{32}$
$G_1()$	1	$\dfrac{25}{26}$	$\dfrac{15}{16}$	$\dfrac{15}{16}$	$\dfrac{15}{16}$	$\dfrac{15}{16}*\dfrac{25}{26}$

Figure 4.16. The efficiency matrix for Example 4.1.

The explicit processor assignment vector (with the exact number of processors assigned to each loop) is computed as a side effect of the computation of G_1. When a particular G_1 is chosen as optimal, the corresponding assignment vector can be trivially reconstructed. In order to illustrate the computational details of the algorithm we give below a simple example involving four DOALLs and $P = 2^5$ processors. It should be noted that this approach not only finds the optimal assignment of the given P processors to a particular loop nest, but it also finds the optimal assignments of $P/2$, $P/4$, $P/8$, $P/16, \ldots,$ 1 processors to the same loop. We can therefore determine the minimum number of useful processors with little extra cost.

Example 4.1: Consider the loop $L_{1,4} = (N_1=15,\ N_2=17,\ N_3=17,\ N_4=25)$ of Figure 4.15 and let $P=2^5$ be the number of available processors. The optimal assignment of P to $L_{1,4}$ is computed as follows: First the 5×4 efficiency matrix M is computed. At the first step for i=4 we have $G_4(2^r) = \epsilon_4^{2^r}$ for $(r=0,\ 1,\ \ldots,\ 5)$. The computations for the remaining three steps are shown analytically below. In each case the maximum element appears in bold letters. For each of the four steps the optimal assignments are tabulated in the table shown in Figure 4.16. Each row of the table corresponds to each of the four steps.

Step 2

$$G_3(2) = \max\left\{ \mathbf{G_4(2)},\ \epsilon_3^2 G_4(1) \right\}$$

$$G_3(4) = \max\left\{ G_4(4),\ \epsilon_3^2 \mathbf{G_4(2)},\ \epsilon_3^4 G_4(1) \right\}$$

$$G_3(8) = \max\left\{ G_4(8),\ \epsilon_3^2 \mathbf{G_4(4)},\ \epsilon_3^4 G_4(2),\ \epsilon_3^8 G_4(1) \right\}$$

$$G_3(16) = \max\left\{ \mathbf{G_4(16)},\ \epsilon_3^2 G_4(8),\ \epsilon_3^4 G_4(4),\ \epsilon_3^8 G_4(2),\ \epsilon_3^{16} G_4(1) \right\}$$

$$G_3(32) = \max\left\{ \mathbf{G_4(32)},\ \epsilon_3^2 G_4(16),\ \epsilon_3^4 G_4(8),\ \epsilon_3^8 G_4(4),\ \epsilon_3^{16} G_4(2),\ \epsilon_3^{32} G_4(1) \right\}$$

Step 3

$$G_2(2) = \max\left\{ \mathbf{G_3(2)},\ \epsilon_2^2 G_3(1) \right\}$$

$$G_2(4) = \max\left\{ \mathbf{G_3(4)},\ \epsilon_2^2 G_3(2),\ \epsilon_2^4 G_3(1) \right\}$$

$$G_2(8) = \max\left\{ G_3(8),\ \epsilon_2^2 \mathbf{G_3(4)},\ \epsilon_2^4 G_3(2),\ \epsilon_2^8 G_3(1) \right\}$$

$$G_2(16) = \max\left\{ G_3(16), \ \epsilon_2^2 G_3(8), \ \epsilon_2^4 G_3(4), \ \epsilon_2^8 G_3(2), \ \epsilon_2^{16} G_3(1) \right\}$$

$$G_2(32) = \max\left\{ G_3(32), \ \epsilon_2^2 G_3(16), \ \epsilon_2^4 G_3(8), \ \epsilon_2^8 G_3(4), \ \epsilon_2^{16} G_3(2), \ \epsilon_2^{32} G_3(1) \right\}$$

Step 4

$$G_1(2) = \max\left\{ G_2(2), \ \epsilon_1^2 G_2(1) \right\}$$

$$G_1(4) = \max\left\{ G_2(4), \ \epsilon_1^2 G_2(2), \ \epsilon_1^4 G_2(1) \right\}$$

$$G_1(8) = \max\left\{ G_2(8), \ \epsilon_1^2 G_2(4), \ \epsilon_1^4 G_2(2), \ \epsilon_1^8 G_2(1) \right\}$$

$$G_1(16) = \max\left\{ G_2(16), \ \epsilon_1^2 G_2(8), \ \epsilon_1^4 G_2(4), \ \epsilon_1^8 G_2(2), \ \epsilon_1^{16} G_2(1) \right\}$$

$$G_1(32) = \max\left\{ G_2(32), \ \epsilon_1^2 G_2(16), \ \epsilon_1^4 G_2(8), \ \epsilon_1^8 G_2(4), \ \epsilon_1^{16} G_2(2), \ \epsilon_1^{32} G_2(1) \right\}$$

The optimal assignment in this example is therefore the one that assigns 16 processors to loop $N_1=15$ and 2 processors to loop $N_4=25$. The processor assignment profile is reconstructed as follows. First we look at the maximum element of $G_1(32)$. This element is $\epsilon^{16} G_2(2)$ which indicates that loop N_1 receives 16 processors, and the remaining processors are allocated to $G_2(2)$. The maximum element of entry $G_2(2)$ is $G_3(2)$ which indicates that loop N_2 receives 1 processor. Continuing in the same way, the maximum element of entry $G_3(2)$ is $G_4(2)$ which again tells us that loop N_3 is assigned 1 processor, and therefore loop N_4 is assigned the remaining 2 processors.

4.4.2.3. The General Algorithm

Although most real multiprocessor systems have $P=2^k$ for some integer k, OPTAL can be used to generate optimal processor assignments for any integer P. It also handles arbitrarily complex nested parallel loops. Before we describe the details of the general algorithm however, we need to define the concepts of DOACROSS and loop nesting more precisely.

As mentioned in Chapters 2 and 8, a DOACROSS loop can be informally defined as a parallel loop in which data dependences allow for partial overlap of execution of successive iterations. That is, if iteration i starts at time t on a given processor, iteration $(i+1)$ can start at time $t+d$, where d is a constant. Constant d is called the delay and represents the difference in execution time between initiations of successive iterations. If B is the size (serial execution time) of the loop body, then d/B is defined to be the percentage of overlap, (or doacross percentage). When $d=B$ the loop is serial, while if d=0 the loop is a DOALL. In DOALL loops all iterations may start execution simultaneously. DOALL and serial loops are therefore special cases of DOACROSS loops. The parallel execution time of a DOACROSS loop with N_i iterations, a delay of d_i, and a body size of B_i that executes on P processors is given by the following expression [PoBa87].

$$T_P^i(B_i) = \left(\left\lceil \frac{N_i}{P} \right\rceil - 1 \right) * \max\{B_i, Pd_i\} + d_i * \Big((N - 1) \mod P \Big) + B_i . \qquad (4.15)$$

In order to simplify the notation in the following discussion, we assume that a block of assignment statements (BAS) can be considered as a DOACROSS loop with $N_i=1$, and $d_i=0$.

An arbitrarily complex nested loop can be uniquely represented as a $k-$ level tree where k is the maximum nest depth. The leaves of the tree correspond to BASs and intermediate nodes correspond to (DOACROSS) loops. Obviously the total number of nodes in a loop tree is $\lambda+\mu$ where λ is the number of individual loops in the structure and μ the number of BASs. An example of a nested loop and its tree representation are shown in Figure 4.17. Intermediate tree nodes at level m correspond to loops at nest depth m. We assume that individual loops in an arbitrarily nested loop are numbered increasingly, in lexicographic order.

In the general case, loops are not perfectly nested and therefore the efficiency index as defined in Section 4.4.2.1 is not useful. In this case it is convenient to define the assignment function to measure directly parallel execution time. Therefore the max term of the assignment function in the previous section becomes min in this case since our objective now is to minimize overall execution time.

The steps of the general algorithm are almost identical to the case of perfectly nested loops. The example of Figure 4.17 is used whenever it helps illustrate the computations involved. A $\lambda \times P$ table can be used to store intermediate values. During the first step we compute the parallel execution time of the DOACROSS loops at level k on the tree, where k is the maximum nest level. This is done as follows:

$$G_k^i(q) = T_q^i(B_i) \ , \qquad (q = 1, \ 2, \ \ldots, \ P) \qquad (4.16)$$

$$\text{and for all leaves } i,$$

where T_q^i is given by (4.15). The general step is defined recursively as in the perfectly nested loop case. The optimal assignment of P processors to loops in levels i through k ($i<k$), (assuming the optimal assignment of P to loops at level $i+1$ is known), is then computed by:

$$G_i^j(q) = \min_{1 \le r \le q} \left\{ T_r^j \left(\sum_{n \text{ child of } j} G_{i+1}^n(\lfloor q/r \rfloor) \right) \right\} \qquad (4.17)$$

$$\text{and for } (q=1, \ 2, \ 3, \ \ldots, \ P)$$

where (4.17) is computed for all nodes (loops) j at level i, and $T(*)$ is given by (4.15). The summation in (4.17) accounts for all nodes at level $i+1$ that are descendants of node j, that is, all loops nested inside loop N_j. The optimal assignment of P processors to a given loop is given by $G_1^L(P)$. Recall from the example of the previous section that the detailed processor assignment vector is automatically constructed

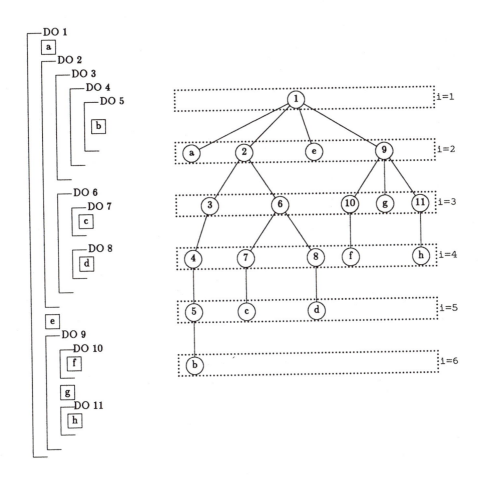

Figure 4.17. A nested loop and its tree representation. Squares and leaves denote BASs.

during the evaluation of (4.17). For each loop the number of processors assigned to that loop correspond to the minimum term is (4.17). A formal description of the algorithm is given in Figure 4.18.

It should be noted that all optimal assignments of $1, 2, \ldots, P-1$ processors to a loop $L_{1,m}$ are computed as intermediate results of the computation of $G_1^L(P)$. We therefore have the following.

Algorithm **OPTAL**

Input:
A loop L of nest depth nest k and P processors.

Output:
An optimal processor allocation profile of P to L.

Method:

- 1. For all loops j at level k of the loop tree, and
  For all $q = 1, 2, 3, \ldots, P$, compute the allocation function:
  $$G_k^j(q) = T_q^j(B_j)$$

- 2. For $i = (k - 1)$ to 1 Compute:
  For all loops j in nest depth i compute:

  $$G_i^j(1) = T_1^j\left(\sum_{n \text{ child of } j} G_j^n(1) \right)$$

  $$G_i^j(2) = \min\left\{ \left[T_1^i\left(\sum_{n \text{ child of } j} G_{i+1}^n(2) \right) \right], \left[T_2^i\left(\sum_{n \text{ child of } j} G_{i+1}^n(1) \right) \right] \right\}$$

  $$\cdot \quad \cdot \quad \cdot$$
  $$\cdot \quad \cdot \quad \cdot$$

  $$G_i^j(P) = \min\left\{ \left[T_r^j\left(\sum_{n \text{ child of } j} G_{i+1}^n(\lfloor P/r \rfloor) \right) \right], |\text{ for } r=1,2,3,\ldots,P \right\}$$

  and store the results in the j-th row of table T.
- 3. Output the processor allocation profile computed by $G_1^L(P)$.

Figure 4.18. A procedural description of OPTAL.

Corollary 4.3. Given P processors for a loop $L_{1,m}$, the maximum number of useful processors is the minimum Q, such that $1 \leq Q \leq P$ and $G_1^L(Q) = G_1^L(P)$.

Theorem 4.8. For any loop $L_{1,m}$ of maximum nest depth m, and any integer P, OPTAL terminates after m iterations and generates the optimal assignment of P processors to $L_{1,m}$.
Proof: The proof is by induction on i. Since i is decreasing in successive steps, we apply induction "backwards". For i=m (the innermost loop) we have by definition an optimal allocation given by $G_m(P)$. Suppose that for i=k + 1, $G_{k+1}^j(q)$, (q= 1, 2, ..., P) is optimal, for all loops j at nest level k+1. We

will show that for i=k, $G_k^j(q)$, (q= 1, 2, ..., P) is also optimal. For every q, G_k is defined by (4.17) and without loss of generality we can assume that,

$$G_k^j(q) = T_r^j \left(\sum_{n \text{ child of } j} G_{k+1}^n(\lfloor q/r \rfloor) \right) \quad (4.18)$$

Since $G_{k+1}^n(q/r)$ is optimal for all n by the induction hypothesis, and since (4.18) is the minimum term in (4.17), it follows that $G_k^j(q)$ is optimal for q and thus $G_k^j(P)$ is optimal. We then conclude that $G_1^1(P)$ gives the optimal allocation of P processors to loop $L_{1,m}$. ∎

The complexity of the algorithm can be easily determined. The assignment function G_i^j is computed P times for each node (loop) in the tree, or a total of λP times. Each evaluation of the assignment function also involves finding the minimum of an average of $P/2$ terms. The complexity therefore (without counting additions) is $O(\lambda P^2/2)$. The complexity can be reduced to $O(\lambda P \log P)$ by executing OPTAL itself in parallel. The maximum speedup resulting from the optimal assignment of P processors to a loop $L_{1,m}$ is given by,

$$S_P = \frac{G_1^L(1)}{G_1^L(P)}.$$

An interesting point of this approach is that although loops at the same nest level are allocated the same total number of processors, each loop manages (assigns) its own processors to its own iterations in an independent way. For example, suppose that loops 3 and 6 of Figure 4.17 are allocated 8 processors each. A possible allocation then may assign 1 processor to loops 3 and 4, and 8 processors to loop 5, while in the second case we may have 2 processors assigned to loop 6, and 4 processors to each of the loops 7 and 8. It is clear that loops on the same nest level must be assigned the same total number of processors when executing on a parallel processor system. Otherwise we have suboptimal parallel execution times since some processors will be forced to remain idle.

This algorithm generates optimal static processor assignments if the loop bounds are known at compile-time. This is frequently the case in numerical software where loop bounds usually reflect the problem size. However there are cases where the loop bounds are not known at compile-time and default values are used instead. In such cases the algorithm fails to generate optimal assignments. Loops with unknown loop bounds at compile-time are, for example, triangular loops, whose bounds are actually indices of other loops. By unrolling loops that surround triangular loops we obtain a sequence of loops with constant upper bounds that can be handled optimally. This unrolling does not need to lexically take place but processor assignment can be performed assuming an implicit loop unrolling at compile-time.

Loop upper bounds that cannot be estimated at compile-time are those that are determined by a function call or by the value of an array element, for example. This problem is alleviated at run-time however, where loop bounds must be known before the loop is entered. It would thus be appropriate to perform processor assignment at run-time just before we start executing a loop. Of course more information is available at run-time but the overhead of run-time assignment would also be very significant.

4.4.3. Experiments

We implemented this processor assignment algorithm in the Parafrase compiler. Processor assignment is performed after DOALL and DOACROSS loops are recognized. In our experiments we measured speedup values for some subroutines of the EISPACK and IEEE DSP packages.

Speedup values were computed as discussed in Chapter 8. In our case T_p, the parallel execution time, was measured for P=32, P=256, and P=2048 processors, and for loop bounds set to 40. In some EISPACK subroutines where loop bounds correspond to the bandwidth of a matrix, we used loop bounds of 1 or 4. The speedup values measured for the three different numbers of processors are shown in Tables 4.2 and 4.3. The subroutines from the two packages used in these experiments were randomly selected.

From the speedup values we observe that for 32 processors the average speedup is almost linear for both EISPACK and IEEE subroutines. For 256 processors the average speedup for EISPACK subroutines is about 137, or more than P/2. In other words, we have an efficiency of more than 50% for P=256. For the IEEE subroutines we observe an even higher average efficiency for the same number of processors. The third column in the tables corresponds to an unlimited number of processors. Since most of the EISPACK subroutines deal with square matrices, for 40X40 arrays the maximum expected speedup is 1600. Taking into account several loops with bounds of 1 or 4 and the number of one–dimensional loops, the average maximum speedup should be expected to be considerably lower than 1600. The average speedup of the third column of Table 4.2 is about 310, which corresponds to an average efficiency of about 15%. Since at most 1600 processors would be useful for most of the EISPACK routines, in reallity we would have an efficiency of about 20%. The corresponding values for the third column of Table 4.3 are quite higher than those of EISPACK. Generally, supercomputers deliver a wide range of performances from program to program. This is true of real machines [Dong85], and has been observed in our earlier experimental work [Kuck84]. It appears, from the experiments we have conducted so far, that when the above algorithm is used there is very little variation when programs are run with limited number of processors (i.e, when the number of processors is proportional to array sizes).

Considering the fact that efficiencies in the range of 20% are characterized very satisfactory in modern supercomputers, we can claim that optimal processor assignments to parallel loops result in high speedups for most cases. Processor allocations to independent code segments can increase the average speedup at least by a factor of two [Veid85].

Figures 4.19, 4.20, 4.21, and 4.22 show the improvement in speedup for the same set of EISPACK and IEEE/DSP subroutines. Experiments were conducted using the processor allocation heuristic previously employed in Parafrase [Cytr84], and OPTAL. The horizontal axis in the plots correspond to subroutines arranged in order of increasing speedup. The vertical axis display actual speedups. The solid lines plot the speedup spectrum obtained by using OPTAL. The dotted lines plot speedups obtained by the previous method [Cytr84].

We compare the performance improvement using the two methods for p=32 and p=2048. As mentioned above, the problem size was chosen so that p=2048

Subroutine Name	S_{32}	S_{256}	S_{2048}
ELMBAK	31.9	242.0	668.0
ELMHES	31.7	33.6	33.6
ELTRAN	29.3	71.3	84.5
HQR2	18.0	26.0	28.0
TRED1	31.0	235.0	240.0
MINFIT	28.0	130.0	181.0
TRED2	18.3	36.5	39.5
CBABK2	30.0	53.5	57.4
CH	25.0	66.9	85.0
COMBAK	31.9	248.5	721.0
CORTB	32.0	254.0	1250.0
CORTH	32.0	252.0	501.0
BANDV	31.0	98.0	98.0

Table 4.2: Speedup values for 32, 256, and 2048 processors for EISPACK subroutines.

Subroutine Name	S_{32}	S_{256}	S_{2048}
INISHL	32.0	255.8	1021.0
WFTA	32.0	255.8	2036.9
TRBIZE	30.8	128.6	128.6
PCORP	31.9	246.3	537.0
POWER	26.4	68.2	79.6
COSYFP	22.2	54.4	65.7
FREDIC	31.9	162.0	190.0
FLPWL	30.9	169.4	363.0
DIINIT	28.0	89.5	119.4
SRINIT	21.3	48.6	56.8
SMINVD	31.9	120.6	186.0
DEFIN4	19.2	37.6	37.6
FFT	30.8	191.0	505.0
LOAD	22.0	36.3	36.3
COVAR1	31.5	68.0	76.5
CLHARM	27.7	91.8	120.0
FLCHAR	31.0	188.3	458.8
REMEZ	10.0	12.1	12.3
D	31.3	210.0	670.0
LPTRN	11.0	13.9	14.8

Table 4.3: Speedup values for 32, 256, and 2048 processors for IEEE DSP subroutines.

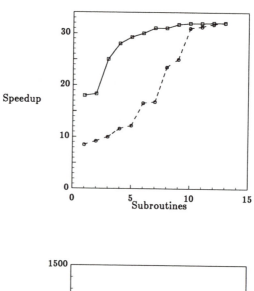

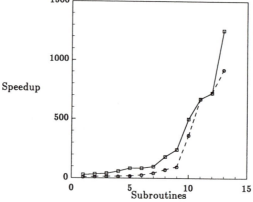

Figures 4.19 and 4.20. New and previous speedups for EISPACK for 32 and 2048 processors.

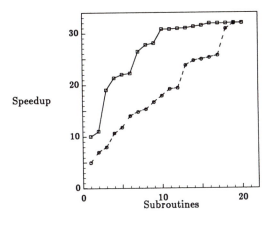

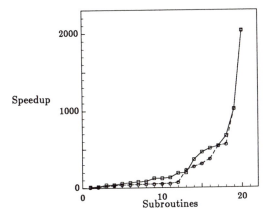

Figure 4.21 and 4.22. New and previous speedups for IEEE/DSP for 32 and 2048 processors.

approaches the unlimited processor case. We observe that for $p=32$ the speedup improvement is very significant for both EISPACK and IEEE/DSP routines. This is the case because when the number of processors is small relative to the problem size, nonoptimal allocations have a significant negative impact on performance. In other words when the number of processors is relatively small we can not afford to underutilize even a few processors. When the number of processors is large, the inefficiency introduced by poor utilization of a few processors is amortized and has less impact on overall performance. This becomes evident in the plots of Figures 4.20 and 4.22 where the number of processors is 2048. In this case the improvement in performance is significantly less than in the case of $p=32$ (Figures 4.19 and 4.21). The relative performance improvement for $p=256$ lies in between.

CHAPTER 5

RUN–TIME OVERHEAD

5.1. INTRODUCTION

The overhead involved with the simultaneous application of many processors to the same task can be very significant [PoKu87], [Poly86], [Rein85], [Cytr85]. So far most of the existing parallel processor systems have not addressed the overhead issue adequately nor have they taken it into account either in the compiler or in the hardware. In Chapter 3 we discussed in length the impact of run–time overhead on usable parallelism. The more the overhead, the less one can exploit the parallelism of a given program. There are two issues pertaining to run–time overhead. The first concerns the design of parallel machines and their software around the goal of minimizing run–time overhead which is incurred during parallel execution. The second issue concerns methodologies for the best utilization of existing parallel computers. In a given machine–program combination, the limitations (overhead etc.) are known and they cannot be altered. The former issue was analyzed in Chapter 3 from the software point of view. The latter case is the focus of this chapter.

First, we give upper bounds on the execution time of parallel loops and tasks. We see that in the absence of run–time overhead, these bounds are very tight even for random scheduling schemes. This gives another indication that run–time overhead is more detrimental on performance than scheduling itself. Next, we analyze two widely used models of overhead and their impact on the degree of parallelism that can be exploited. Using these models we can compute an approximation to the optimal number of processors for a given parallel task. This is also equivalent to computing the minimum size of an allocatable task. With these models we then perform some measurements using simple parallel loops. Finally we discuss ways of computing approximate execution times of tasks at compile time.

5.2. BOUNDS FOR DYNAMIC LOOP SCHEDULING

Theorem 5.1. Let L be a DOALL loop with N iterations and a loop–body that takes a maximum of B units of time to execute. Then the execution time ω_L using any self–scheduling scheme is bounded by

$$\omega_L \leq \left\lceil \frac{N}{p} \right\rceil B. \qquad (5.1)$$

Proof: Let us assume that $N > p$. During self–scheduling iterations are scheduled on demand. When a processor becomes free it dispatches a new iteration or a block of iterations. (Since the latter case can be reduced to the case where iterations are assigned one by one, we consider the former case.) In a DOALL there are no cross-iteration dependences. Therefore new processes are always available until L is completely dispatched. In other words there are no "gaps" in the execution profile.

Assume that all p processors start at time 1. Let t be the time the first of the p processors finishes completely (i.e., it finds an empty Q). Then no new iteration (process) can start execution at time greater than or equal to t. Therefore all other processors will complete before time $t + B$ and thus

$$\omega_L \leq t + B. \qquad (5.2)$$

There is at least one (out of the p) processor that by time t has been assigned at most $\lceil N/p \rceil - 1$ iterations. This is true because otherwise (i.e., if each processor has been assigned at least $\lceil N/p \rceil$ iterations by time t) the total number of iterations x assigned up to time t would be $x \geq p\lceil N/p \rceil \geq N$ which is impossible (unless p divides N which again proves the theorem). It follows therefore that

$$t \leq \left(\left\lceil \frac{N}{p} \right\rceil - 1 \right) B \quad \text{or} \quad t + B \leq \left\lceil \frac{N}{p} \right\rceil B \qquad (5.3)$$

and if we substitute t in (5.2) we finally have

$$\omega_L \leq \left\lceil \frac{N}{p} \right\rceil B. \qquad \blacksquare$$

Consider again a DOALL loop L with N iterations, or equivalently a set of N independent serial tasks. Let B and b be the execution times of the longest and shortest iterations of L respectively. Then if ω_o is the optimal schedule length of L on p processors and ω_L the schedule lenght of L on p processors under any dynamic (demand–driven) scheduling scheme (assuming no overhead of any kind), we have the following.

Corollary 5.1. ω_L can never be B/b times worse than the optimal, that is

$$\frac{\omega_L}{\omega_o} \leq \frac{B}{b}.$$

Proof: From the previous theorem it follows that

$$\left\lceil \frac{N}{p} \right\rceil b \leq \omega_o \leq \omega_L \leq \left\lceil \frac{N}{p} \right\rceil B, \quad \text{or}$$

$$\frac{\omega_L}{\omega_o} \leq \frac{\lceil N/p \rceil B}{\omega_o} \leq \frac{\lceil N/p \rceil B}{\lceil N/p \rceil b} = \frac{B}{b}.$$

For example if all iterations of L have equal execution times $\omega_L = \omega_o$, i.e., any demand–driven scheme is optimal, excluding again overhead. ■
Another upper bound which in general is more tight than that of Corollary 5.1 is given by the following.

Corollary 5.2. $\dfrac{\omega_L}{\omega_o} \leq 1 + \dfrac{p}{N} * \dfrac{B}{b}.$

Proof: Since t is the time the first processor completes execution on L (Theorem 5.1), it is obvious that

$$\omega_o \geq t \geq \left\lfloor \frac{N}{p} \right\rfloor b. \tag{5.4}$$

From the previous theorem we also have,

$$\omega_L = T_p \leq t + B. \tag{5.5}$$

From (5.4) and (5.5) it follows that

$$\frac{\omega_L}{\omega_o} \leq \frac{t + B}{\omega_o} \leq \frac{t + B}{t} = 1 + \frac{B}{t} \leq 1 + \frac{B}{\lfloor N/p \rfloor b} \leq 1 + \frac{p}{N} * \frac{B}{b} \tag{5.6}$$

which proves the corollary. ■

5.3. OVERHEAD OF PARALLEL TASKS

If T_1 and T_p are the serial and parallel execution times (on p processors) for a program PROG respectively, then we define the *speedup* S_p of PROG on a p processor system to be $S_p = T_1/T_p$. The *efficiency* of execution of PROG is then defined by $E_p = S_p/p$ (Chapter 1). It is usually hard to precisely compute T_1 and T_p at compile–time. However, close approximations are adequate in estimating overhead and performing related optimizations. The terms "task" and "process" which are used in this chapter were defined in Chapter 3.

We will consider the worst–case overhead incurred with the parallel execution of processes. This is the familiar fork/join operation which is employed, for instance, in generating several processes from a parallel DO loop. Such parallel loops can be specified by the programmer or can be the result of program restructuring. The iterations of a DOALL loop are data independent and therefore can be assigned to different processors and can be executed in any order. A DOALL loop defines a task; one or more iterations executing concurrently on the same processor define a process. Parallelism at the task level can be utilized by executing different tasks simultaneously.

The issue of interest here is the estimation of the critical process size or CPS as defined in Chapter 3. Informally, the CPS can be defined as the minimum size of a process for which the execution time on a single processor is equal to the associated overhead. When a parallel task is distributed to several processors at run–time, it incurs a penalty or overhead that limits the degree of exploitable task granularity. Consider the parallel execution of a DOALL loop whose iterations are spread across processors at run–time. Run–time overhead may include several activities that do not occur during serial execution. All processors involved, for example, will have to access the ready–task queue in a serial mode since it is a critical section. Different processors will get different iterations of the same loop. At the end of the loop all processors involved must pass through a barrier to determine that the loop has been executed and that they are allowed to proceed with the next task. The fetching of instructions at run–time can also be considered part of the overhead. Especially with self–scheduling, instruction prefetching cannot work since, by definition, it is impossible to predict which processor will execute the next task or the next iteration of a loop. All these activities prolong the parallel execution time of a program. None of the above occurs during serial execution. This overhead, as would be expected, makes it inefficient to execute in parallel small tasks or to use a very large number of processors on even large parallel tasks. If the task is not large enough to amortize the overhead, we may end up with a parallel execution time which is larger than the serial execution time.

As mentioned in Chapter 3, minimizing the overhead incurred from communication, synchronization and scheduling is a non–trivial optimization problem, and attempts to minimize such overheads usually result in reducing the degree of program parallelism. Most instances of this optimization problem have been proven to be NP–Complete [GaJo78]. A heuristic algorithm would attempt to minimize the communication cost by merging nodes of the graph together to avoid the overhead involved in communicating data from one processor to another. This however often reduces the degree of available vertical parallelism (Chapter 6).

As an example of node merging, consider two loops L_1 and L_2 in our restructured program model, with data dependences going from L_1 to L_2. The dependences restrict the two loops to execute in this order since data computed in L_1 are used by L_2. In this case only parallelism inside each loop can be exploited. If we do not coordinate the processors chosen for the execution of L_1 and L_2, then data computed inside L_1 will have to be stored in a shared memory upon completion of L_1, and then fetched from that memory to the processors executing L_2. If on the other hand we consider the two loops as a single task, then we can bind iterations of L_1 and corresponding iterations of L_2 to specific processors (loop spreading). In this manner data computed by a particular iteration of L_1 and used by the corresponding iteration of L_2 need only be stored in fast registers of the processor, thus avoiding the overhead of redundant store and fetch operations. For relatively small loops the savings by such "task merging" can be very significant.

Task merging can also be used to decrease scheduling overhead that is involved when we distribute different program nodes across different processors. This scheduling overhead is in addition to the synchronization overhead and may become disastrous especially for very small tasks. For the Cray X–MP for example, the overhead involved with scheduling two parallel tasks can be several *msecs* [Cray85]. This overhead imposes a minimum size on parallel tasks, below which the speedup becomes rather a slowdown (i.e., $S_p < 1$). This is the critical task size.

If during the execution of a program we schedule a set of parallel tasks, the parallel execution time is augmented by O_T, where O_T is the scheduling overhead. The maximum expected speedup therefore is given by

$$S_p = \frac{T_1}{T_1/p + O_T}. \qquad (5.7)$$

In order to have a speedup of at least 1, we must have $T_1 \geq T_1/p + O_T$, i.e., $T_1 \geq p*O_T/p-1$ which gives the critical task size as a function of the overhead and the number of processors. More generally, the minimum program size T_{min} required to obtain a given speedup S^* on p processors should satisfy:

$$\frac{T_{min}}{T_{min}/p+O_T} \geq S^*, \quad \text{or} \quad T_{min} \geq \frac{p*O_T*S^*}{p-S^*}. \qquad (5.8)$$

The tasks involved in an instance of high level spreading can be thought of as iterations of a DOALL loop whose loop–body contains conditional statements, and therefore different iterations have different execution times. Therefore high level spreading can be reduced to the parallel loop case where the number of iterations equals the number of independent tasks in that set. Since it is impossible to precisely estimate the execution time of a loop body with conditional statements, either at compile–time or at run–time, we assume an average or a worst case value. For the moment let us assume that the loop–body for a given parallel loop has a constant execution time.

Consider a DOALL loop with N iterations whose body execution time is B units, and which is to be executed on a system with p processors. In Section 3.2.4.2 we computed an approximation to the CPS, i.e., the minimum number of iterations k (chunk) which must be packed together and form a process large enough to amortize the overhead σ involved during dispatching. This was

$$k > \frac{\sigma}{B(p-1)}. \qquad (5.9)$$

If $N \leq k$ then that loop must be executed serially; any parallel execution would be worse than its serial one. In the following sections we compute the optimal number of processors for a given loop–overhead model combination; a measure which is equivalent to the "optimal chunk size".

5.4. TWO RUN–TIME OVERHEAD MODELS

To analyze the run–time overhead we use two conjectures that have been backed by empirical results [Cytr85], [LeKK86], [Ston87]. The first conjecture states that during the parallel execution of a task the run–time overhead is linearly proportional to the number of processors involved. The second conjecture states that the run–time overhead is logarithmically proportional to the number of processors. Let us consider two examples where these two conjectures are valid.

Consider the execution of a DOALL loop on a set of p processors connected to a common bus. If the iterations of this DOALL are spread among the p processors, then all p processors must execute a join operation before they are allowed to proceed with the next task. If two lexically adjacent DOALLs L_1 and L_2 operate on the same array, it will be necessary (in general) to execute a barrier synchronization (join) between L_1 and L_2. Thus all processors executing L_1 must finish before they start on L_2. Clearly the execution of a barrier operation on a bus–based multiprocessor involves O (p) steps in the worst case [Ston87]. In a dynamic scheduling environment this overhead will also occur during dispatching of iterations, assuming all processors start on a loop at the same time.

If the same example is used for p processors interconnected in a tree structure, the barrier operation will take O (logp) steps to complete. A more real–world example of logarithmic run–time overhead are shared memory multiprocessors such as the Cedar and the Ultracomputer which employ multistage interconnection networks. If no special hardware is used and if synchronization is done through the shared memory, then the logarithmic overhead case applies here as well. The results presented in this section can be used by the compiler to draw exact or approximate conclusions for each task in a program, and can be used at run–time to avoid inefficient processor allocations.

5.4.1. Run–time Overhead is O (p)

As mentioned above we can identify a parallel task with a DOALL loop without loss of generality. Let T_1 and T_p denote, as usual, the serial and parallel execution time of a given task. Let N be the number of iterations of a DOALL loop and B the execution time of the loop–body. If the loop–body has a varying execution time the procedure of Section 5.5 can be used to derive a worst case or average value for B.

In this section we consider the case where the run–time overhead is linearly proportional to the number of processors assigned to a parallel loop. Let σ_o be the run–time overhead constant which in general depends on the characteristics of the code and the machine architecture. The compiler can supply the value of σ_o for each loop (parallel task) in the program. The serial execution time of a loop with N iterations and a loop–body execution time of B would be $T_1=NB$. The parallel execution time then on p–processors would be

$$T_p = \left\lceil \frac{N}{p} \right\rceil B + \sigma_o p. \tag{5.10}$$

Consider (5.10) as a function of p. If overhead was zero, (5.10) would be an integer–valued decreasing function. Since (5.10) is not continuous it is not amenable to analytical study. We can approximate the function in (5.10) by a continuous function, by eliminating the ceiling. We thus get

$$T (p) = NB/p + \sigma_o p. \tag{5.11}$$

T (p) is a continuous real function in the interval (0, $+\infty$), with continuous first and second derivatives. Therefore we can study its shape and determine the point where overhead becomes minimal. In other words we want to find the value of p for which (5.10) becomes minimum and therefore the speedup of that task is maximized. The minimum value is given by the following theorem.

Theorem 5.2. T (p) in (5.11) is minimized when the task is executed on a number of processors given by

$$p_0 = \sqrt{NB \, / \, \sigma_0}. \tag{5.12}$$

Proof: First we show how (5.12) is derived and then prove that it is indeed the optimal value for that task (loop). Consider (5.11) which is an approximation to the parallel execution time defined by (5.10). $T(p)$ has a first derivative

$$\frac{dT(p)}{dp} = T'(p) = -\frac{NB}{p^2} + \sigma_0. \tag{5.13}$$

The local extreme points of (5.11) are at the roots of its first derivative, that is, at

$$p_{0,1} = \pm\sqrt{NB \, / \, \sigma_0} \tag{5.14}$$

and since we are only interested for values in the interval $(0, +\infty)$, we discard the negative root p_1. The second derivative of $T(p)$ is

$$\frac{d^2T(p)}{dp^2} = T''(p) = \frac{2NB}{p^3} > 0. \tag{5.15}$$

$T''(p)$ is always greater than zero and therefore the extreme at $(p_0, T(p_0))$ is a minimum, where p_0 is given by (5.14). If p_0 is an integer that divides N, then the parallel execution time T_p is also minimized and it is given by

$$T_{p_0} = \frac{NB}{\sqrt{NB/\sigma_0}} + \sigma_0\sqrt{NB \, / \, \sigma_0} =$$

$$\sqrt{NB\sigma_0} + \sqrt{NB\sigma_0} = 2\sqrt{NB\sigma_0}. \tag{5.16}$$

Indeed if T_p is the parallel execution time for any other p, then p can be expressed as $p = c\sqrt{NB/\sigma_0}$ where c is a positive rational number. Then $T_{p_0} < T_p$, or equivalently,

$$2\sqrt{NB\sigma_0} < \sqrt{(NB)^2\sigma_0 \, / \, c^2(NB)} + \sqrt{c^2\sigma_0^2(NB) \, / \, \sigma_0} \tag{5.17}$$

and if we substitute $x = NB\sigma_0$ in (5.17) we have

$$2\sqrt{x} < \sqrt{x/c^2} + \sqrt{c^2x} \quad \longrightarrow \quad 0 < x(1 + c^4 - 2c^2)$$

and since $x > 0$, we get $(1 - c^2)^2 > 0$ which is always true. ∎
Therefore p_0 is the optimal value for $T(p)$ and in certain cases the optimal value for T_p.

Corollary 5.3. For $\sigma_0 \geq (NB)/4$ the approximation function $T(p)$ defined in (5.11) satisfies

$$T(p) \geq NB \tag{5.18}$$

for any integer $p \neq 0$.

Proof: By substituting $T(p)$ from (5.11) in (5.18) we have

$$\frac{NB}{p} + \sigma_0 p > NB \quad \text{or} \quad \sigma_0 p^2 + p(NB) + NB > 0. \tag{5.19}$$

(5.19) is a quadratic equation of p and since $\sigma_0 > 0$, the inequality in (5.19) is always true if the determinant D of the equation in (5.19) is negative, i.e.,

$$D = (NB)^2 - 4\sigma_o (NB) < 0 \quad \text{which gives us} \quad \sigma_o > \frac{NB}{4}. \blacksquare$$

Corollary 5.4. If $\sigma_o \geq (NB)/k$ then the parallel execution time for $p \geq k$ is greater than the serial execution time, i.e., $T_p > T_1$.

5.4.2. Run–Time Overhead is $O(\log p)$

Let us assume that the run–time overhead is logarithmically proportional to the number of processors assigned to a parallel task. Therefore, in this case the parallel execution time is given by

$$T_p = \left\lceil \frac{N}{p} \right\rceil B + \sigma_o \log p. \tag{5.20}$$

To determine the optimal number of processors that can be assigned to a parallel task, we follow the same approach as in the previous case. Again since (5.20) is not a continuous function we approximate it with

$$T(p) = \frac{NB}{p} + \sigma_o \log p \tag{5.21}$$

which is continuous in $(0, +\infty)$, with continuous first and second derivatives. The corresponding theorem follows.

Theorem 5.3. The approximate parallel execution time defined by (5.21) is minimized when

$$p_o = \frac{NB}{\sigma_o}.$$

Proof: The first derivative of (5.21) is given by

$$\frac{dT(p)}{dp} = T'(p) = -\frac{NB}{p^2} + \frac{\sigma_o}{p}. \tag{5.22}$$

$T'(p)$ has an extreme point at

$$p_o = \frac{NB}{\sigma_o}. \tag{5.23}$$

The second derivative of (5.21) at p_o is

$$T''(p) = \frac{2NB - \sigma_o p}{p^3} \quad \text{and} \quad T''(NB/\sigma_o) = \frac{\sigma_o^3}{(NB)^2} > 0$$

Therefore $T(p)$ has a minimum at $p = p_o$. $\blacksquare$

However p_o is not necessarily a minimum point for (5.20). We can compute an approximation to the optimal number of processors for (5.20) as follows. Let $\epsilon = \lceil p_o \rceil - p_o$ where $0 < \epsilon < 1$. Then the number of processors p_o' that "minimizes" the parallel execution time T_p in (5.20) is given by

$$p_o' = \begin{cases} \lfloor p_o \rfloor & \text{if } \epsilon \leq 0.5 \\ \lceil p_o \rceil & \text{if } \epsilon > 0.5 \end{cases} \tag{5.24}$$

where $p_o = NB/\sigma_o$. In the next section we see that (5.24) is a very close approximation to the optimal number of processors for (5.20). The overhead problem was studied in a similar context in [Cytr85].

5.4.3. Measurements

We can use the above models to derive an approximate estimate of the effect of run–time overhead on the degree of usable parallelism, and thus on execution time. We used (5.10) to compute the actual execution time of a parallel task, and (5.11) to compute its approximation function for the linear overhead case. Similarly (5.20) and (5.21) were used for the logarithmic overhead case.

Figure 5.1 illustrates the execution time versus the number of processors for a DOALL with N=150 and B=8 under (a) linear overhead, and (b) under logarithmic overhead. Figures 5.2, 5.3, and 5.4 illustrate the same data for three different DOALLs, whose N and B values are shown in each figure. The solid lines plot the values of T_p, the actual parallel execution time. Dashed lines give the approximate execution times $T(p)$. For these measurements a value of $\sigma_o = 4$ was used. The overhead constant although optimistically low, is not unrealistically small for (hypothetical) systems with fast synchronization hardware. In all cases we observe that as long as $p \leq N$ (which is the case of interest), the difference between the values of the approximation function $T(p)$ and the actual parallel execution time T_p is negligible.

Looking at Figures 5.1a and 5.3a we observe that when the loop body is small, the associated overhead limits severely the number of processors that can be used on that loop. For these two cases for example, only 1/10 and 1/40 of the ideal speedup can be achieved. When B is large however the overhead has a less negative impact on performance. For the case of Figure 5.2a for instance, 1/2 of the maximum speedup can be obtained in the presense of linear overhead. The same is true for Figure 5.4a. In all cases the logarithmic overhead had significantly less negative impact on speedup.

5.5. DECIDING THE MINIMUM UNIT OF ALLOCATION

Estimating the projected execution time of a piece of code (on a single processor) can be done by the compiler or the run–time system with the same precision. Let us take for example the case of a DOALL loop without conditional statements. All that needs to be done is estimate the execution time of the loop body, and let it be B. For our purpose, the exact number of loop iterations need not be known at compile–time. Since we know the overhead for the particular machine and the structure of a particular loop, we can find the critical block size for that DOALL that is, the minimum number X of iterations that can be allocated to a single processor such that $S_p > 1$. This number X can be "attached" to that DOALL loop as an attribute at compile–time. During execution the run–time system must assign to an idle processor X or more iterations of that loop (but no less). In case $X \leq N$ the loop is treated as serial.

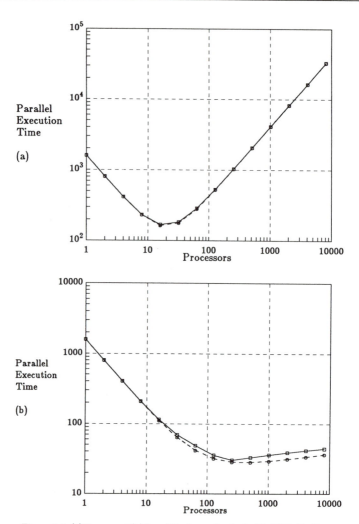

Figure 5.1. (a) linear and (b) logarithmic overheads for N=200, B=8.

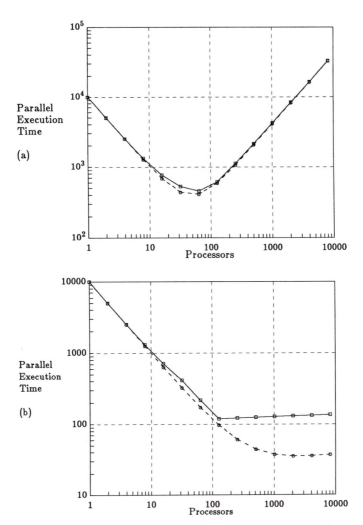

Figure 5.2. (a) linear and (b) logarithmic overheads for N=100, B=100.

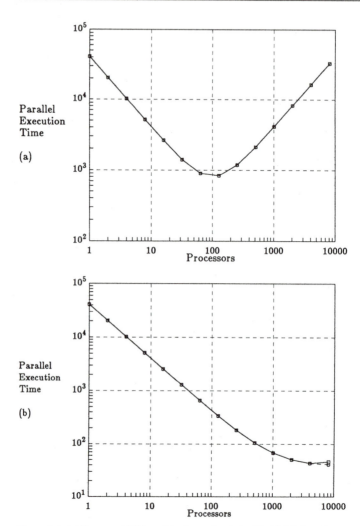

Figure 5.3. (a) linear and (b) logarithmic overheads for N=4096, B=10.

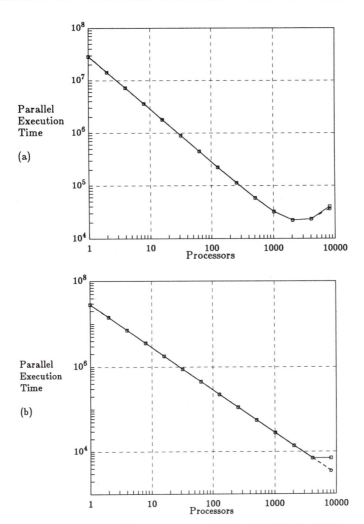

Figure 5.4. (a) linear and (b) logarithmic overheads for N=4096, B=7000.

```
1:   B₁
     if C₁ then B₂
     else B₃
     B₂
     if C₂ then goto 1
     else if C₃ then B₄
               else B₅
     exit
     B₃
     if C₄ then B₆
     else B₇
```

Figure 5.5. An example of conditional code.

Let us consider the code inside a DOALL loop. The control–flow graph of a code module with conditional statements can be uniquely represented by a directed graph.

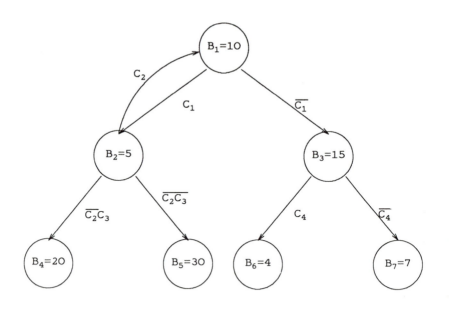

Figure 5.6. The control flow tree of Figure 5.5.

Consider for example the code module of Figure 5.5 which constitutes the loop body of some DOALL. The corresponding control–flow graph is shown in Figure 5.6. Since there is no hope of accurately estimating the execution time either in the compiler or at run–time, we choose to follow a conservative path. The execution time of each basic block $B_1, \ldots, B_7$ can be estimated quite precisely. We take the execution time of the loop body to be equal to the execution time of the shortest path in the tree.

The shortest path can be found by starting from the root of the tree and proceeding downwards labeling the nodes as follows. Let t_i be the execution time of node v_i, and l_i be its label. The root v_1 is labeled $l_1 = t_1$. Then a node v_i with parent node v_j is labeled with $l_i = l_j + t_i$. As we proceed we mark the node with the minimum (so far) label. In case we reach a node that has already been labeled (cycle) we ignore it. Otherwise we proceed until we reach the leaves of the tree. Note that the labeling process does not have to be completed: If at some point during the labeling process the node that has the minimum label happens to be a leaf, the labeling process terminates. The path π that consists of the marked nodes is the shortest execution path in that code. The number of iterations required (conservatively) to form the critical size is a function of the number of processors as it is indicated by (5.9). B, the execution time of π, is given by the label of the last node of path π. A less conservative approach would be to take the average path length, assuming all branches in the code are equally probable. In the example of Figure 5.6 the above procedures give us B = 12 and B = 33.33 respectively.

CHAPTER 6

STATIC PROGRAM PARTITIONING

6.1. INTRODUCTION

In this chapter we attempt to define more precisely the problems of program partitioning and interprocessor communication, to model them, identify the variables involved and quantify them. We mentioned earlier that program partitioning, interprocessor communication, parallelism, and data dependences are all closely related. In shared memory parallel machines, interprocessor communication is not explicit but it happens through sharing of specific memory locations. Processors read from and write to shared memory under the control of synchronization which enforces a predetermined order. However, in message passing systems (e.g., hypercube architectures), communication between processors takes place through the use of explicit send/receive of packets of data. Since there is no shared memory in such systems, data is requested by a given processor from another specific processor in the distributed system. The latter processor must then assemble a packet with the requested data and forward it to the requesting processor. The message may be routed through other intermediate processors before it reaches its destination. Thus communication overhead is far more critical on distributed systems than it is on shared memory systems. As discussed in Chapter 3, a consequence of this is that parallel tasks in distributed systems are of coarse granularity.

The models and techniques which are discussed here may be applicable, at least in principle, to both shared and distributed memory systems. However, since communication is less important than other types of run–time overheads in shared memory machines, simpler partitioning schemes (like the ones described in Chapter 3) may be as effective or even better than optimal or near–optimal static partitioning. In distributed systems, dynamic partitioning involves the creation, assignment and migration of tasks in real–time. These activities may be too expensive to effectively utilize the parallelism in programs without tasks of large granularity. In such cases a fully static partitioning may be the only alternative solution.

Let us consider initially the problem of interprocessor communication for the case of a 2–processor system. During the parallel execution of a program, different program modules will execute on different processors. Since both processors work on the same program there should be some coordination among them. One processor must "inform" the other at certain instances about specific events. The process of information exchange between two or more processors executing the same program is called *interprocessor communication*. We can distinguish two types of interprocessor communication: *Data communication*, during which one processor receives data that it needs from other processors, and *control communication*, where processors exchange control information, for example to announce an event or to coordinate execution. Data communication is mostly program dependent. Control communication depends highly on the architecture of the machine and is necessary only because it is needed to impose an order under which specific events must take place (e.g. order of execution). Both types of interprocessor communication are significant because both are reflected as overhead in the total execution time of a program. Control communication is involved in activities such as barrier synchronization, semaphore updates, or invocations of the operating system. For the most part in this chapter, we ignore control communication or assume that it takes a constant amount of time to check/update a semaphore, set a flag, or activate a process.

As mentioned in Chapter 1 from the DDG of a program we can derive different compact DDGs with nodes representing blocks of code (instead of statements) and arcs representing collections of dependences between nodes. Each different CDDG defines a different program partition. Let G(V, E) be a compact data dependence graph of a given program. This directed graph G(V, E) is called the *program task graph* or simply the *task graph*. The nodes V of G are the tasks of the program and arcs E represent data dependences among tasks. Each node $v_i \in V$ makes a request for r_i processors (i.e., task v_i can use at most r_i processors). We have serial and parallel tasks when $r_i = 1$ and $r_i \geq 1$ respectively. During program execution a parallel task spawns two or more processes. A parallel loop for example can be considered a parallel task with one or more iterations forming a process. A task graph may be connected or disconnected. The cardinality of G is the number of connected subgraphs in G. If $|G| = |V|$ then any parallel execution of G will involve an interprocessor communication of zero. The *indegree* of a node of G is the number of dependence arcs pointing to it, or equivalently, the number of immediate predecessors of that node. Similarly we define the *outdegree* of a node to be the number of immediate successors or the number of arcs originating from that node. The indegree of a subgraph G' of G is the number of arcs $u \rightarrow v$ such that u does not belong to G' and $v \in G'$. The *outdegree* of G' is the number of arcs of G such that $u \rightarrow v$, $u \in G'$ and v does not belong to G'. A node or subgraph of G is said to be *ready* if its indegree is zero. All nodes of a subgraph with zero indegree can be executed in parallel. Consider the two loops of Figure 6.1. The second loop is data dependent on the first loop. However we can still execute them in parallel, each on a different processor assuming synchronized write/read access to array A by each processor.

6.1.1. Communication and Parallelism Trade–offs

Communication overhead obviously occurs at run–time, but we want to deal with the problem at compile–time (the reason being that any extra run–time activity will incur additional overhead). We will consider techniques which when applied to the source program at compile–time, result in the reduction of communication at run–time. The main goal is to design these schemes such that when applied to a given program, they do not reduce the degree of potential parallelism in that program. In other words, if $PROG_1$ and $PROG_2$ denote a parallel program before and after optimization of communication is done, the execution time of $PROG_2$ on a p–processor machine under any scheduling policy will be less than or equal to the execution time of $PROG_1$ under the same scheduling policy.

Now let us see how communication takes place between two tasks u and v where v is data dependent on u. If during execution u and v run concurrently on different processors, data computed in u must be sent to v and the overhead involved is explicitly taken into account. Another alternative is to execute u to completion and thereafter execute v on the *same* processor(s). Thus data computed in u and used by v can reside in the corresponding processor(s), and therefore no explicit communication through the interconnection network is needed. Yet another alternative is to execute v after u has completed, and possibly on a different set of processors. In this case we assume the existence of *prefetching* capabilities in the system (e.g., Cedar machine), i.e., the data computed in u and used by v are written into the shared memory (upon completion of u) and prefetched (for example to registers)

```
DO   i=1,n
     . . .
S1:  A(i) = B(i) * C(i)
     . . .
ENDO


DO   i=1,n
     . . .
S2:  D(i) = A(i) + E(i)
     . . .
ENDO
```

Figure 6.1. Example of data communication.

before v starts executing. The communication overhead in this case will also be zero. Note that this latter approach allows other tasks to execute between the time u completes and the time v starts. It also takes care of local memory limitations, e.g. when the processor(s) executing u is unable (due to memory limitations) to keep the data needed by v until v starts executing. In general, we can not avoid overheads due to real–time communication that occurs when tasks execute concurrently, but by using appropriate techniques one can eliminate or reduce this overhead when the tasks involved execute on different time intervals.

One possible approach is to reduce interprocessor communication by disallowing high level spreading whenever it appears to be harmful. It is clear that by prohibiting high level spreading we reduce the degree of potential program parallelism. As shown later however, this is done only when it can be guaranteed that the savings in interprocessor communication outweight the potential loss of parallelism irrespectively of the scheduling scheme used.

In what follows when we explicitly prohibit two or more (data dependent) tasks from executing concurrently, we say that these tasks are *merged*. Thus task merging does not actually merge tasks but it implies that the merged tasks can execute on the same or different sets of processors, but on different time intervals. This restriction can be relaxed for certain cases as shown later. For our purposes we assume that merged tasks execute on adjacent time intervals (one after the other), and the data computed by one task reside in local memory until the successor task can use them. During execution each task is assigned a set of processors which remains fixed throughout execution of that task, or varies dynamically during execution.

The process of merging defines a *partition* of the program into disjoint code modules or tasks. One should start from a structure that represents a program without "hiding" any of its parallelism. This structure should be a low–level representation of the program, and in our case the best one is the data dependence graph. Any other higher level program graph can be derived from the DDG by merging some of its nodes. Merging however may hide some of the parallelism inherent in the DDG. The extreme case is considering the entire program (DDG) as a single node (task). (It should be emphasized that we are not concerned about how to schedule a program graph at this point; and the material of this chapter is applicable to any scheduling scheme.) Since merging reduces the degree of parallelism, it should be done only when it can be proved that the (resulting) reduced graph will have a shorter execution time than that of the previous graph, under any scheduling scheme. Clearly independent tasks can never be merged, unless scheduling overhead is taken into account. First we consider an idealized program model consisting of atomic operations, and without coarse grain constructs. All atomic operations have equal execution times. Then we consider the case of Fortran–like programs and show how some of the above ideas can be applied to real programs.

6.1.2. More on Communication and Partitioning

For the rest of this chapter interprocessor communication refers to data communication alone, unless stated otherwise. Let u_i denote the task (program module) assigned to processor i, in a parallel processor system with p processors. Then interprocessor communication, or data communication from processor i to processor j, takes place if and only if u_j is data or flow dependent on u_i. Anti–dependences and output dependences can be satisfied through control communication only. Therefore data communication refers to interprocessor communication that involves explicit transmission of data between processors.

Let us define the *unit of data* to be a scalar value, and the *communication unit* τ to be the time it takes to transmit a unit of data between two processors. Then the time spent for communication during the concurrent execution of the two loops of Figure 6.1 on two processors would be $\tau*n$.

Real–time interprocessor communication takes place only during the parallel execution of data dependent tasks. By executing such tasks in parallel we may reduce the execution time if the amount of communication is not too high. Clearly there is a tradeoff between parallelism and communication. Communication is minimized when all tasks execute on the same processor; parallelism however is also minimized in such a case. Parallelism on the other hand tends to be maximized (or equivalently execution time tends to be minimized) when each task executes on a different processor. This however maximizes interprocessor communication. The problem of simultaneously maximizing parallelism and minimizing communication is a hard optimization problem that has been proved NP–Complete [Ston77], [GaJo79], [GiPo88a]. Communication takes place to satisfy data dependences. Another way of viewing this relation is the following: communication quantifies the notion of flow dependence between different tasks.

We can intuitively define the *degree of parallelism* as the number of ready tasks (processes) at any given moment. Obviously in a system with p processors we want the degree of parallelism to always be at least p. In general, the degree of parallelism and interprocessor communication are incompatible. The goal during program partitioning is to decompose the program as much as possible to keep the degree of parallelism close to p, and at the same time to have as many independent tasks as possible to keep interprocessor communication low. Usually it is impossible to optimize both objectives since optimizing one counteroptimizes the other. For certain cases however there is an "equilibrium" point that minimizes the parallel execution time.

6.2. METHODS FOR PROGRAM PARTITIONING

There are two approaches for partitioning a program. The *top–down* approach starts with a single task which is the entire program. Then following some rules it decomposes the program into smaller tasks in a recursive way. The second is a *bottom–up* approach. Starting with the lowest level graph representation of the program, it tries to merge nodes together to form larger tasks. The best low level representation of a program is the DDG. In both cases we have to split or merge nodes repeatedly until 1) we have enough tasks to assign to p processors at each moment during execution, and 2) the splitting/merging creates tasks with as few interdependences as possible. Heuristic algorithms could be used to obtain a suitable partition. In terms of available information, the bottom–up composition is superior to the top–down decomposition. This is true since during decomposition of the entire program we do not have information about its internal structure, and extensive searching must take place. During composition however, we have information about the global structure of the program (that can be easily maintained by the compiler) as well as about its basic components. We can therefore perform local optimizations that may be impossible or very expensive to do in the top–down approach. For what follows we assume that program partitioning is performed through composition starting from the data dependence graph of the program.

Let $G_i \equiv G_i(V_i, E_i)$ be a directed graph. A possible approach to program partitioning is to start from G_1, the DDG of the program, and through a series of transformations that create a sequence of CDDGs $G_2, G_3, \ldots, G_{k-1}$, construct G_k which gives the program task graph and therefore the final partition. Since the construction of the program graph is done through composition we have $|V_1| \leq |V_2| \leq \cdots \leq |V_k|$ and $|E_1| \leq \cdots \leq |E_k|$. Presumably, G_k will have enough tasks to keep all p processors busy while minimizing interprocessor communication. Nodes are merged only if data communication is very high. In this way we reduce only the necessary degree of parallelism to keep communication at tolerable levels. The next section describes the model that can be used to construct G_k.

6.2.1. A Model for Quantifying Communication

For simplicity, let us assume that communication is done serially and only one pair of processors can communicate at any point in time (consider, for example, a machine with p processors that are connected through a bus to a shared memory). The model starts with a representation of the program as a directed task graph as defined in the previous section. Candidates for merging are nodes whose possible parallel execution involves a large amount of data communication.

Let G_1 be the DDG of a program. The first composition of tasks finds all strongly connected components of G_1. Each strongly connected component forms a task and let G_2 be the resulting task graph. The arcs of G_1 and G_2 are labeled with weights called the *communication traffic* or *weight* such that the weight w_i of arc $e_i = (v_i, v_j)$ is given by

$$w_i = \tau * m$$

where m is the number of data items that need to be transmitted from task v_i to task v_j, and τ is the communication constant. For example the communication traffic between the two loops of Figure 6.1 is $\tau * n$. During the reduction of G_1 to G_2 the composition of new tasks is performed as follows:

Let $V_1 = \{u_1, u_2, \ldots, u_n\}$ be the tasks of G_1 and t_{v_i}, (i=1, $\cdots$,n) be their serial execution times. Suppose now that subgraph $H_i \subseteq G_1$ is a strongly connected component of G_1. Then H_i is replaced by a node u^H with execution time

$$t_i = \sum_{v \in H_i} t_v.$$

Arcs are merged using the following procedure: For each task v not in H_i, replace all arcs $e_1^v, e_2^v, \ldots, e_j^v$ originating from v and such that $e_i^v = (v, u_k)$, and $u_k \in H_i$, (i=1, 2, $\ldots$, j) with an arc $e^v = (v, u^H)$ which has a weight w^u given by

$$w^u = \sum_{i=1}^{j} w_i^v.$$

After the first reduction the resulting graph G_2 is a connected or disconnected graph without nontrivial strongly connected components. Therefore G_2 is a directed acyclic graph or DAG.

During parallel execution of G_2, two (or more) independent or data dependent nodes may execute simultaneously. Let $u_i \rightarrow u_j$ be two data dependent tasks. If u_i and u_j execute simultaneously on two processors, the total execution time T will be

$$T = \max(T_1^i, T_1^j) + w_{ij}.$$

This is a reasonable assumption since the processors are connected through a bus and bus transactions are serial. The communication time w_{ij} is reflected in the total execution time since the processor executing u_i incurs an overhead to transmit the data, and the processor executing u_j must wait until the data arrives.

Let us assume that the total overhead is equal to the time it takes to transmit the data. Therefore if tasks u_i and u_j execute on the same processor, the communication can be done through the local memory inside each processor and it is ignored. The execution time in that case will be

$$T_1 = T_1^i + T_1^j.$$

We also assume that tasks are collections of atomic operations, and if u is a parallel task and T_1^u is its serial execution time, then the parallel execution time T_p^u of u on $p \leq T_1^u$ processors will be

$$T_p^u = \frac{T_1^u}{p}. \tag{6.1}$$

Consider a set of two tasks $\{u, v\}$. We use the notation (set-x/task-x) to describe the execution of u and v, where x can be *serial* or *parallel*. *Task–serial* (or t–s) means that both u and v execute serially. *Task–parallel* (or t–p) indicates that at least one of u and v executes on more than one processor. *Set–serial* (or s–s) means that both u and v execute on the same *set* of processors (perhaps each in parallel). If both execute on p processors, then u will complete execution before v starts. If u executes on p and v on p' processors and $p < p'$, then p' processors are given to the set and u and v start simultaneous execution with u executing on the first p processors and v executing on the remaining $p'-p$ processors. When u finishes executing, all p' processors are taken over by v. *Set–parallel* (or s–p) means that u and v are executed concurrently on disjoint sets of processors. Therefore there are four possible ways of executing u and v. (s-s/t-s) describes the case where both u and v execute serially on the same processor. (s-s/t-p) when each of u and v executes in parallel but on the same set of processors. (s-p/t-s) is the case of u and v executing serially but each on a different processor. Finally (s-p/t-p) denotes the case where each of u and v executes in parallel and both execute concurrently on disjoint sets of processors.

As mentioned above, interprocessor communication is ignored for the case of (s-s/t-s) or (s-s/t-p) when all tasks execute on the same number of processors. For the case of two tasks u and v the total execution time is defined as follows:

$$(s\text{-}s/t\text{-}s) \quad \rightarrow \quad T_1^u + T_1^v \tag{6.2}$$

$$(s\text{-}s/t\text{-}p) \quad \rightarrow \quad T_p^u + T_p^v \tag{6.3}$$

(if both execute on the same p processors)

$$(s\text{-}p/t\text{-}s) \quad \longrightarrow \quad \max(T_1^u, T_1^v) + w_e \qquad (6.4)$$

$$(s\text{-}p/t\text{-}p) \quad \longrightarrow \quad \max(T_p^u, T_{p'}^v) + w_e \qquad (6.5)$$

where w_e is the weight of the arc $e = (u, v)$ (if any) and p, p' are disjoint sets of processors used by u and v, respectively.

Note that for the $(s\text{-}s/t\text{-}p)$ case, if u and v execute on a different number (but have a common subset) of processors, say p and p' respectively, then the total execution time is defined as follows: Suppose $p < p'$, i.e., both tasks will execute on a common set of p processors but task v will use an extra $p' - p$ processors. Suppose also that task v will finish execution after task u has completed. Both tasks start executing concurrently, u on p processors and v on $p' - p$ processors. When u terminates, task v takes over the remaining p processors and executes on p' processors until it completes. Since the overlap (i.e. set serialization) is not perfect some interprocessor communication will occur in this case. We assume that the data communication is proportional to $p' - p/p'$. In other words if the total amount of data communication from u to v is w, the amount of data that must be explicitly transmitted will be inversely proportional to the the number of common processors. In the above case the data communication that must be transmitted through the bus will be $(p' - p/p')\,w$. When $p' = p$ (total set serialization), the communication is zero. When p' and p are disjoint sets of processors (set parallel), then $p = 0$ and therefore the data communication is w as would be expected based on the previous definitions. Therefore the total execution time for the case of $(s\text{-}s/t\text{-}p)$ where u and v execute on p and p' processors respectively is

$$t_{u,v} = T_p^u + \frac{T_1^v - (p' - p)\,T_p^u}{p'} + \left(\frac{p' - p}{p'}\right) w. \qquad (6.6)$$

Since this case is not truly set–serial let us denote it with $(s\text{-}\tilde{s}/t\text{-}p)$. The above model describes four basic *schedules*. We can compare basic schedules, i.e., the corresponding schedule lengths (or execution times) using the following notation.

$$(s\text{-}?/t\text{-}?) \quad \bullet \quad (s\text{-}?/t\text{-}?)$$

where $? \in \{\text{serial, parallel}\}$ and $\bullet \in \{ <, \leq, >, \geq, =, \neq \}$. We can augment the basic schedule notation with a tuple that specifies the number of processors assigned to each task. For the case of the previous example $(s\text{-}s/t\text{-}p)\ (p, p)$, indicates that u will execute on p processors followed by the execution of v on the same p processors. The schedule corresponding to (6.6) can be uniquely characterized by $(s\text{-}\tilde{s}/t\text{-}p)\ (p, p')$. We can now state the following lemma.

Lemma 6.1. If u and v are two adjacent tasks connected by $e = (u, v)$ with a communication weight of w_e, and

$$(s\text{-}s/t\text{-}s) \leq (s\text{-}p/t\text{-}s) \quad \text{or} \quad T_1^u + T_1^v \leq \max(T_1^u, T_1^v) + w_e \qquad (6.7)$$

then it is also true that

$$(s\text{-}s/t\text{-}p) \leq (s\text{-}p/t\text{-}p) \quad \text{or} \quad T_p^u + T_p^v \leq \max(T_p^u, T_p^v) + w_e. \qquad (6.8)$$

Equivalently if the execution time of u and v when they execute serially on the same processor is smaller than when they execute simultaneously on two different processors, then the combined parallel execution time when they execute on the same set of p processors is smaller than when each executes on its own set of p processors and their execution is concurrent.

Proof: Since (6.7) is true, it follows directly that

$$w_e \geq \min(T_1^u, T_1^v) .$$

Since by definition $T_p^u \leq T_1^v$ and $T_p^v \leq T_1^v$ we have

$$w_e \geq \min(T_p^u, T_p^v) \tag{6.9}$$

and by adding the same term to both sides of (6.9) we get

$$w_e + \max(T_p^u, T_p^v) \geq \min(T_p^u, T_p^v) + \max(T_p^u, T_p^v) . \tag{6.10}$$

But the right handside of (6.10) is by definition equal to $T_p^u + T_p^v$, therefore (6.8) is also true. ∎

Theorem 6.1. For a set of tasks { u, v } and an unlimited number of processors, the following is a generalization of Lemma 6.1.

$$\text{if} \qquad (s\text{-}s/t\text{-}s) \leq (s\text{-}p/t\text{-}s)$$

$$\text{then} \qquad (s\text{-}s/t\text{-}p)\,(p,\ p') \leq (s\text{-}p/t\text{-}p)\,(p,\ p')$$

or equivalently (from (6.2), (6.4), (6.5), and (6.6))

$$\text{if} \qquad T_1^u + T_1^v \leq \max(T_1^u,\ T_1^v) + w_e \tag{6.11}$$

$$\text{then} \qquad T_p^u + \frac{T_1^v - (p' - p)\,T_p^u}{p'} \leq \max(T_p^u,\ T_{p'}^v) + \frac{p}{p'}w_e . \tag{6.12}$$

Proof: We have two cases depending on which of u and v is larger.
Case 1: $T_1^u \geq T_1^v$, (i.e., task u is greater than or equal to task v). Then from (6.11) we have

$$T_1^v \leq w_e . \tag{6.13}$$

From (6.12) and (6.1) we have,

$$pT_1^v - \left\lfloor \frac{p' - p}{p} \right\rfloor T_1^u \leq pT_1^v \leq pw_e$$

which is true due to (6.13).
Case 2: $T_1^u < T_1^v$ (i.e., task u is smaller than v). Therefore from (6.11) we have

$$T_1^u \leq w_e . \tag{6.14}$$

Here there are two subcases.
Subcase 2.1: $T_{p'}^v \geq T_p^u$. \tag{6.15}
Then after we carry out the calculations in (6.12) we have

$$pT_p^u \leq pw_e \qquad \text{or} \qquad T_p^u \leq w_e$$

which is (6.15) and therefore true.
Subcase 2.2: $T_{p'}^v < T_p^u$. \tag{6.16}
Again from (6.12) we have

$$T_1^v - (p' - p)\, T_p^u \leq pw_e \qquad \text{or,} \qquad pT_1^v - (p' - p)\, T_1^u \leq p^2 w_e$$

and finally

$$\frac{T_1^v}{T_1^u} \leq pw_e + \frac{p' - p}{p}. \tag{6.17}$$

But from (6.16) we have

$$\frac{T_1^v}{p'} \leq \frac{T_1^u}{p} \qquad \text{or,} \qquad \frac{T_1^v}{T_1^u} \leq \frac{p'}{p} \tag{6.18}$$

and therefore to show (6.17) it is enough to show that

$$\frac{p'}{p} \leq p^2 w_e + \frac{p' - p}{p}, \qquad \text{or,} \qquad w_e \geq \frac{1}{p}$$

which is true since $w_e \geq T_1^u > 1/p$. ∎

Lemma 6.1 and Theorem 6.1 can be used to partition a program in a bottom–up approach, starting from its DDG representation and composing larger tasks by merging nodes of the DDG together whenever appropriate. But task merging reduces the possibilities for high level spreading and therefore the degree of parallelism. However by using Lemma 6.1 and Theorem 6.1 we can merge only those tasks that do not affect the degree of parallelism. More precisely if G is a program task graph and u, v are tasks in G, then let G' be the graph derived from G by merging nodes u and v into a single node w. The merging of u and v takes place if and only if the execution time of G' is less than or equal to the execution time of G under any scheduling scheme and any number of processors. In other words we merge tasks together only when it is "safe" under any circumstances.

We can merge tasks of a graph G in any order by checking repeatedly pairs of tasks in G. If a pair of tasks satisfies the conditions of Lemma 6.1 or Theorem 6.1, the two nodes in the pair are merged and form a single task. If for a given task there is more than one adjacent task for which the conditions are met, the order of merging becomes significant. Only in special cases one can find the optimal order and thus the optimal partition. However any merging that is based on the above tests is bound to reduce G into a task graph G' that will have an execution time less than or equal to that of G, irrespectively of the scheduling scheme used. For example an initial partition of the graph in Figure 6.2a will be formed by merging the first three nodes labeled 5, 10, and 15 into a single node labeled 30. This will be accomplished in two steps. The same partition will be obtained if we start from the leftmost or rightmost node. For special types of graphs the optimal merging can be found.

6.3. OPTIMAL TASK COMPOSITION FOR CHAINS

This section considers partitioning of chains, a restricted type of directed graphs. Due to the simple structure chains, an optimal partition can be computed in polynomial time. Chains model a large number of real applications especially at higher granularity levels. For example, an inherently serial application can be represented by a sequence (chain) of subroutine calls, or by the most time consuming path in the procedure call tree.

A *chain* graph is a directed graph $G(V, E)$ with $V=\{1, 2, \ldots, k\}$ and $E=\{e_i=(i, i+1) \mid i=1, \ldots, k-1\}$ (Figure 6.2a). Each node i is associated with a weight t_i which is its serial execution time. Each arc $e_i=(i, i+1)$ is labeled with a weight w_{e_i} which gives the amount of communication traffic from node i to node $i+1$.

Consider a chain graph G, and let v_o and v_k be its first (source) and last (sink) node respectively. Let $V_G = \{1, 2, \ldots, k\}$ be the tasks in chain G. We construct a layered graph L_G consisting of k layers $L_1, L_2, \ldots, L_k$. Nodes in L_G are represented by ordered pairs (i, j) such that $1 \leq i, j \leq k$ and $i \leq j$. A node (i, j) denotes the merging of nodes i through j (inclusive) into a single node. Each node (i, j) in L_G is labeled with t_{ij} defined by

$$t_{ij} = \sum_{m=i}^{j} t_m \qquad (6.19)$$

where t_m is the label (serial execution time) of node m in G. The optimal partition will contain nodes which represent contiguous subsets of the original graph. Let the partitioned chain be $\{(1, i_1), (i_1+1, i_2), \ldots, (i_{r-1}+1, i_r=k)\}$. $T(\pi)$ denotes the execution time of the partitioned chain and it is defined recursively as follows. $T_1=t_{1i_1}$, $T_s=\max(T_{s-1}, t_{i_{s-1}+1, i_s}) +w_{i_{s-1}}$, for $2 \leq s \leq r$, and $T(\pi) =T_r$.

We construct a layered graph L_G consisting of k layers $L_1, L_2, \ldots, L_k$. Nodes in L_G are represented by ordered pairs (i, j). Each node (i, j) in L_G is labeled with $t_{i, j}$ defined by (6.19). The layers of L_G are constructed as follows. $L_1 = \{(1, j) \mid j = 1, 2, \ldots, k\}$, i.e., L_1 contains the nodes corresponding to all combinations of merging tasks 1 through j, for $(j = 1, 2, \ldots, k)$. There are k such nodes. Then for $(i = 2, 3, \ldots, k)$ we construct $k - 1$ layers L_i which are defined as follows.

$$L_i=\left\{(i,i), (i,i+1), (i,i+2), \ldots, (i,k), (i+1,i+1), \ldots, (i+1,k), \ldots, (k-1,k), (k,k)\right\}.$$

The leftmost and rightmost nodes of L_i (with the exception of L_1) are (i, i) and (k, k) respectively. The L_G for the example of Figure 6.2a is shown in Figure 6.2b. The ordered pair (i, j) at the left hand side of each node in Figure 6.2b denotes the tasks included (merged) into that node (i.e., tasks i through j inclusive).

Arcs in L_G exist only between successive layers and only connect nodes (i, j) and (m, l) such that $i \leq j$, $m \leq l$ and $m=j+1$. In layer L_i the first node is (i, i) and the number of different merging combinations that start from node i is $k-i+1$. Similarly all merging combinations that start from node $(i+1)$ are $k-(i+1)+1$. In general, the number of nodes in layer L_i, $(i=2, 3, \ldots, k)$ is

$$|L_i| = (k-i+1) + (k-(i+1)+1) + (k-(i+2)+1) + \cdots + (k-(k-1)+1) + (k-k+1)$$

or

$$|L_i| = \frac{(k-i+1) * (k-i+2)}{2}.$$

For the first layer of L_G we have $|L_1|=k$, since the first layer consists of all nodes

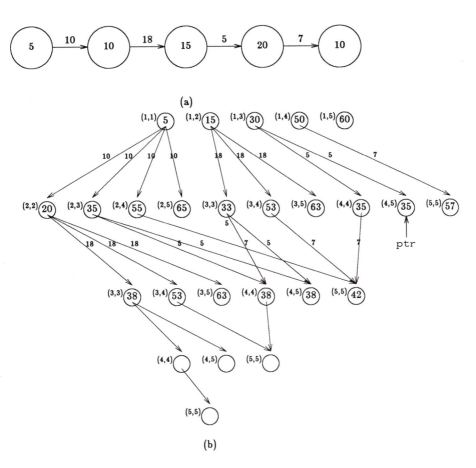

(a)

(b)

Figure 6.2. (a) An example of a chain graph and (b) Its layered graph
with the optimal partition indicated by ptr.

$(1, i)$, for $(i=1, 2, \ldots, k)$. The outdegree of node $(1, 1)$ is $k-1$, of node $(2, 2)$
$k-2$, and in general the outdegree of node (i, i) is $k-i$. Note that in each layer L_i
the node with the largest outdegree is (i, i). In fact if the nodes inside each L_i are
in order as shown in Figure 6.2b, then the outdegree of each node from left to right
is $[(k-i), (k-i-1), (k-i-2), \ldots, 1, 0], [(k-i-1), (k-i-2), \ldots, 1, 0], \ldots,$
$[1, 0], [0]$.

The arcs in L_G are labeled as follows. From each node (i_1, i) we have $(k-i)$
arcs originating from it and pointing to nodes of the form $(i+1, j)$, for $i < j$ in

the next layer. All these arcs are labeled with w_{e_i}, i.e., the communication weight of arc $e_i = (i, i+1)$ in G.

The nodes of the first layer L_1 are labeled according to (6.19). Then the algorithm relabels all nodes and arcs of L_G starting from L_2. In general, if the nodes of and arcs originating from layers $L_1, \ldots, L_{r-1}$ have been labeled, the nodes of layer L_r, $(r < k)$ are labeled as follows. Let (m, i) be a node of L_r connected to a number of nodes of the form $(h_r, m-1)$ of L_{r-1} (for $h_r \leq m-1 < m \leq i$ and all h_r). Let x_{h_r} be the label of $(h_r, m-1)$ and w_{h_r} be the weight of arc $(h_r, m-1) \rightarrow (m, i)$. Also let t_{mi} be defined by (6.19). The label x_m of node (m, i) is chosen from the labels of all nodes $(h_r, m-1)$ of L_{r-1} pointing to (m, i) as follows.

$$x_m = \min_r \left\{ w_{h_r} + \max(x_{h_r}, t_{mi}) \right\}. \tag{6.20}$$

The arc from which the node (m, i) was labeled is marked.

A global pointer ptr is maintained which at any given moment points to a node with the minimum label. The algorithm terminates when one of the following two conditions is met.

• All nodes of L_G are labeled, or

• All nodes at a given layer L_i have labels greater than the node
  pointed to by ptr, and ptr points to a node (j, k) of a previous layer.

After the algorithm terminates, the optimal merging of the tasks in G is given by following backwards the marked arcs starting from the node pointed to by ptr. The nodes in this path are of the type $(1, i_1), (i_1+1, i_2), \ldots, (i_m+1, k)$ where $1 \leq i_1 < i_2 < i_3 < \cdots < i_m < k$, and they uniquely define an optimal solution. A procedural description of the algorithm is given in Figure 6.3.

The application of this algorithm for the example of Figure 6.2a is shown in Figure 6.2b. Note that the algorithm terminated when all labels of the third layer were found to be greater than that of ptr. The optimal solution for this example is $(1, 3)(4, 5)$, i.e., tasks 1, 2, and 3 form a new task and tasks 4 and 5 form another composite task.

The construction of the layered graph L_G and the partitioning process can be performed simultaneously. Each layer in L_G has at most $O(k^2)$ nodes and each node has an outdegree of at most $O(k)$. Since there are k layers in L_G the worst case performance of the algorithm is $O(k^4)$ and the average complexity is $O(k^3)$ where k is the number of tasks in the original chain G.

This algorithm can also be used to find the optimal schedule of a set of k data dependent tasks on p processors. In such a case the layered graph will consist of p layers and the path starting from ptr will give us the schedule that minimizes parallel execution time taking into account interprocessor communication cost.

Input: A chain with $V=\{1,2,\ldots,k\}$, $E=\{e_i=(i,i+1) \mid i=1,2,\ldots,k-1\}$, task execution times t_i, $(i=1,2,\ldots,k)$ and arc weights w_{e_i}, $(i=1,2,\ldots,k-1)$.

Output: The optimal partition, or the optimal schedule of G on $p\leq k$ processors.

Method:
- From G construct a layered graph L_G with k layers $(L_1, L_2, \ldots, L_k)$. Nodes in layers are ordered pairs (i, j) such that $i \leq j$ representing the merging of nodes i through j of G. Layers are defined by the following sets:

$$L_1=\{(1,i) \mid i = 1,2,\ldots,k\}$$

. . .

$$L_1=\{(m,i) \mid \text{ such that } m\leq i, m=1,1+1,\ldots,k, \text{ and } i=1,1+1,\ldots,k\}$$

. . .

$$L_k=\{(k,k)\}.$$

- FOR (all nodes (i,j), $i \leq j$, $i,j = 1,2,\ldots,k$ of L_G) DO
    - label (i, j) with $x_i = \sum_{m=i}^{j} t_i$

ENDFOR

- FOR (all nodes $(1, i)$ of L_1) DO
    - label all arcs originating from $(1, i)$ with w_{e_i}.
    - ptr points to node $(1, i)$ with minimum x_i.

ENDFOR

- FOR $(r = 2, \text{to } (k - 1))$ DO
    FOR (every node (m, i) in L_r) DO
    - By searching all nodes $(h, m-1)$ of L_{r-1} connected to (m, i) through e_h compute the label x_m of (m, i):
        $$x_m = \min_h \{ w_{e_h} + \max(x_h, t_{mi}) \}$$
    - Mark the arc e_h corresponding to the minimum value, and label all arcs originating from (m, i) with $w_{e_\bullet}$
    - If ptr $> x_m$ then ptr $\leftarrow x_m$
    ENDFOR
    ENDFOR
- label node (k, k) of L_G with t_k.
- Reconstruct the optimal solution from ptr.

Figure 6.3. The task composition algorithm for chains.

6.4. DETAILS OF INTERPROCESSOR COMMUNICATION

The assumption about constant communication weights used previously is not very realistic when we consider real programs. Communication per se, i.e., the number of data items that must be transmitted between two given tasks is indeed constant. However in multiprocessor systems the time it takes to transmit the same

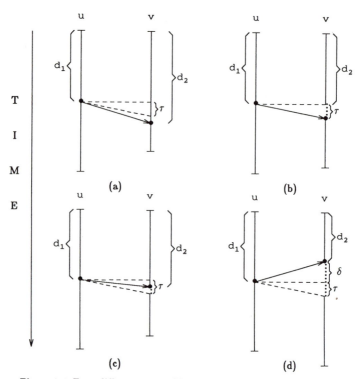

Figure 6.4. Four different cases of interprocessor communication.

amount of data at two different instances may vary. In our case we want to measure the effect of communication on program speedup, that is, in terms of processor latencies, or execution time. Consider for example two tasks u and v, where v is data dependent on u. The number of data items that will be sent from u to v is constant for each such pair of tasks. In order to measure communication overhead precisely using a deterministic model, we must assume that the time it takes to transmit a unit of data between two processors is constant. Delays in processor initiation caused by communicating these data however vary and depend on several factors. One such factor is the relative position of the source of a dependence in the code of task u, and its sink in the code of task v.

Consider for example the parallel execution of tasks u and v of the previous paragraph, when both tasks start executing at the same moment each on a different processor. Let τ be the time it takes to transmit a unit of data between two processors. Assume that each statement in u and v takes a unit of time to execute. Consider now a data dependence from u to v caused by a variable X which is defined in u and used in v. Let d_1 be the execution time of the segment of u between its first statement and the statement defining X, inclusive. Correspondingly d_2 denotes the execution time of the code of task v between its first statement and the statement using X, exclusive. Depending on the relative positions of the use and the definition statements of X in v and u respectively, we have the four cases described below and shown in Figure 6.4.

Case 1: X is computed in u before it is used in v. Figure 6.4a shows the case where $d_2 > d_1 + \tau$. The communication overhead in this case is zero, that is, no extra delays will occur in the processor executing v, since the value of X will be available when needed.

Case 2: Figure 6.4b shows the case where X is computed in u when it is needed in v. That is, $d_2 = d_1$ and in this case the communication overhead is τ, the time it takes to transmit X between the two processors.

Case 3: In Figure 6.4c X is used after it is computed but $d_2 - d_1 < \tau$, and the overhead in this case is $(d_1 - d_2) + \tau$.

Case 4: In this case (Figure 6.4d) X needs to be used before it is computed. This case involves the largest overhead, and the processor latency is given by $(d_1 - d_2) + \tau$.

It is clear that the communication overhead in all four cases is given by

$$\delta = \max(0, \ d_1 - d_2 + \tau),$$

and the execution time of u and v when they execute concurrently on two processors is given by

$$\max(T_1^u, \ T_1^v + \delta).$$

The two tasks u and v should therefore be merged if and only if

$$T_1^u + T_1^v \leq \max(T_1^u, \ T_1^v + \delta)$$

or equivalently if and only if $T_1^u \leq \delta$. The same analysis can be done when each of u and v execute on several processors, and both start executing concurrently. In this case we assume that each task is distributed equally among p processors, and each processor executes $\lceil T_1^u/p \rceil$ and $\lceil T_1^v/p \rceil$ part of u or v respectively. The corresponding timing in this case would use $\lceil d_1/p \rceil$ and $\lceil d_2/p \rceil$ in place of d_1 and d_2 respectively.

The data communication overhead caused by several dependences can be determined in a similar way. Consider again the tasks u and v of Figure 6.4. Only "parallel" dependences, that is dependences that lexically do not intersect need to be considered. This implicitly assumes that in the worst case we can transmit $\lceil \tau/\epsilon \rceil$ data items simultaneously through an interconnection network without conflicts (where ϵ is the execution time of a single statement). Clearly this is a realistic assumption for a parallel processor system. When two or more dependence arcs cross each other, the arc whose sink precedes all other (sinks) is preserved and all other dependences are ignored (as far as processor initiation delays are concerned, but are accounted for in the amount of communication). An example with two dependence arcs is shown in

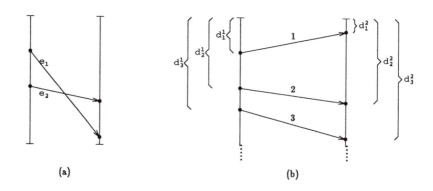

(a)   (b)

Figure 6.5. (a) A cross dependence example. (b) Parallel tasks with several dependences.

Figure 6.5a. A communication overhead may be caused by e_2 but not by e_1 and therefore e_1 is discarded as far as overhead is concerned.

Thus in the general case we have nonintersecting dependences from u to v that may prolong the execution time of v as shown in Figure 6.5b. (Since strongly connected components are always merged, as discussed below, the case with dependences going both directions never arises.) If d_i^1 and d_i^2 denote the execution times for the segments of u and v defined by the i-th dependence arc, as shown in Figure 6.5b, then we have the following proposition.

Proposition 6.1. If there are n dependences from u to v and the two tasks execute concurrently on two different processors, the total communication overhead will be

$$\delta_n = \max \left[0, \ (d_n^1 - d_n^2) + \tau + \delta_{n-1} \right]$$

where $\delta_0 = 0$.

Proof: The formula can be easily proved using induction on n. (For example, $\delta_1 = \max(0, \ d_1^1 - d_1^2 + \tau)$ is obviously true as it was shown above for the case of Figure 6.4.) ∎

The execution time is then given by

$$\max(T_1^u, \ T_1^v + \delta_n)$$

and the two tasks are merged if and only if $T_1^u \leq \delta_n$.

Assuming that the compiler is used to measure interprocessor communication as described above, the task composition approach can be used to find optimal or near-optimal partitions for certain types of task graphs.

CHAPTER 7

STATIC TASK SCHEDULING

7.1. INTRODUCTION

Depending on the granularity of the different parts of a program we have low and high level spreading for fine and coarse grain program modules respectively. Most instances of the spreading problem are NP–Complete [GaJo79]. In this chapter we discuss optimal solutions for some instances of high level spreading, and efficient heuristics for the intractable cases.

Recall that the data dependence graph is a directed graph with nodes representing statements of the program and arcs representing data and control dependences. The compiler can build a similar graph called the task graph with nodes representing higher level blocks of code such as BASs and loops, and arcs representing collections of dependences between these higher blocks. Chapter 3 discussed how basic program statements can be grouped together to form higher level blocks called tasks.

Ideally, high level spreading should be applied to a set of program modules that are free of control or data interdependences. In such a case any assignment of modules to processors would be "legal" and no extra precautions need to be taken to assure correct execution. There are several such instances of independent program modules in real numerical programs. As an example Figures 7.1, 7.2, and 7.3 show the task graphs of three numerical subroutines (Denelcor benchmarks) that are commonly used in different application areas. Subroutine SETDT in Figure 7.1 consists of thirteen independent DOALL loops. The notation nD shows the dimensionality of

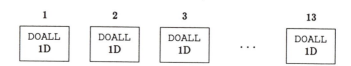

Figure 7.1. Task graph for subroutine SETDT.

each loop, i.e., the number of nest levels. Figure 7.2 shows a type of task graph that occurs frequently in numerical programs. The entire graph is surrounded by two serial loops. If we unroll these serial loops we get a series of uniform task graphs. In Chapter 3 we considered unrolling loops and argued against the practicality of this approach. Figure 7.3 shows a more complex task graph (DAG) for subroutine THREEDH. Performing high level spreading for such arbitrary graphs is much more complex than for uniform graphs of the type of NOLI's. Of course we can still use simple heuristics to optimize high level spreading for random graphs locally. For example the optimal algorithm of the next section could be used to perform high level spreading for the first two levels of tasks in the graph of Figure 7.3. As we shall later see however, optimizing schedules locally may result in non-efficient global schedules. Spreading can also be applied to lexically disjoint program modules that are "connected" with any type of dependences. For example, we can still execute concurrently the two last modules of Figure 7.3. In such a case though synchronization instructions should be used to coordinate the execution of these modules such that interdependences are satisfied in the correct order.

In this chapter we focus on both instances of spreading, i.e., spreading of independent program modules, and spreading of program modules with interdependences. First we look at the problem of spreading a set of independent tasks where the number of processors is larger than the number of tasks, each task may request any number of processors up to the maximum available, and all tasks are to be executed simultaneously. Several instances of spreading in real programs belong to this category. We solve this instance optimally in polynomial time. A fast heuristic algorithm is also presented for the case of independent tasks where the number of processors is smaller than the number of tasks and each task requests exactly one processor. This algorithm is also useful for scheduling a set of ready jobs in a multiprogramming environment where load balancing in the processors is our objective. Finally we discuss spreading of dependent tasks and scheduling of complete program task graphs. An efficient heuristic is also presented for the latter case.

7.2. OPTIMAL ALLOCATIONS FOR HIGH LEVEL SPREADING

In this section we consider the instance of spreading where the number of processors is larger than the number of tasks, all tasks are to be executed concurrently, and each task may request any number of processors up to the maximum available.

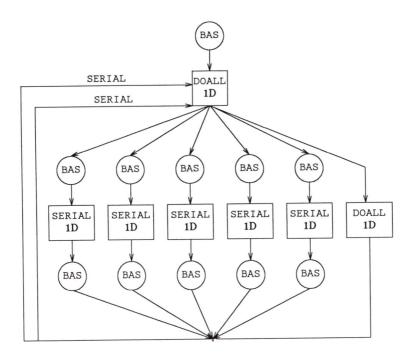

Figure 7.2. Task graph for subroutine NOLI .

All tasks are independent, i.e, intertask dependences of any kind are not allowed. Let us suppose that we are given a set $S = \{M_1, M_2, \ldots, M_m\}$ of m disjoint program modules (tasks) from a given program PROG. Then $M_i \cap M_j = \emptyset$, for $i \neq j$, and $\bigcup_{i=1}^{m} M_i \subseteq$ PROG. Since no dependences exist between any pair (M_i, M_j) of tasks, all elements of S may be executed simultaneously. Let us also suppose that PROG is to be executed on a parallel processor system with P processors, and that each program module M_i requests $p_i \leq P$, $(i=1, 2, \ldots, m)$ processors (the maximum it can use). In order to simplify the following discussion we always assume that $p_i \geq P$. The results that we derive below can be trivially extended for the general case where $p_i \leq P$.

As shown below, algorithm OPTAL from Chapter 4 can be used to solve this instance of high level spreading optimally. Let T_r^i denote the parallel execution time of module M_i on r processors. We can now define the allocation function G of OPTAL for this case, and show how the same algorithm computes optimal processor

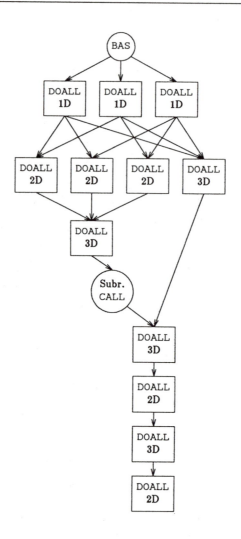

Figure 7.3. Task graph for subroutine THREEDH.

allocations for high level spreading. Starting from the last task M_m in S we define:

$$G_m(q) = T_q^m, \qquad \text{for} \qquad q=1, 2, \ldots, P.$$

Then for $1 \leq i < m$ the allocation function (which in this case measures parallel execution time) is defined as

$$G_i(q) = \min \left\{ \max\ (T^i_r,\ G_{i+1}(q-r))\ /\quad r = 1,\ 2,\ldots,\ q \right\} \quad (7.1)$$

$$\text{and} \qquad (q = 1,\ 2,\ldots,\ P).$$

Following the same approach as in Chapter 4, it can be proved that $G_1(P)$ will compute the optimal allocation of P processors to the independent program modules $M_1,\ M_2,\ \ldots,\ M_r$. The processor allocation vector giving the optimal assignment of processors to tasks is computed similarly to Example 4.1 of Chapter 4. In this case however the subscripts of T^i's are used in place of the exponents of the ϵ terms in Example 4.1.

A point that has not been clarified yet is how we compute T^i_q for a given M_i and for different values of q. There are two alternatives for computing the parallel execution time of a task. The most precise one would be to have the compiler recompute T^i_q for each different value of q. This however may be an expensive process. A less accurate but very close (and inexpensive) approximation, would be to compute T^i_q from T^i_1, the serial execution time of M_i, as shown in (7.2).

$$T^i_q = \left\lceil \frac{T^i_1}{q} \right\rceil \qquad \text{for} \quad q = 1,\ 2,\ldots,\ \min(P,\ p_i). \qquad (7.2)$$

The parallel execution time defined by (7.2) is very accurate when M_i is a loop for example, which is often the case. Each step of the algorithm involves an average of $P/2$ comparisons. There are m phases and therefore the complexity of OPTAL for high level spreading is $O(1/2mP^2)$.

When $P < m$ and $p_i = 1$, $(i = 1,\ 2,\ldots,\ m)$, i.e., when each task is allowed to execute on exactly one processor and there are more tasks than processors, the problem becomes NP-Complete [GaJo79]. Although this case does not occur very often during parallel processing of a single program, especially when the granularity of the tasks is fairly coarse, it arises frequently in multiprogramming environments where a set of serial jobs are to be scheduled on the processors of a system, such that processor loads are kept balanced. Since this is a special case of high level spreading at the program level we discuss it in the following section. Because of the intractability of this problem only heuristic algorithms that work in polynomial time are possible.

7.3. SCHEDULING INDEPENDENT SERIAL TASKS

In this section we consider the problem of spreading a set of independent serial tasks across a number of processors in order to minimize the total execution time. Since each task may use exactly one processor, and if the number of processors is larger than the number of tasks the problem becomes trivial. We examine the case where the number of processors is smaller than the number of tasks. This problem is a classical NP-Complete problem [GaJo79] and the best known approximation algorithm so far is Multifit [CoGJ79] which uses bin-packing as its core routine. In this section we present a new heuristic algorithm for this problem that has essentially the same complexity as Multifit. Experimental results show that our algorithm outperforms Multifit in most cases. Even though this algorithm is primarily designed for spreading a set of independent serial tasks on a parallel processor system, it can also be used for load balancing on a multiprogrammed parallel processor system where individual jobs are the unit of workload.

The *Divide-and-Fold* or D&F algorithm which is discussed below operates in two phases. Before we describe D&F in detail let us introduce the necessary definitions and nomenclature. Let us suppose that we have a set of n tasks that are ordered by execution time: $S = \{t_1 \geq t_2 \geq \cdots \geq t_n\}$. We use the execution time t_i to represent the i-th task. Our problem here is to spread the tasks in S across p processors, so that the total execution time of S is minimized. Let τ represent the execution (completion) time of S for a given distribution of tasks, i.e, the time it takes the processor with the heaviest load to process its workload. If preemption is allowed we can easily spread for the optimal τ in polynomial time. Therefore we assume that S contains nonpreemptive tasks. This is a practical restriction since, in most real cases, S consists of a set of relatively small BASs, and the overhead involved with process swapping during preemptive execution of BASs would more than eliminate the benefits of spreading.

A *list* of tasks from S is an ordered subset of tasks that are assigned to the same processor. A list of size m is represented as an m-tuple, $(t_{i+1}, t_{i+2}, \ldots, t_{i+m})$. Let

$$T = \sum_{i=1}^{n} t_i, \qquad T_{cp} = \max_{1 \leq i \leq n} \{t_i\} = t_1$$

and ω be the optimal execution time or schedule length. Then it is easy to prove the following lemma.

Lemma 7.1. $\tau \geq \omega \geq \max \{\lceil T/p \rceil, T_{cp}\} = LB.$

The motivation here is to generate a schedule with a length τ as close to ω as possible, by spreading the tasks of S so that the load in each processor is balanced around LB. D&F consists of two phases. During Phase I the set of tasks is partitioned into subsets of tasks and subsets are merged together until the number of subsets is equal to p. Thus generating a set of p lists. By assigning one list to each processor we have the first "first-cut" assignment of tasks to processors. Subsequently, Phase II moves tasks between processors according to a specific procedure to obtain a finer degree of balancing. The two phases of the D&F algorithm are described below in detail.

Phase I

During this phase the set of tasks S is partitioned into $q = \lceil n/p \rceil$ subsets $S_1^1, S_2^1, \ldots, S_q^1$ with each subset but (possibly) the last containing p tasks. If q is odd, we add a "dummy" subset S_{q+1}^1 that consists of p tasks of zero execution time at the end of the list, and set $q \leftarrow q+1$. After the initial partitioning, Phase I proceeds with a series of folding steps. During the first folding we concatenate subsets S_i^1 and S_{q-i+1}^1, $(i=1, 2, \ldots, q/2)$ such that, if $S_i^1 = \{t_1^i, t_2^i, \ldots, t_p^i\}$ and $S_{q-i+1}^1 \equiv S_j^1 = \{t_1^j, t_2^j, \ldots, t_p^j\}$, the resulting subset S_i^2 consists of p lists of size two, i.e.,

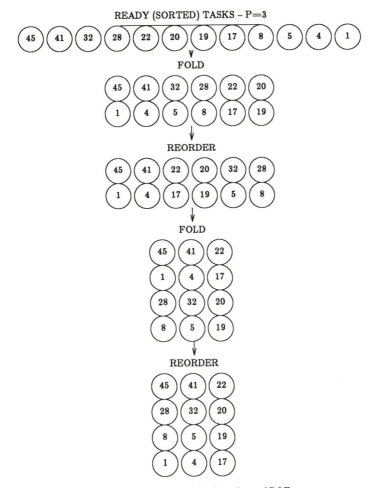

Figure 7.4: Example of the first phase of D&F.

$$S_i^2 = (S_i^1, S_j^1) = \left\{ (t_1^i, t_p^j), (t_2^i, t_{p-1}^j), \ldots, (t_p^i, t_1^j) \right\}$$

for $i = 1, 2, \ldots, q/2.$

After the first folding step we have $q/2$ subsets $S_1^2, S_2^2, \ldots, S_{q/2}^2$ with each consisting of p lists of size two. Between successive folding steps we reorder the subsets by list (accumulated) execution time. At the end of each folding step an empty subset is appended if the resulting number of subsets is odd. We proceed in the same way until, after $f = \lfloor \log_2 n \rfloor$ steps, the configuration is reduced to a single subset $S_1^f \equiv S^f$ which consists of p lists. Each list contains $\lceil n/p \rceil$ tasks from the original set. Figure 7.4 illustrates the steps of Phase I for $p = 3$ and for the set of tasks shown at the top of Figure 7.4. The tasks inside each list are sorted at the end of Phase I in order of decreasing execution time. In each of the p lists we add an empty task of zero execution time needed for the tests of Phase II.

Phase II

Phase II of D&F reassigns tasks to processors selectively in order to further balance the load inside each processor, and thus reduce the overall completion time. The previous phase constructed $S^f = \{l_1, l_2, \ldots, l_p\}$ where each list l_i contains $\lceil n/p \rceil$ tasks and has been assigned to the i-th processor ($i = 1, 2, \ldots, p$). Phase II performs a single pass through the loads of the p processors considering a pair of processors (i, $p-i+1$) at a time for ($i = 1, 2, \ldots, \lfloor p/2 \rfloor$). For each pair of processors it performs three tests and, based on the outcome of these tests, makes one reassignment. For the list l_i or processor i let T_i be the total execution time of the tasks in l_i, ($i=1,2,\ldots,p$). Then for each pair (i, $j=p-i+1$) of processors perform the following: Let $\tau_1 = \max\{T_i, T_j\}$.

Test 1: Find the smallest task t_k^i of l_i for which $T_i - t_k^i \leq LB$. If such task does

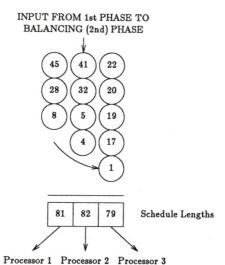

INPUT FROM 1st PHASE TO
BALANCING (2nd) PHASE

| 81 | 82 | 79 | Schedule Lengths

Processor 1   Processor 2   Processor 3

Figure 7.5: Example of the balancing (2nd) phase of D&F.

not exist let t_k^i be the largest (topmost) task of l_i. Let t_{k-1}^i be the next smallest task and compute

$$M1 = \max\left(T_i - t_k^i, \ T_j + t_k^i\right)$$

$$M2 = \max\left(T_i - t_{k-1}^i, \ T_j + t_{k-1}^i\right)$$

$$\tau_2 = \min(M1, M2) .$$

Test 2: Find the smallest sum W_k^i of the first k smallest tasks in l_i for which $T_i - W_k^i \leq LB$, and let $W_{k-1}^i = W_k^i - \{t_k^i\}$. Then perform the following computations.

$$N1 = \max\left(T_i - W_k^i, \ T_j + W_k^i\right)$$

$$N2 = \max\left(T_i - W_{k-1}^i, \ T_j + W_{k-1}^i\right)$$

$$\tau_3 = \min(N1, N2) .$$

Test 3: This test finds the optimal single exchange of tasks between the two processors. Let

$$D_i = \left\lfloor \frac{T_i - T_j}{2} \right\rfloor$$

be the difference in loads between processors i and $j = p-i+1$. For $q = \lceil n/p \rceil$, compute

$$\tau_4 = \min\left\{\left|\left|D_i - (t_{k_1}^i - t_{k_2}^j)\right|\right| \ \text{for} \ 1 \leq k_1, \ k_2 \leq q\right\}.$$

From the three tests we find the smallest value between τ_2, τ_3, τ_4 and τ_1 (that corresponds to no action) and perform the reassignment of tasks that is implied by the test for that τ. For example, if τ_2 is the minimum then if $\tau_2 = M_1$, task t_k^i is dequeued from processor i and queued in processor $j = p-i+1$; otherwise t_{k-1}^i is reassigned to the j-th processor. If τ_3 is the minimum and $\tau_3 = N_1$, the first k smallest tasks from processor i are transferred to processor j; otherwise the first $k-1$ tasks are transferred. Finally if τ_4 is the minimum among the three, a mutual exchange of tasks between processors i and j takes place. This exchange is the one that best balances the loads in the two processors. This rebalancing procedure is performed once for each pair of processors $(i, \ p-i+1)$, $(i = 1, \ 2, \ldots, \ q)$. Figure 7.5 shows a trivial case of rebalancing for the example of Figure 7.4.

Since the tasks are ordered inside each l_i, test 3 takes an average of q comparisons for each pair of processors. The most expensive activity in Phase II is the 3rd test. Assuming that tasks are initially ordered by execution time, Phase I takes $O(\log_2(n/p))$ steps to complete. Phase II of D&F is performed once but it is the bottleneck since its average complexity is $O(n^2/p^2)$. If the balancing phase is restricted to use only the first of the three tests, the complexity of Phase II is $O(p)$.

In order to test the performance of D&F against Multifit, we implemented both schemes and performed the same experiments for the two cases. The implementation of D&F has a balancing phase (II) that uses only the first of the three tests described above. Thus a full implementation of D&F as described in this chapter should perform at least as well as the current implementation. In order to compare our experiments with those for Multifit reported in [CoGJ78], the same approach was used to generate our tests. The execution times of tasks were randomly generated using normal distribution and the same size of tests as the ones reported in [CoGJ78].

More specifically we conducted two types of experiments. For Experiment 1 we performed 20 runs. Each run consisted of 128 tasks randomly generated with task execution times following the normal distribution with values in the range [1...100]. The 20 runs used different numbers of processors ranging from 2 to 21. Table 7.1 summarizes the results of the first experiment. $\overline{D\&F}$ and $\overline{Multifit}$ denote the average schedule lengths over all 20 runs. In the second experiment the number of processors was kept constant to p=10 and again 20 runs were performed each with a different number of tasks. The task execution times were also generated randomly in the range [1...100]. The number of tasks in each of the twenty sets was 20, 30, 40, 50,..., 210 respectively. Table 7.2 summarizes the results of the second experiment.

	Wins	Losses	Ties	Optimal Schedules
D&F	19	0	1	19
Multifit	0	19	1	0

$$\frac{\overline{D\&F}}{opt.} = 1.0005, \qquad \frac{\overline{Multifit}}{opt.} = 1.013$$

Table 7.1. Results of 1st experiment.

	Wins	Losses	Ties	Optimal Schedules
D&F	18	1	1	14
Multifit	1	18	1	0

$$\frac{\overline{D\&F}}{opt.} = 1.012, \qquad \frac{\overline{Multifit}}{opt.} = 1.022$$

Table 7.2. Results of 2nd experiment.

So far we have discussed and presented algorithms for spreading independent serial or parallel tasks. High level spreading however can be applied to sets of tasks that exhibit intertask dependences and thus form, in the general case, a direct graph. Such directed task graphs can be generated for a given program by the compiler. Performing spreading for a directed graph is the most difficult case of spreading, and all instances of this problem for $p > 2$ and task execution times of greater than 1 are NP-Hard [GaJo79]. In the following sections we consider high level spreading for directed task graphs and present efficient heuristics for assigning processors to minimize execution time and maximize efficiency.

7.4. HIGH LEVEL SPREADING FOR COMPLETE TASK GRAPHS

7.4.1. Processor Allocation for p–Wide Task Graphs

Suppose that a parallel program is represented by a task graph $G \equiv G(V, E)$, where the set of nodes V represents the tasks and the set of arcs E represents inter-task dependences. For each such graph G we can construct its corresponding layered graph. The mechanism for deriving the layered graph of a DAG is described in Chapters 3 and 8. Since each node of the layered G may be a complex module of code it may be executable on one or more processors.

Below we present a simple linear time heuristic algorithm for allocating processors to general task graphs. We call this *Proportional Allocation* heuristic since it allocates to each node a number of processors which is proportional to the size of the node. The idea behind proportional allocation is to allocate processors to the task graph on a layer–by–layer basis, so that the load in each layer is evenly distributed across the available processors, resulting in a suboptimal execution time.

Let V_i, ($i=1, 2, \ldots, k$) represent the layers in G and v_j, ($j=1, 2, \ldots, n$) the nodes of $V = \bigcup\limits_{i=1}^{k} V_i$. Let also c_i be the cardinality (number of tasks) of layer V_i. We define the *width* of G to be the maximum number of nodes in any of its k layers. If p is the number of available processors a p–wide graph is thus a graph in which each layer contains at most p nodes. In this section we discuss high level spreading for p–wide graphs. A generalization of this algorithm that handles graphs of any width is given later in this chapter. Each node v_j of G may request $r_j \leq p$, ($j = 1, 2, \ldots, n$) processors. For each layer V_i, ($i=1, 2, \ldots, k$) of G we carry out the following steps. (The notation $x \leftarrow a$ used below indicates the assignment of an expression a to variable x.)

Step 1. Each node $v_j \in V_i$ is allocated one processor. If $|V_i| = q_i$, then the number of remaining processors is $p_R = p - q_i$. The tasks in V_i are arranged in order of decreasing size.

Step 2. The remaining $p' = p_R$ processors are allocated to the nodes of V_i with $r_j > 1$ so that each node receives a number of processors proportional to its size. For a node v_j in V_i with $r_j > 1$, the serial execution time is t_j. Let $\tau_i = \sum\limits_{v_j \in V_i} t_j$ denote the total execution time of all nodes $v_j \in V_i$ with $r_j > 1$. Then, for all

---

```
      DOALL 1 I1 = 1, 7
          } 1
  1 ENDOALL

      DOALL 2 I2 = 1, 14
          } 8
  2 ENDOALL

      DOALL 3 I3 = 1, 5
          } 5
  3 ENDOALL

      DOALL 4 I4 = 1, 20
          } 4
  4 ENDOALL

      DOALL 5 I5 = 1, 24
          } 6
  5 ENDOALL
```

| Number of processors allocated to each loop ||
Loop Number	No. of Processors
1	1
2	9
3	3
4	7
5	12
Total	32

Figure 7.6. A simple program with DOALLs and the processor allocation profile.

---

such nodes perform:

$$p_j = \left\lceil p' * \frac{t_j}{\tau_i} \right\rceil \tag{7.3}$$

$$p_j \leftarrow \min(r_j - 1, \ p_j) \tag{7.4}$$

$$p_R \leftarrow p_R - p_j \tag{7.5}$$

where p_j is the number of processors allocated to node v_j. Steps (7.3), (7.4), and (7.5) are repeated until all processors are allocated ($p_R = 0$), or all nodes in V_i are processed. It should be noted that if at the end $p_R > 0$, then $p_j + 1 = r_j$, ($j = 1, 2, \ldots, q_i$). A procedural description of the proportional allocation heuristic is given in Figure 7.8. A simple example of the application of this algorithm to a single layer with DOALL loops, is shown in Figures 7.6 and 7.7. The number of processors allocated to each loop by our algorithm is shown in the table of Figure 7.6. Figure 7.7a shows the processor/time diagram when loops are executed one by one on an unlimited (in this case) number of processors, with a total execution time of 24 units. Figure 7.7b shows the processor/time diagram for the allocation performed by proportional allocation heuristic. Processors were allocated so that both horizontal and vertical parallelism are utilized; 16 units is the total execution time in this case. The total program speedup on p processors that results from the application of the above heuristic is given by Theorem 8.4 of Chapter 8.

7.4.2. List Scheduling Heuristics

The only parallel processor scheduling problem for DAGs that has been solved optimally in polynomial time is the case where p=2 and all tasks in the graph have unit execution time. Hardly any practical cases fall into this category. In most real cases we have p>2 and tasks that have varying execution times. A family of heuristic algorithms that have been developed for more general cases are the *list scheduling* algorithms [Coff76]. The most popular of them is the *critical path* heuristic. The basic idea behind list scheduling is to arrange the tasks of a given graph in a priority list and assign tasks with highest priority each time a processor becomes idle. The critical path heuristic finds the critical path of the graph, and gives priority to those tasks that compose the critical path. To find the critical path of a graph we label the nodes starting from the topmost node. Each node is labeled with the accumulated execution time of the longest path (in terms of execution time) to the first node of G.

The CP/IMS heuristic in [KaNa84] is acclaimed to be the best heuristic yet for scheduling general DAGs. This scheme is identical to the Critical Path heuristic with the following enhancement: tasks that do not belong to the critical path are given priority based also on the number of their successors i.e., the more the successor nodes of a task, the higher the priority it is assigned. As is the case with all scheduling heuristics, CP/IMS handles only graphs with serial nodes, the point being that parallel nodes can be broken down to a set of serial nodes. However this assumption is not practical. Usually program task graphs supplied by the compiler consist of a few tens of nodes. Decomposing parallel tasks even for small program graphs could create thousands of nodes that even fast heuristics could not process in a reasonable amount of time.

In the following section we discuss a scheduling heuristic that processes program graphs with parallel nodes without decomposing them. This heuristic is more general than both the critical path and the CP/IMS heuristics. Later we see how this heuristic can be coupled with the proportional allocation heuristic to form an efficient algorithm for scheduling task graphs of any width with parallel nodes.

7.4.3. The Weighted Priority Heuristic Algorithm

The unique characteristic of this algorithm that distinguishes it from the CP or CP/IMS heuristics is that it covers a continuous spectrum of scheduling algorithms. In other words the *weighted priority (WP)* heuristic is a parameterized scheduling algorithm whose performance can be tuned by choosing values for a set of

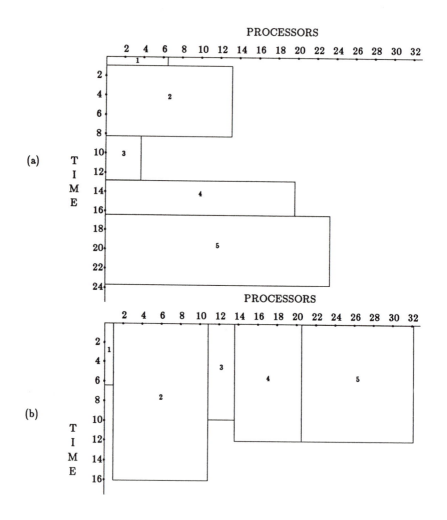

Figure 7.7. (a) The processor/time diagram for the program of Figure 7.6.
(b) The processor/time diagram after the application of the algorithm.

P–ALLOCATION HEURISTIC

INPUT: The layered task graph $G(V, E)$ of a transformed program and the number of available processors p.

OUTPUT: A processor assignment profile for the nodes of $G(V, E)$.

FOR (All layers V_i of $G(V, E)$) DO

- Allocate one processor to each node v_j of layer V_i.

- If $q_i = |V_i|$ then set $p' = p_R \leftarrow p - q_i$, and compute $\tau_i = \sum t_j$ for all $v_j \in V_i$ with $r_j > 1$. t_j is the serial execution time of v_j and p_R the number of remaining processors.

- Sort tasks of V_i in decreasing size.

    FOR (All $v_j \in V_i$ with $r_j > 1$) AND WHILE ($p_R > 0$) DO

    - For node v_j compute:

    $$p_j = \left\lceil p' * \frac{t_j}{\tau_i} \right\rceil$$

    $$p_j = \min(r_j - 1, \ p_j)$$

    - Allocate p_j processors to node v_j.

    - $p_R = p_R - p_j$.

    ENDFOR

- Task $v_j \in V_i$ is allocated $p_j + 1$ processors, $(j = 1, 2, \ldots, q_i)$.

ENDFOR

Figure 7.8. The Proportional Allocation Heuristic.

parameters or weights. Before we describe the WP heuristic let us see how we can construct the critical path for a task graph with parallel nodes.

Let G be a task graph with n nodes that is to be scheduled on p processors, and r_i the number of processors requested by the i-th task, (i=1, 2, . . ., n). An *initial* node in the graph is a task that has no predecessors and a *final* node one without successors. If a task graph has more than one initial or final node we can always change it so that it has a single initial and a single final node. This can be done by adding an empty task at the top of the graph and connecting it to all nodes without predecessors. Similarly we can add an empty final node and connect it from all nodes without successors. Starting from the initial node then we label the nodes in G visiting them in a Breadth First manner. Let t_i be the execution time of the i-th task, (i=1, 2, . . ., n). The initial node receives a label 0. All nodes immediately reachable from the initial node are labeled with their execution times. In general if node v_i is visited from node v_j, and x_j is the label of v_j then v_i is labeled with $x_j + \lceil t_i/r_i \rceil$. If v_i had been already labeled by an earlier visit and x_i is its old label, then the visit from v_j will relabel it with $\max(x_i, x_j + \lceil t_i/r_i \rceil)$. We continue in the same way until the final node is labeled.

To find the critical path of G we start from the bottom of the graph constructing the critical path (CP) as a set of nodes. The final node v_j is added to CP. Next we add to CP the immediate predecessor of v_j with the largest label. We proceed in the same way until the initial node of the graph is added to the critical path. Obviously if ω_o is the optimal completion time of G on an unlimited number of processors then

$$\omega_o \geq \sum_{v_i \in CP} \left\lceil \frac{t_i}{r_i} \right\rceil .$$

The WP algorithm considers a subset of the tasks in G at a time. It computes priorities for these tasks and then allocates processors to the tasks with the highest priorities. In fact in WP "highest priority" means lowest numeric priority.

Let L_i be the set of executable tasks of G, i.e., the set of tasks that have no predecessor nodes. The algorithm schedules the tasks in L_i until all tasks of G have completed. There are k discrete steps in WP and each step processes the tasks of list L_i, (i=1, . . ., k). The tasks of L_{i+1} cannot start executing until all tasks of L_i have completed. We want to schedule tasks so that those that constitute a bottleneck are given preference over less critical tasks. We also want to maintain a fairness criterion. In other words more processors should be allocated to tasks that are time consuming and demand many processors. The criteria are listed below and we see later how they are embedded in the WP algorithm.

Our scheme assumes nonpreemptive schedules where each task is assigned a priority, and tasks execute in ascending priority (lowest priority tasks first). The heuristic computes priorities using the following three rules of thumb:

- Give priority to tasks that belong to the critical path.

- Give priority to those tasks that have the longest
  execution times.

- Give priority to those tasks that have the largest
  number of immediate successors (i.e., break as many
  dependences as possible and as soon as possible).

- Give priority to those tasks that have successors
  with long execution times.

Below we show how to compute these three individual priorities, and from them the composite priority for each task.

At each moment during program execution, we have a set $L \subseteq V$ of runnable or executable tasks i.e., those that have no predecessors (not including the ones currently running). Suppose that the m tasks in L have execution times t_1, t_2, $\cdots$, t_m respectively. Let a_i, ($i=1,2,\ldots,m$) be the number of successor tasks for each t_i, ($i=1,2,\ldots,m$) and t_1^i, t_2^i, $t_{a_i}^i$ be the execution times of the a_i successors of task t_i. Then we define the following:

$$A=\sum_{i=1}^{m} a_i \quad (7.6) \qquad T=\sum_{i=1}^{m} t_i \quad (7.7)$$

$$T_i=\sum_{j=1}^{a_i} t_j^i \quad (7.8) \qquad T_a=\sum_{i=1}^{m} T_i \quad (7.9)$$

and using (7.6), (7.7), (7.8), and (7.9) we define the three individual priorities in the following way (low numbers correspond to high priorities):

- Tasks with longest execution times first:

$$p_1^i=\left\lceil \frac{T}{t_i} \right\rceil \qquad (i=1,2,\ldots,m) \qquad \text{(P1)}$$

- Tasks with largest number of successors first:

$$p_2^i=\left\lceil \frac{A}{a_i} \right\rceil \qquad (i=1,2,\ldots,m) \qquad \text{(P2)}$$

- Tasks with largest successor–tasks first:

$$p_3^i=\left\lceil \frac{T_a}{T_i} \right\rceil \qquad (i=1,2,\ldots,m) \qquad \text{(P3)}$$

The composite priority $P(i)$ of task t_i is then computed from (P1), (P2), and (P3) as,

$$P(i)=(\lambda_1 p_1^i + \lambda_2 p_2^i + \lambda_3 p_3^i) \qquad \text{(P4)}$$

where $0 \leq \lambda_1$, λ_2, $\lambda_3 \leq 1$ and $\lambda_1+\lambda_2+\lambda_3=1$. We call parameters λ_1, λ_2 and λ_3 the *priority weights* since they reflect the weight (significance) we give to each of these three individual priorities. Tasks on the critical path are given the highest absolute priority i.e., if L contains a task on the critical path, that task will be given priority over all other tasks in L. It is trivial to prove that at each time the set of executable tasks L contains at most one task of the critical path. This is true since, by definition, there is always a dependence between any two successive tasks (t_i, t_{i+1}) of the critical path.

After all tasks of L have been assigned a priority $P(i)$, $(i=1,2,\ldots,m)$ for some predefined values of λ_1, λ_2 and λ_3, the processor allocation is performed as follows.

The tasks of L are ordered in increasing priority and let $L=\{t_1, t_2, \ldots, t_m\}$ be the new order. Each t_i requests r_i processors. We choose the first k tasks from L such that

$$\sum_{i=1}^{k} r_i \leq p \leq \sum_{i=1}^{k+1} r_i.$$

Processor allocation will now be performed for the k selected tasks of L. It should be noted that if a task of the critical path belongs to L it is selected for allocation automatically no matter what its composite priority $P(i)$ is. Each of the k tasks receives one processor and the remaining $p_R = p' = p-k$ processors are allocated as shown below. Let

$$T_k = \sum_{i=1}^{k} t_i \quad \text{and} \quad p_i = \left\lceil p' * \frac{t_i}{T_k} \right\rceil$$

Then task t_i, $(i=1,2,\ldots,k)$ receives $\min(r_i - 1, p_i)$ processors and we reset $p_R \leftarrow p_R - \min(r_i - 1, p_i)$, $(i = 1, 2, \ldots, k)$. The assignment of processors is repeated for all k tasks that were selected. If $k=m$ then we delete the nodes of L from the task graph G together with the dependences (arcs) originating from them. Those tasks that had predecessors only in L become now the new executable tasks and are added to L. This process is repeated until all n tasks of G are assigned processors. If $k<m$ then only the first k tasks of L are deleted from G as described above. The remaining m-k tasks together with any new executable tasks compose the new set L of executable tasks.

Another version of the WP heuristic is when only one priority is used to order tasks within each list as follows. Let T_1^i be the serial execution time of the i-th task in list L_j, and r_i the number of requested processors (maximum number of processors it can use). Then the priority for each task is defined as $P(i) = \lceil T_1^i / \min(r_i, p) \rceil$, where p is the number of processors in the system. Tasks are ordered inside each L_j in order of decreasing priority and processor allocation is performed in exactly the same way as above. Note that this version orders the tasks in order of decreasing minimum parallel execution time. The priorities as defined above measure the minimum possible time it takes to execute each task on p processors. This approach accomplishes two desirable goals: It gives priority to large tasks, and simultaneously, groups together tasks whose parallel execution time after proportional allocation is approximately the same (minimizing therefore idle processor time).

We can use many combinations of boundary values (0's and 1's) for the λ's to derive different heuristics. For example, if we set $\lambda_3=0$ then only task execution time and number of successors contribute to the composite priority. Another special case of this heuristic (for $\lambda_1=0$, $\lambda_2=1/2$, $\lambda_3=0$) is the CP/IMS heuristic [KaNa84] which is the best known so far. Since CP/IMS is a special case of the WP algorithm, WP performs at least as well as CP/IMS.

In the worst case where $r_i > p$, $(i=1, 2, \ldots, n)$ the complexity of WP is $O(nq)$ where q is the width of the task graph. If in addition $r_i = cp$, $(i=1, 2, \ldots, n)$ for some integer c, it can be shown that the WP heuristic generates the optimal processor allocation for G. In general, when the processors requested by each node are uniformly distributed the complexity of WP is $O(n)$.

7.5. BOUNDS FOR STATIC SCHEDULING

In the previous sections we presented algorithms for allocating processors at compile–time to high level program modules. Only one of the algorithms is provably optimal even though the heuristics which handle the general problem generate schedules which can be very close to optimal. In this section we derive a worst case bound for any random scheduling heuristic. Coffman has shown that when dealing with serial task graphs (where nodes are serial tasks) any random heuristic can generate schedules which are at most less than twice as long as the optimal ones. In deterministic scheduling of parallel task graphs however, this worst case bound is much larger. The reason is that when we allocate several processors to several different parallel nodes, all processors should become idle before we may reassign them. (Since we process nodes in groups and in order to satisfy dependences an implicit type of barrier synchronization must be used between successive groups of nodes that are scheduled.) This may result in several idle processors in successive steps when a "purposely bad" heuristic is used. Of course intelligent heuristics should have a worst case performance which is always close to the optimal. Although the worst case bound that we prove below should not characterize any reasonable heuristic we include it for the sake of completeness.

An *atomic* operation is an indivisible operation that takes one unit of time to execute. Let PROG be a program that consists of n atomic operations and ω_0 and ω be the optimal completion time, and the completion time of PROG for a specific scheduling algorithm and for p processors. Then we have the following theorem.

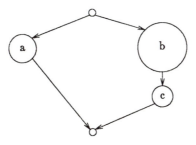

Figure 7.9. Example of a scheduling anomaly.

Theorem 7.1. $\quad \dfrac{\omega}{\omega_o} \leq p.$

Proof: Consider the extreme case where PROG consists of n independent atomic operations and it is to be executed on a parallel processor system with p processors. Then it is clear that

$$\omega_o \geq \frac{n}{p} \tag{7.10}$$

Now consider how we can achieve the worst case schedule for PROG on p processors. Since all p processors must be utilized at least once, the worst case schedule would be the one that assigns a single atomic operation to each of the first p-1 processors, and the remaining of the program to the last p-th processor. The completion time of such an assignment would thus be

$$\omega \leq n - (p - 1). \tag{7.11}$$

From (7.10) and (7.11) we have

$$\frac{\omega_o}{\omega} \geq \frac{\dfrac{n}{p}}{n - p + 1} \qquad \rightarrow \qquad \frac{\omega_o}{\omega} \geq \frac{1}{p} \cdot \frac{n}{n - p + 1}$$

and for $n \rightarrow \infty$ we have

$$\frac{\omega_o}{\omega} \geq \frac{1}{p} \qquad \text{or} \qquad \frac{\omega}{\omega_o} \leq p. \tag{7.12}$$

Therefore the worst case schedule can be asymptotically p times longer than the optimal. ∎

In fact the worst case bound of Theorem 7.1 can be asymptotically reached for non–trivial programs. Consider for example the task graph of Figure 7.9, which is surrounded by a serial loop with k iterations. Nodes a and b are parallel consisting of

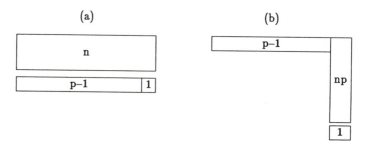

Figure 7.10. The optimal and the worst case allocation for the graph of Figure 7.9.

p-1 and np atomic operations respectively, and node c is a single atomic operation. Figure 7.10a shows the execution profile for the optimal allocation of G on p processors. Figure 7.10b illustrates the worst case schedule of G on p processors. From Figure 7.10 it is easy to see that $\omega_o = k(n + 1)$ while $\omega = k(np + 1)$. Therefore for $n \rightarrow \infty$ we have

$$\frac{\omega}{\omega_o} = \frac{np + 1}{n + 1} \rightarrow p.$$

Thus static scheduling heuristics that are based on local information to obtain locally optimal solutions may fail in certain cases.

CHAPTER 8

SPEEDUP BOUNDS FOR PARALLEL PROGRAMS

8.1. INTRODUCTION

In this chapter we consider a more idealized model according to which a program consists of a series of atomic operations. Based on this model we discuss how one can compute speedup values for inter and intra–task parallelism. Then we consider nested doacross loops and give a generalized speedup formula. Let us state the assumptions and describe the model before we proceed to the derivation of speedup formulas.

An assignment statement is a statement of the form x=E, where x is a variable and E an expression. A DOACR loop with *delay* d has the form

```
L : DOACR I = 1, N
        B
    END
```

where d, N are integer constants, I an integer variable with the range {1, 2, . . . , N }, B a sequence of assignment statements and DOACR loops, and it is understood that the iterations of L can be partially overlapped as long as there is a delay of at least d units of time from the start of iteration i to the start of iteration i + 1, (i = 1, 2, . . . , N - 1). For L, the index variable is I, the number of iterations is N, and the loop–body is B.

Consider now the two extreme cases of overlapping. If d = 0, there is complete overlapping, i.e. all the iterations of L can be executed simultaneously. In this case the DOACR loop is a DOALL loop. If $d = b$, where b is the execution time (assumed to be independent of I) of the loop–body B, then there is no overlapping, i.e. the iterations of L must be executed serially, one after another. In this case the DOACR loop is a standard serial loop, and we write DOSERIAL for DOACR. A BAS or a block of assignment statements is a special kind of serial loop, namely a loop with a single iteration. (A BAS may also be regarded as a special case of a DOALL loop.)

A program is a sequence of steps where each step consists of one or more operations that can be executed simultaneously. A program is *serial* if each step has exactly one operation; otherwise it is *parallel*. Two programs are semantically *equivalent* if they always generate the same output on the same input. Parallel programs are conveniently represented in terms of DOACR loops (Section 8.3).

Let $PROG_1$, $PROG_2$ be two equivalent programs and let their execution times on a p–processor machine be $T_p(PROG_1)$ and $T_p(PROG_2)$ respectively. Then the speedup obtained (on this machine) by executing $PROG_2$ instead of $PROG_1$ is denoted by $S_p(PROG_1, PROG_2)$ and is defined by

$$S_p(PROG_1, PROG_2) = \frac{T_p(PROG_1)}{T_p(PROG_2)}.$$

An immediate consequence of this definition is the following lemma.

Lemma 8.1. If $PROG_1, PROG_2, \ldots, PROG_n$ is a sequence of programs any two of which are equivalent, then

$$S_p(PROG_1, PROG_n) = \prod_{i=1}^{n-1} S_p(PROG_i, PROG_{i+1}).$$

We usually write S_p for the speedup when the two programs involved are understood. Of special interest to us is the case where $PROG_1$ is a serial program and $PROG_2$ is an equivalent parallel program obtained by restructuring $PROG_1$. In this chapter we assume that the execution time of a program is determined solely by the time taken to perform its operations, and that the total number of operations in a program is never affected by any restructuring. These assumptions are not very far from the truth; they help to keep the formulas simple, and yet let us derive important conclusions. If T_1 is the number of operations in the serial program $PROG_1$, then T_1 is also the execution time of $PROG_1$ on the basic sequential machine, or on any parallel machine (i.e., $T_1 = T_p(PROG_1)$). The equivalent parallel program $PROG_2$ also has T_1 operations, but now these operations are arranged in fewer than T_1 steps. We call T_1 the *serial execution time* of $PROG_2$ and it can be obtained simply by counting the operations in $PROG_2$. The execution time $T_p \equiv T_p(PROG_2)$ of $PROG_2$ on the p–processor machine will depend on the structure of the program, the magnitude of p, and the way the p processors are allocated to different parts of $PROG_2$. To distinguish it from T_1, T_p is referred to as the parallel execution time of $PROG_2$ (Chapter 1).

For a given program, we have the *unlimited* processor case when p is large enough so that we can always allocate as many processors as we please. Otherwise, we have the *limited* processor case. These two cases will be often discussed separately.

There are several factors affecting the speedup of a given program. For example, different compiler implementations or different compiler algorithms used on the same problem may result in different speedups. Given a particular parallel machine $M_i \in M$, where M is the universal set of machine architectures, and a set A of equivalent algorithms (all of which receive the same input and produce the same output), we can define a mapping:

$$E_{M_i}: \quad A \quad \longrightarrow \quad R_0^+$$

where R_0^+ is the set of the nonnegative real numbers and $E_{M_i}(A_j) = T_j$ is the execution time of algorithm A_j on machine M_i. Let $A_o \in A$ be the algorithm for which $E_{M_i}(A_o) = \min_j \{E_{M_i}(A_j)\}$ and A_c be the algorithm we currently have available. Then the speedup we can achieve by selecting A_o, (the most appropriate algorithm for the specific architecture) would be:

$$S_c = \frac{E_{M_i}(A_c)}{E_{M_i}(A_o)}.$$

The selection of the fastest algorithm is the user's responsibility and it seems unlikely that this process will be automated at least in the foreseeable future.

In our program model we assume that parallelism is explicitly specified in the form of tasks (disjoint code segments) which are parallel loops (DOALL or DOACR). Each branch of an IF or GOTO statement is assigned a *branching probability* by the user, or automatically by the compiler [Kuck84]. We can therefore view any program as a sequence of assignment statements, where each statement has an accumulated *weight* associated with it. All loops in a program are automatically *normalized*, i.e., loop indices assume values in [1, N] for some integer N. As in the case of branching statements, unknown loop upper bounds are either defined by the user, or automatically by the compiler (using a default value).

In a restructured program we may observe two types of parallelism: *horizontal* and *vertical*. Horizontal parallelism results by executing a DOACR loop on two or more processors, or equivalently, by simultaneously executing different iterations of the same loop. Vertical parallelism in turn, is the result of the simultaneous execution of two or more different loops (tasks). Two or more loops can execute simultaneously only if there does not exist control or data dependence between any two of the loops. In the general case the program task graph exposes both types of parallelism.

8.2. GENERAL BOUNDS ON SPEEDUP

In this section we consider an arbitrary parallel program, and think of it simply as a sequence of steps where each step consists of a set of operations that can execute in parallel. The total number of operations (and hence the serial execution time) is denoted by T_1. Let p_0 denote the maximum number of operations in any step.

Suppose first we are using a p–processor system with $p \geq p_0$. (This is the unlimited processor case). Let $\phi_i T_1$ denote the number of operations that belong to steps containing exactly i operations, $(i = 1, 2, \ldots, p_0)$. Then ϕ_i is the fraction of the program that can utilize exactly i processors, and we have $\sum_{i=1}^{p_0} \phi_i = 1$. We call

$f= \sum\limits_{i=2}^{p_0} \phi_i$ the *parallel part* of the program or the *fraction of parallel code,* and

$1-f=\phi_1$ the *serial part* of the program or the *fraction of serial code.* (At least p-p_0 processors will always remain unused.)

Consider now a limited processor situation with a p–processor machine where $p<p_0$. The steps with more than p operations have to be folded over and replaced with a larger number of steps with p operations. (For simplicity, we are assuming that each new step has exactly p operations, although one of them may actually have fewer than p). Let $f_i \equiv f_i(p)$ denote the fraction of the modified program that can utilize exactly i processors, $(i=1, 2, \ldots, p)$. Then we have

$$f_i = \phi_i \qquad (i = 1, 2, \ldots, p-1), \qquad \text{and} \qquad f_p = \sum_{i=p}^{p_0} \phi_i.$$

As long as $p \geq 2$, the parallel part f is given by $\sum\limits_{i=2}^{p} f_i$ and the serial part $1-f$ by f_1.

An arbitrary p–processor machine is assumed in the following. The first two results are well–known [Bane81], [Lee77].

Theorem 8.1. $\qquad \dfrac{1}{S_p} = \sum\limits_{i=1}^{p} \dfrac{f_i}{i}.$

Proof: When executing on a p–processor machine, the fraction of the program that uses exactly i processors is $f_i T_1$, $(i = 1, 2, \ldots, p)$. Hence, the number of steps where i processors are active is $\dfrac{f_i T_1}{i}$. The total number of steps is then given by

$$T_p = \sum_{i=1}^{p} \frac{f_i T_1}{i} = T_1 \sum_{i=1}^{p} \frac{f_i}{i}.$$

Since T_1 is the serial and T_p the parallel execution time of the program, we get

$$\frac{1}{S_p} = \frac{T_p}{T_1} = \sum_{i=1}^{p} \frac{f_i}{i}. \qquad \blacksquare$$

Corollary 8.1. $\qquad 1 \leq S_p \leq p.$

Proof: We have $f_i \geq \dfrac{f_i}{i} \geq \dfrac{f_i}{p} \qquad (i=1, 2, \ldots, p)$. Hence

$$\sum_{i=1}^{p} f_i \geq \sum_{i=1}^{p} \frac{f_i}{i} \geq \sum_{i=1}^{p} \frac{f_i}{p}$$

$$\text{or,} \qquad 1 \geq \sum_{i=1}^{p} \frac{f_i}{i} \geq \frac{1}{p}$$

$$\text{so that} \quad 1 \geq \frac{1}{S_p} \geq \frac{1}{p},$$

i.e. $1 \leq S_p \leq p.$ $\blacksquare$

Corollary 8.2. $\qquad S_p \leq 1/f_1.$

Corollary 8.3.   The speedup S_p, the number of processors p and the fraction of parallel code f satisfy (for $p > 1$)

$$S_p \leq \frac{p}{f + (1 - f)p},\qquad(8.1)$$

$$f \geq \frac{S_p - 1}{S_p} * \frac{p}{p - 1},\qquad(8.2)$$

$$\text{and}\quad p \geq \frac{fS_p}{1 - (1 - f)\,S_p}.\qquad(8.3)$$

Proof: These three inequalities are equivalent; from any one the other two can be derived easily. Note that

$$\sum_{i=1}^{p} \frac{f_i}{i} = f_1 + \sum_{i=2}^{p} \frac{f_i}{i} \geq f_1 + \sum_{i=2}^{p} \frac{f_i}{p} = 1 - f + \frac{f}{p},$$

since $f = \sum_{i=2}^{p} f_i$ and $f_1 = 1 - f$. Then by Theorem 8.1, $\frac{1}{S_p} \geq 1 - f + \frac{f}{p}$, so that $S_p \leq \frac{p}{f + (1 - f)p}$. ∎

Now, assume we have a program that can use a maximum number of p_0 processors. If the fraction ϕ_1 of serial code in it is very small, we can choose p (> 1) processors such that $f_p = \sum_{i=p}^{p_0} \phi_i \approx 1$. Then, since

$$\frac{1}{S_p} = \sum_{i=1}^{p-1} \frac{f_i}{i} + \frac{f_p}{p}\qquad\text{we get}$$

$$\left| \frac{1}{S_p} - \frac{f_p}{p} \right| = \left| \sum_{i=1}^{p-1} \frac{f_i}{i} \right| \leq \sum_{i=1}^{p-1} f_i = 1 - f_p \approx 0,$$

or equivalently, $S_p \approx p/f_p \approx p$. Thus, if for some $p > 1$, $\sum_{i=p}^{p_0} \phi_i \approx 1$, then the program runs very efficiently on a p–processor system giving an almost linear speedup. In this case, given the coefficients ϕ_i for the particular program, we can always determine the maximum number of processors that would get a linear speedup.

Because of Corollary 8.2, Amdahl and other researchers thereafter questioned the usefulness of very large MES systems, since, according to their argument, the majority of programs have an average of more than 10% serial code and therefore their speedup on any MES machine is bounded above by 10.

We conducted some experiments to measure the fraction of parallel code f in LINPACK, a widely used numerical package for solving systems of linear equations. Knowing the serial execution time T_1, the parallel execution time T_p and the number of processors p that were used during the execution of a subroutine, we can easily compute a lower bound for f from (8.2). All the above parameters are supplied by Parafrase. On the other hand, if the value of f for a particular subroutine is known

Sub. Name	f	Sub. Name	f	Sub. Name	f
SPOFA	0.9997	SSIFA	0.9862	SPBFA	0.9257
SQRDC	0.9988	SPODI2	0.9853	SGBFA	0.9189
SPBDI1	0.9975	SGESL1	0.9807	SGBSL2	0.9164
SGBDI1	0.9974	SSISL	0.9806	SGBCO	0.8561
SGEDI2	0.9961	STRSL0	0.9773	SPBCO	0.8314
SQRDC1	0.9961	STRSL1	0.9773	SSIDI3	0.7353
SSIDI2	0.9961	SPOSL	0.9767	SGBSL1	0.6545
SSVDC1	0.9954	SGESL2	0.9762	STRCO	0.6113
SPODI1	0.9950	STRSL2	0.9753	SPBSL	0.5659
SSICO	0.9905	STRSL3	0.9753	SGTSL	0.5295
SQRSL1	0.9900	SPOCO	0.9751	SPPDI	0.5064
SQRSL2	0.9900	SPPCO	0.9746	SSPSL	0.4010
SQRSL4	0.9900	SSIDI1	0.9746	SPTSL	0.3799
SQRSL5	0.9900	SGEDI1	0.9745	SSPDI	0.3615
SSPCO	0.9896	SGECO	0.9664	SSPFA	0.1348
SQRSL3	0.9868	SPPSL	0.9629		
SGEFA	0.9862	SPPFA	0.9350		

Table 8.1. Values of f for LINPACK subroutines.

and we want to achieve a specific speedup S_p for this subroutine, then (8.3) gives us a lower bound on the number of processors that we must use.

The sorted lower bounds of f are shown in Table 8.1. The measurements were done on LINPACK subroutines after they had been restructured by Parafrase. From Table 8.1 we observe that the majority of subroutines have a very high fraction of parallel code. For the first 37 subroutines (out of 49), the average fraction of parallel code was $\overline{f} \geq 0.9784$. Almost 76% of the subroutines have f > 0.9 and only 18% have f < 0.8.

Considering that LINPACK is a typical numerical package not very amenable to restructuring, the results of Table 8.1 are very encouraging. EISPACK for example (another numerical package), should be expected to have a much higher value of $\overline{f}$ than LINPACK [Kuck84]. Since several numerical packages are more amenable to restructuring than LINPACK, we should be more optimistic when designing large multiprocessor systems. The claim for the non–effectiveness of systems with large numbers of processors is mostly based on programs that exhibit an f < 0.9.

Secondly, we should consider all possible operating modes of a multiprocessor. There is no question that there exist numerical programs that could fully exploit hundreds or thousands of processors. For programs that utilize only a few processors, MES systems can be operated in a multiprogramming mode to keep system utilization high. The question then breaks down to whether we can have sites with enough users (workload) to keep system utilization at acceptable levels. The answer to this

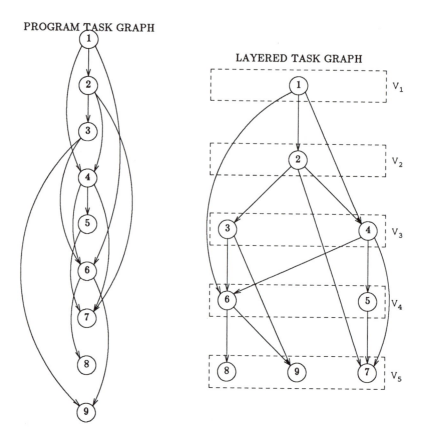

PROGRAM TASK GRAPH

LAYERED TASK GRAPH

Figure 8.1. A example of a program task graph and its corresponding layered graph.

question is rather obvious.

8.3. SPEEDUP MEASURES FOR TASK GRAPHS

We consider here an arbitrary parallel program represented by a task graph $G \equiv G(V, E)$. Recall from Chapter 3 that this graph is defined on a restructured program with nodes representing outermost DOACR loops, and arcs representing data and control dependences among loops. Let there be n nodes in V: $v_1, v_2, \ldots, v_n$. These nodes can be partitioned into disjoint layers $V_1, V_2, \ldots, V_k$, such that

(1) all nodes in a given layer can execute in parallel, and (2) the nodes in a layer V_{i+1} can start executing as soon as all the nodes in layer V_i have finished, $(i = 1, 2, \ldots, k - 1)$. To construct this layered graph of G, we use a modified Breadth First Search scheme for labeling the nodes of the graph. Initially, the first node of the graph (corresponding to the lexically first loop of the program), is labeled 1 and queued in a FIFO queue Q. At each following step, v_j, the node at the front of Q is removed, and if i is its label, all nodes adjacent to v_j are labeled $i + 1$, and are queued in Q. Note that a node may be relabeled several times but its final label is the largest assigned to it. When Q becomes empty, the labeling process terminates and we get the layered graph by grouping all nodes with label i into layer V_i. An example of a program task graph and its corresponding layered task graph is shown in Figure 8.1. We consider below three execution models of a layered task graph on a p–processor MES machine. The most general and the two extreme cases are discussed.

As usual T_1 denotes the total number of operations in the whole program. For a node v_j, let $g_j T_1$ denote the number of operations in the node and T_{pj} its parallel execution time, $(j = 1, 2, \ldots, n)$. Then $\sum_{j=1}^{n} g_j = 1$. The *absolute speedup* S_{pj}^A of v_j is the speedup obtained by considering the node separately as a program and is given by $S_{pj}^A = g_j T_1 / T_{pj}$.

Case 1. (Horizontal parallelism). Let $k = n$ and each layer V_i consist of a single node v_i, $(i = 1, 2, \ldots, n)$. To get the maximum speedup for the whole program on p processors, we need to get the maximum speedup for each node. Detailed formulas are given below.

The *relative speedup* S_{pi}^R of v_i is the speedup of the whole program when only v_i is executed in parallel and all other nodes are executed serially. Thus

$$S_{pi}^R = \frac{T_1}{T_1 - g_i T_1 + T_{pi}}.$$

Lemma 8.2. The absolute and relative speedups of a node v_i are connected by the equation

$$\frac{g_i}{S_{pi}^A} = \frac{1}{S_{pi}^R} - 1 + g_i \qquad (i = 1, 2, \ldots, n).$$

Proof: It follows directly from the above definitions. ∎

Theorem 8.2. The speedup S_p of the whole program (when all nodes are executed in parallel) is related to the absolute and relative speedups of the individual nodes by the following equations:

$$\frac{1}{S_p} = \sum_{i=1}^{n} \frac{g_i}{S_{pi}^A} = \sum_{i=1}^{n} \frac{1}{S_{pi}^R} - n + 1.$$

Corollary 8.4. If all n nodes give the same absolute speedup S_p^A, then $S_p^A = S_p$. If all n nodes give the same relative speedup S_p^R, then

$$S_p^R \leq \frac{np}{np-p+1} < \frac{n}{n-1}.$$

Proof: The first assertion follows immediately from the above theorem, since $\sum_{i=1}^{n} g_i = 1$. For the second, we see that when the relative speedups are all equal

$$\frac{1}{S_p} = \sum_{i=1}^{n} \frac{1}{S_p^R} - n + 1 = \frac{n}{S_p^R} - n + 1.$$

Since $S_p \leq p$, this implies

$$\frac{n}{S_p^R} - n + 1 \geq \frac{1}{p} \quad \text{or}$$

$$S_p^R \leq \frac{np}{np - p + 1} = \frac{n}{n - 1 + \frac{1}{p}} < \frac{n}{n - 1}. \blacksquare$$

Each node of the graph can be an arbitrarily complex nested loop containing DOSERIAL, DOALL, and DOACR loops. The problem of optimal static processor allocation to such nodes was discussed in Chapter 4.

Corollary 8.4.1. A program can not be partitioned into n disjoint segments so that the relative speedups are $1, 2, \ldots, n$ respectively, for $n \geq 3$.

Proof : If there was a program with the above property, then from Theorem 8.2 we would have,

$$\frac{1}{S_p} = \sum_{i=1}^{n} \frac{1}{i} - (n - 1) = H_n - (n - 1)$$

where H_n is the n–th harmonic number and therefore,

$$S_p = \frac{1}{H_n - (n - 1)} < 0$$

because for $n \geq 3$ we have $H_n < (n - 1)$. $\blacksquare$

Corollary 8.4.2. If a program is partitioned into n disjoint segments with all segments having a relative speedup $S^R = \frac{1}{n} S_p$, and if $n \leq p - 1$, then

$$S_p = n + 1 \qquad \text{and therefore} \qquad S^R = \frac{n + 1}{n} \qquad (8.4)$$

Proof: By substituting S^R in Theorem 8.2 we get,

$$\frac{1}{S_p} = \frac{n - (n - 1) S^R}{S^R} = \frac{n^2 - (n - 1) S_p}{S_p}$$

and after simplification we have $n^2 - (n - 1) S_p - 1 = 0$. Solving for S_p, we finally get $S_p = n + 1$. $\blacksquare$

Case 2. (Vertical parallelism). Let the task graph be *flat,* i.e. let there be a single layer V consisting of n nodes. This is the case when no dependences exist between any pair of nodes. Here we may exploit vertical parallelism by executing all program nodes simultaneously. We consider the extreme case where each node requests exactly one processor. Since each node is allocated one processor, if $n \leq p$ the execution time is dominated by the largest task. In the general case bin–packing can be used to evenly distribute the n nodes into p bins. In Chapter 7 we discussed D&F, a heuristic algorithm for this case. Then, if $b_i, 1 \leq i \leq p$ denotes the largest bin, we have the following theorem.

Theorem 8.3. The total speedup resulting from the parallel execution of an n–node flat graph on p processors, where each node is allocated one processor, is given by

$$S_p = \frac{1}{\sum\limits_{v_j \in b_i} g_j}.$$

Proof: The proof follows directly from the definition of speedup and the assumptions stated above. ∎

Corollary 8.5. If $n \leq p$ then

$$S_p = \frac{1}{\max(g_1, g_2, \ldots, g_n)}.$$

Proof: This follows from the previous theorem since each bin contains one node. ∎

Case 3. (Horizontal and vertical parallelism). In the most general case we have a program that exhibits both types of parallelism, horizontal and vertical. In other words, the task graph consists of k (> 1) disjoint layers $V_1, V_2, \ldots, V_k$ with at least one layer containing two or more nodes (Figure 8.1). If $|V_i|$ is the cardinality of the i-th layer, we assume that $|V_i| \leq p$, ($i = 1, 2, \ldots,$ k). (In the case of $|V_i| > p$ we fold and fuse nodes such that $|V_i| \leq p$ (Chapter 7).) Our aim in this case is to exploit horizontal and vertical parallelism in the best possible way. Maximizing speedup is equivalent to minimizing parallel execution time. For each node of the task graph v_j, we define r_j to be the maximum number of processors that the node could use. When $r_j=1$, ($j = 1, 2, \ldots,$ n) our problem is reduced to the classical multiprocessor scheduling problem, which has been proved NP–Complete [GaJo78]. Our general problem can be reduced to the latter one by decomposing each node v_j into r_j independent sub–nodes of equal size. This trivially proves that our problem is also NP–Complete. Heuristic solutions are therefore the only acceptable approach to solving the problem suboptimally in polynomial time.

In Chapter 7 we discussed a linear–time heuristic algorithm (PA) for allocating processors to general task graphs. The total program speedup on p processors that results from the application of this heuristic is given by the following theorem.

Theorem 8.4. The total program speedup that results from the parallel (vertical and horizontal) execution of a k–layer task graph on p processors is given by

$$S_p = \frac{1}{\sum\limits_{i=1}^{k} \lambda_i} \qquad \text{where} \qquad \lambda_i = \max_{v_j \in V_i} \left\{ \frac{g_j}{S_{p_j}^A} \right\} \qquad (8.5)$$

where $S_{p_j}^A$ is the absolute speedup of node v_j when p_j processors are allocated to it.

Note that Theorems 8.2 and 8.3 are special cases of Theorem 8.4. If the graph is reduced to a flat graph, then $k=1$ and Corollary 8.5 holds. On the other hand, if each layer contains one node (linearized) then $q_i=1$ in (8.5), $(i= 1, 2, \ldots, k)$, and thus Theorem 8.2 holds true.

8.4. SPEEDUP MEASURES FOR DOACR LOOPS

In this section we focus on a single node of the task flow graph representing the given program, i.e. a DOACR loop. We extend and generalize the do across model, to

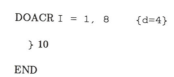

$$\text{DOACR } I = 1, 8 \qquad \{d=4\}$$

$$\} \ 10$$

$$\text{END}$$

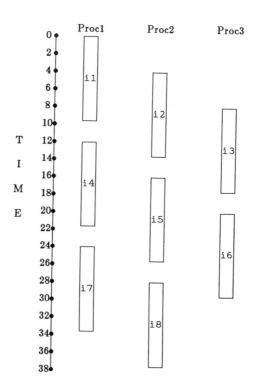

Figure 8.2. An example of the application of Theorem 8.5 for $p = 3$.

allow for idle processor time caused by do across delays. In [Cytr84] it is assumed that no processor may become idle unless it completes all iterations assigned to it. This is true only in certain special cases. As we shall see later by means of an example, each processor may have to idle between successive iterations. The following theorem generalizes the do across model and accounts for idle processor time.

Theorem 8.5. Consider a DOACR loop with N iterations and delay d, and let b denote the execution time of the loop–body. Then p processors can be allocated to the iterations of the loop in such a way that the speedup is given by $S_p = Nb/T_p$, where

$$T_p = \left(\lceil N/p \rceil - 1\right) \max (b, pd) + d((N-1) \bmod p) + b \qquad (8.6)$$

Proof: Let us number the iterations 1, 2, ..., N in their natural order and the processors 1, 2, ..., p in any order. The processors are allocated to the iterations as follows. Assume first that N > p. Iteration 1 goes to processor 1, iteration 2 goes to processor 2, ..., iteration p goes to processor p. Then iteration (p + 1) goes to processor 1, etc., and this scheme is repeated as many times as necessary until all the iterations are completed. We can now think of the iterations arranged in a $\lceil N/p \rceil \times p$ matrix, where the columns represent processors. If N $\leq$ p, we employ the same scheme, but now we end up with a 1 $\times$ N matrix instead.

Let t_k denote the starting time of iteration k, (k = 1, 2, ..., N), and assume that t_1 = O. Let us find an expression for t_N. First, assume that N > p. For any iteration j in the first row, the time t_j is easily found:

$$t_j = (j - 1)d \qquad (j = 1, 2, ..., p).$$

Now iteration (p + 1) must wait until its processor (i.e., processor 1) has finished executing iteration 1, and d units of time have elapsed since t_p, the starting time of iteration p on processor p. Hence

$$t_{p+1} = \max (b, t_p + d) = \max (b, pd).$$

The process is now clear. If we move right horizontally (in the matrix of iterations), each step amounts to a time delay of d units. And if we move down vertically to the next row, each step adds a delay of max(b, pd) units. Thus the starting time t_k for an iteration that lies on row i and column j will be given by

$$t_k = (i - 1) \max (b, pd) + (j-1)d.$$

For the last iteration, we have i = $\lceil N/p \rceil$ and

$$j = \begin{cases} N \bmod p & \text{if } N \bmod p > O \\ p & \text{otherwise} \end{cases}$$

Since j - 1 can be written as (N - 1) mod p, we get

$$t_N = \left(\lceil N/p \rceil - 1\right) \max (b, pd) + d((N - 1) \bmod p).$$

Now let N $\leq$ p. It is easily seen that

$$t_N = (N - 1)d$$

$$= \left(\lceil N/p \rceil - 1\right) \max (b, pd) + d((N - 1) \bmod p).$$

Finally, since the parallel execution time T_p is given by $T_p = t_N + b$, the proof of the theorem is complete. ■

Figure 8.2 shows an example of the application of Theorem 8.5. The DOACR loop of Figure 8.2 has 8 iterations, a delay $d = 4$, and a loop–body size of 10. The total parallel execution time on $p = 3$ processors is 38 units, as predicted by Theorem 8.5. We can maximize the speedup of an arbitrarily nested DOACR loop which executes on p processors by using the optimal processor allocation algorithm described in Chapter 4.

Corollary 8.6. Consider a sequence of m perfectly nested DOALL loops numbered $1, 2, \ldots, m$ from the outermost loop to the innermost. Let S_{p_i} denote the speedup of the construct on a p_i–processor machine when only the ith loop executes in parallel and all other loops serially, $(i = 1, 2, \ldots, m)$. Then the speedup S_p on a p–processor machine, where $p = \prod_{i=1}^{m} p_i$ and p_i processors are allocated to the ith loop, is given by $S_p = \prod_{i=1}^{m} S_{p_i}$.

8.5. MULTIPROCESSORS VS. VECTOR/ARRAY MACHINES

Generally speaking, in a restructured program we have vector constructs that can execute in parallel on an SEA system. Let S_v denote the speedup that results by executing a program PROG, on an SEA machine. Obviously vector statements can be executed in parallel on any MES system as well (perhaps with a significantly higher overhead). Do across loops with $d > 0$ can execute in parallel only on MES systems. Let S_m denote the additional speedup we achieve by executing the DOACR loops of PROG with $d > 0$ in parallel. Finally, let S_o denote the additional speedup that results by overlapping disjoint code modules during execution (vertical parallelism or high level spreading). If S_p is the total speedup we obtain by executing PROG on an MES machine, then from Lemma 8.1 we have

$$S_p = S_v * S_m * S_o$$

It is clear that for SEA systems we always have $S_m = 1$ and $S_o = 1$, while for MES systems all three components may be greater than one. If S_{SEA} (PROG) and S_{MES} (PROG) denote the overall speedups of PROG for SEA and MES systems respectively, then

$$S_{SEA} = S_v \quad \text{and} \quad S_{MES} = S_v * S_m * S_o$$

Assuming no overhead of any type or the same overhead for both systems, the S_v term should have a value that depends on the program characteristics (and is independent of the machine architecture). For each program we can therefore measure the additional speedup offered by MES systems. Let us define α (PROG), the MES *superiority index* as follows.

$$\alpha (PROG) = \frac{S_{MES} (PROG)}{S_{SEA} (PROG)} = S_m * S_o$$

where $1 \leq \alpha (PROG) \leq P$. α is computed on a program basis and can be used as a relative performance index for MES architectures.

REFERENCES

[AbMa86]   W. Abu–Sufah and A. Malony, "Vector Processing on the Alliant FX/8 Multiprocessor", Proceedings of the *1986 International Conference on Parallel Processing*, August 1986, pp. 559–566.

[AhSU86]   A.V. Aho, R. Sethi, and J.D. Ullman, *Compilers: Principles, Techniques, and Tools*, Addison–Wesley, Reading, Massachusetts, 1986.

[AlCo72]   F. Allen and J. Cocke, "A Catalogue of Optimizing Transformations," *Design and Optimization of Compilers*, R. Rustin, Ed. Prentice–Hall, Englewood Cliffs, N.J., 1972, pp. 1–30.

[Allen87]   F. Allen, et. al., "An Overview of the PTRAN Analysis System for Multiprocessing," Proceedings of the *1987 International Conference on Supercomputing*, Springer–Verlag LNCS Vol. 297, February 1988.

[AlKe82]   J.R. Allen and K. Kennedy, "PFC: A Program to Convert Fortran to Parallel Form," Techn. Rept. MASC–TR82–6, Rice University, Houston, Texas, March 1982.

[AlKe87]   R. Allen and K. Kennedy, "Automatic Translation of FORTRAN Programs to Vector Form," *ACM Transactions on Programming Languages and Systems*, Vol. 9, No. 4, October 1987.

[Alli85]   Alliant Computer Systems Corp., "FX/Series Architecture Manual," Acton, Massachusetts, 1985

[Amda67]   G. M. Amdahl, "Validity of the Single Processor Approach to Achieving Large Scale Computing Capabilities," *AFIPS Computer Conference Proc.*, Vol. 30, 1967.

[ANSI86]   American National Standards Institute, *American National Standard for Information Systems. Programming Language Fortran S8 (X3.9–198x)*. Revision of X3.9–1978, Draft S8, Version 99, ANSI, New York, April 1986.

[ArNi87]   Arvind and R. S. Nikhil, "Executing a Program on the MIT Tagged–token Dataflow Architecture," *Proceedings of PARLE conference*, Eindhoven, The Netherlands, Springer–Verlag LNCS 259, June 1987.

[Bain79]   W.L. Bain, "Hardware Scheduling Strategies for Systems with Many Processors," Proceedings of the 1979 *International Conference on Parallel Processing*, August, 1979.

[Bane79]   U. Banerjee, "Speedup of Ordinary Programs," Ph.D. Thesis, University of Illinois at Urbana–Champaign, DCS Report No. UIUCDCS–R–79–989, October 1979.

[Bokh88]   S. Bokhari, "Partitioning Problems in Parallel, Pipelined and Distributed Computing," *IEEE Transactions on Computers*, Vol. 37, No. 1, January 1988.

[Brod81]   B. Brode, "Precompilation of Fortran Programs to Facilitate Array Processing," *Computer 14, 9*, September 1981, pp. 46–51.

[ChCi87]   H.–B. Chen and Y.–G. Ci, "Parallel Execution of Non–DO loops", Proceedings of the *1987 International Conference on Parallel Processing*, August 1987, pp. 512–516.

[Chen83]   S. Chen, "Large–scale and High–speed Multiprocessor System for Scientific Applications – Cray–X–MP–2 Series," *Proc. of NATO Advanced Research Workshop on High Speed Computing, Kawalik(Editor)*, pp. 59–67, June 1983.

[Coff76]   E.G. Coffman, Jr., ed., *Computer and Job–shop Scheduling Theory*, John Wiley and Sons, New York, 1976.

[CoGr72]   E.G. Coffman and R.L. Graham, "Optimal Scheduling on Two Processor Systems," *Acta Informatica*, Vol. 1, No. 3, 1972.

[CoGJ78]   E.G. Coffman, M.R. Garey, D.S. Johnson, "An Application of Bin–Packing to Multiprocessor Scheduling," *SIAM J. Comput.*, Vol. 7, No. 1, February, 1978.

[Cray85]   "Multitasking User Guide," Cray Computer Systems Technical Note, SN–0222, January, 1985.

[Cytr84]   R.G. Cytron, "Compile–Time Scheduling and Optimizations for Multiprocessor Systems," Ph.D. Thesis, Dept. of Computer Science, University of Illinois, Sept., 1984.

[Cytr85]   R. Cytron, "Useful Parallelism in a Multiprocessor Environment", Proceedings of the *1985 International Conference on Parallel Processing*, August 1985, pp. 450–457.

[Cytr86]   R.G. Cytron, "Doacross: Beyond Vectorization for Multiprocessors (Extended Abstract)," *Proceedings of the 1986 International Conference on Parallel Processing*, St. Charles, IL, pp. 836–844, August, 1986.

[Cytr87]   R. Cytron, "Limited Processor Scheduling of Doacross Loops", Proceedings of the *1987 International Conference on Parallel Processing*, August 1987, pp. 226–234.

[DBMS79]   J. J. Dongarra, J.R. Bunch, C. B. Moler, and G. W. Stewart, "Linpack User's Guide," *SIAM Press*, Philadelphia, PA, 1979.

[Dong85]   J. J. Dongarra, "Comparison of the CRAY X–MP–4, Fujitsu VP–200, and Hitachi S–810/20: An Argonne Perspective," Argonne National Laboratory, ANL–85–19, October, 1985.

[FYTZ87]   Z. Fang, P.–C. Yew, P. Tang, and C.–Q. Zhu, "Dynamic Processor Self–Scheduling for General Parallel Nested Loops", Proceedings of the *1987 International Conference on Parallel Processing*, August 1987, pp. 1–10.

[Fox87]   G. C. Fox, "Domain Decomposition in Distributed and Shared Memory Environments. A Uniform Decomposition and Performance Analysis for the NCUBE and JPL Mark IIIfp Hypercubes," Proceedings of the *1987 International Conference on Supercomputing*, Springer–Verlag LNCS Vol. 297, February 1987.

[GaJG88]   D. Gannon, W. Jalby, and K. Gallivan "On the Problem of Optimizing Parallel Programs for Hierarchical Memory Systems", Proceedings of the *1988 ACM International Conference on Supercomputing*, St. Malo, France, July 1988.

[GaJo79]   M.R. Garey and D.S. Johnson, "Computers and Intractability, A Guide to the Theory of NP–Completeness," W.H. Freeman and Company, San Francisco, California, 1979.

[GGKM83]   A. Gottlieb, R. Grishman, C.P. Kruskal, K.P. McAuliffe, L. Rudolph, and M. Snir, "The NYU Ultracomputer — Designing an MIMD Shared Memory Parallel Machine," *IEEE Trans. on Computers*, Vol. C–32, No. 2, February 1983.

[GiPo88a]   M. Girkar and C. D. Polychronopoulos, "Partitioning Programs for Parallel Execution," Proceedings of the *1988 ACM International Conference on Supercomputing*, St. Malo, France, July 4–8, 1988.

[GiPo88b] M. Girkar and C. D. Polychronopoulos, "Compiler Issues for Supercomputers," Technical Report CSRD No. 676, Center for Supercomputing Research and Development, University of Illinois, March 1988.

[GJMY88] K. A. Gallivan, W. Jalby, A. D. Malony, and P.-C. Yew, "Performance Analysis of the Cedar System", Chapter in the book *Performance Evaluation of Supercomputers*, J. L. Martin Editor, North–Holland, January 1988.

[Gokh87] M. B. Gokhale, "Exploiting Loop Level Parallelism in Nonprocedural Dataflow Programs", Proceedings of the *1987 International Conference on Parallel Processing*, August 1987, pp. 305–311.

[GPKK82] D. Gajski, D. Padua, D. Kuck and R. Kuhn, "A Second Opinion on Dataflow Machines and Languages," *IEEE Computer*, February 1982.

[Grah72] R. L. Graham, "Bounds on Multiprocessor Scheduling Anomalies and Related Packing Algorithms," Proceedings of Spring Joint Computer Conference, 1972.

[GuPL88] M. Guzzi, D. Padua and D. H. Lawrie, "Cedar Fortran," Internal Document, Center for Supercomputing Research and Development, University of Illinois, January 1988.

[IEEE79] "Programs for Digital Signal Processing," Edited by Digital Signal Processing Committee, IEEE Press, N. Y., 1979.

[KaNa84] H. Kasahara and N. Seinosuke, "Practical Multiprocessor Scheduling Algorithms for Efficient Parallel Processing," *IEEE Trans. Compt.*, Vol. C–33, No. 11, Nov., 1984.

[Kenn80] K. Kennedy, "Automatic Vectorization of Fortran Programs to Vector Form," Technical Report, Rice University, Houston, TX, October, 1980.

[KKLW80] D.J. Kuck, R.H. Kuhn, B. Leasure, and M. Wolfe, "The Structure of an Advanced Vectorizer for Pipelined Processors," *Fourth International Computer Software and Applications Conference,* October, 1980.

[KKPL81] D.J. Kuck, R. Kuhn, D. Padua, B. Leasure, and M. Wolfe, "Dependence Graphs and Compiler Optimizations," *Proceedings of the 8-th ACM Symposium on Principles of Programming Languages,* pp. 207–218, January 1981.

[KDLS86] D. J. Kuck, E. S. Davidson, D. H. Lawrie, and A.H. Sameh, "Parallel Supercomputing Today and the Cedar Approach," *Science 231*, 4740 February 28, 1986, pp. 967–974.

[Koba81] H. Kobayashi, *Modeling and Analysis,* Second Edition, Addison Wesley, 1981.

[KrWe85] C. Kruskal and A. Weiss, "Allocating Independent Subtasks on Parallel Processors," *IEEE Trans. on Software Engineering,* Vol. SE–11, No. 10, October, 1985.

[Kuck78]   D. J. Kuck, *The Structure of Computers and Computations,* Volume 1, John Wiley and Sons, New York, 1978.

[Kuck84]   D.J. Kuck et. al., "The Effects of Program Restructuring, Algorithm Change and Architecture Choice on Program Performance," *International Conference on Parallel Processing,* August, 1984.

[KuSa87]   D. J. Kuck and A. H. Sameh, "A Supercomputer Performance Evaluation Plan," Proceedings of the *1987 International Conference on Supercomputing,* Springer–Verlag, LNCS Vol. 297, February, 1987.

[Lawr75]   D. H. Lawrie, "Access and Alignment of Data in an Array Processor," *IEEE Transactions on Computers,* vol. C–29, pp. 1145–1155, December 1975.

[Lee 80]   R. B. Lee, "Empirical Results on the Speedup, Efficiency, Redundancy, and Quality of Parallel Computations," *Inter. Conf. on Parallel Processing,* 1980.

[LuBa80]   S.F. Lundstron and G.H. Barnes, "Controllable MIMD Architecture," *Proceedings of the 1980 Conference on Parallel Processing,* pp. 19–27, 1980.

[Mann84]   R. Manner, "Hardware Task/Processor Scheduling in a Polyprocessor Environment," *IEEE Trans. Compt.,* Vol. C–33, No. 7, July, 1984.

[MeRo85]   P. Mehrotra and J. Van Rosendale, "The Blaze Language: A Parallel Language for Scientific Programming," Rep. 85–29, Institute for Computer Applications in Science and Engineering, NASA Langley Research Center, Hampton, Va., May 1985.

[MiPa86]   S. P. Midkiff and D. A. Padua, "Compiler Generated Synchronization for DO loops", Proceedings of the *1986 International Conference on Parallel Processing,* August 1986, pp. 544–551.

[MiPa87]   S. P. Midkiff and D. A. Padua, "Compiler Algorithms for Synchronization," *IEEE Transactions on Computers,* Vol. 36, No. 12, December 1987.

[MiUc84]   K. Miura and K. Uchida, "Facom Vector Processor VP–100/VP–200," *High Speed Computation,* NATO ASI Series, Vol. F7, J.S. Kowalik Ed., Springer–Verlag, New York, 1984.

[Nico84]   A. Nicolau, "Parallelism, Memory Anti–Aliasing and Correctness for Trace Scheduling Compilers," Ph.D. Thesis, Yale University, June 1984.

[Nico88]   A. Nicolau, "Loop Quantization: A Generalized Loop Unwinding Technique", to appear in the *Journal of Parallel and Distributed Computing,* Vol. 5, November 1988.

[Padu79]   D. A. Padua, "Multiprocessors: Discussion of Some Theoretical and Practical Problems," Ph.D. Thesis, University of Illinois at Urbana–Champaign, DCS Report No. UIUCDCS–R–79–990, November, 1979.

[PaKL80]   D.A. Padua Haiek, D.J. Kuck, D.H. Lawrie, "High–Speed Multiprocessors and Compilation Techniques," *IEEE Transactions on Computers*, Vol. C–29, No. 9, September 1980.

[PaWo86]   D.A. Padua, and M. Wolfe, "Advanced Compiler Optimizations for Supercomputers," *Communications of the ACM*, Vol. 29, No. 12, pp. 1184–1201, December 1986.

[PfNo85]   G. F. Pfister, V. A. Norton, "'Hot Spot' Contention and Combining in Multistage Interconnection Networks," *Proceedings of the 1985 International Conference on Parallel Processing*, St. Charles, IL, August, 1985.

[PoBa87]   C. D. Polychronopoulos, U. Banerjee, "Processor Allocation for Horizontal and Vertical Parallelism and Related Speedup Bounds," *IEEE Transactions on Computers*, Vol. C–36, Issue 4, April, 1987.

[PoKu87]   C. D. Polychronopoulos and D. J. Kuck, "Guided Self–Scheduling: A Practical Scheduling Scheme for Parallel Supercomputers," *IEEE Transactions on Computers*, Vol. C–36, No. 12, December, 1987.

[PoKP86]   C. D. Polychronopoulos, D. J. Kuck, and D. A. Padua, "Execution of Parallel Loops on Parallel Processor Systems," Proceedings of the *1986 International Conference on Parallel Processing*, St. Charles, August 1986.

[Poly86]   C. D. Polychronopoulos, "On Program Restructuring, Scheduling, and Communication for Parallel Processor Systems," Ph.D. Thesis, CSRD No. 595, Center for Supercomputing Research and Development, University of Illinois, August, 1986.

[Poly87a]   C. D. Polychronopoulos, "On Advanced Compiler Optimizations for Parallel Computers," *Proceedings of the International Conference on Supercomputing*, (Athens, Greece, June 8–12, 1987), E. Houstis, T. Papatheodorou, and C.D. Polychronopoulos Ed., Springer–Verlag, New York, 1987.

[Poly87b]   C. D. Polychronopoulos, "Loop Coalescing: A Compiler Transformation for Parallel Machines," *Proceedings of the 1987 International Conference on Parallel Processing*, St. Charles, IL, August, 1987.

[Poly88a]   C. D. Polychronopoulos, "Compiler Optimizations for Enhancing Parallelism and Their Impact on Architecture Design," *IEEE Transactions on Computers*, Vol. C–37, No. 8, August 1988.

[Poly88b]   C. D. Polychronopoulos, "The Impact of Run–Time Overhead on Usable Parallelism," to appear in the Proceedings of the *1988 International Conference on Parallel Processing*, St. Charles, IL, August 15–19, 1988.

[Poly88c]   C. D. Polychronopoulos, "Towards Auto–Scheduling Compilers," *The Journal of Supercomputing*, July 1988.

[RaCG72]   C. V. Ramamoorthy, K. M. Chandy and Gonzalez, "Optimal Scheduling Strategies in Multiprocessor Systems," *IEEE Trans. Compt.*, Vol. C–21, Febr., 1972.

[Rein85]   S. Reinhardt, "A Data–Flow Approach to Multitasking on CRAY X–MP Computers," *Proceedings of the 10th ACM Symposium on Operating Systems Principles*, December, 1985.

[Sahn84]   S. Sahni, "Scheduling Multipipeline and Multiprocessor Computers," *IEEE Trans. Compt.*, Vol. C–33, No. 7, July, 1984.

[SBDN87]   K. So, A. S. Bolmarcich, F. Darema, and V. A. Norton, "A Speedup Analyzer for Parallel Programs", Proceedings of the *1987 International Conference on Parallel Processing*, August 1987, pp. 653–662.

[ScGa85]   K. Schwan and C. Gaimon, "Automatic Resource Allocation for the Cm* Multiprocessor," *Proc. of the 1985 International Conference on Distributed Computing Systems*, 1985.

[ShTs85]   C. C. Shen and W. H. Tsai, "A graph Matching Approach to Optimal Task Assignment in Distributed Computing Systems Using Minimax Criterion," *IEEE Trans. Compt.*, Vol. C–34, No. 3, March, 1985.

[Smit81]   B. Smith, "Architecture and Applications of the HEP Multiprocessor Computer System," *Real Time Processing IV, Proc. of SPIE*, pp. 241–248, 1981.

[Ston77]   H. S. Stone, "Multiprocessor Scheduling With the Aid of Network Flow Algorithms," *IEEE Trans. on Software Engineering*, Vol. SE–3, No. 1, Jan., 1977.

[TaYe86]   P. Tang and P. C. Yew, "Processor Self–Scheduling for Multiple–Nested Parallel Loops," *Proceedings of the 1986 International Conference on Parallel Processing*, August, 1986.

[Toma67]   R. M. Tomasulo, "An Efficient Algorithm for Exploiting Multiple Arithmetic Units," *IBM Journal of Research and Development*, Vol. 11, No. 1, January 1967.

[Uht88]   A. K. Uht, "Requirements for Optimal Execution of Loops with Tests", Technical Report No. CS88–116, University of California San Diego, February, 1988, and in Proceedings of the *1988 ACM International Conference on Supercomputing*, St. Malo, France, July 1988.

[Vied85]   A. V. Veidenbaum, "Compiler Optimizations and Architecture Design Issues for Multiprocessors," Ph.D. Thesis, UIUC–DCS–85–8012, CSRD, University of Illinois, March 1985.

[WaGa87]   K.–Y. Wang and D. Gannon, "Applying AI Techniques to Program Optimization for Parallel Computers", Technical Report No. 227, Indiana University, September 1987.

[Wolf82]   M. J. Wolfe, "Optimizing Supercompilers for Supercomputers," Ph.D. Thesis, University of Illinois at Urbana–Champaign, DCS Report No. UIUCCDCS–R–82–1105, 1982.

[ZhYe84]   C. Q. Zhu and P. C. Yew, "A Synchronization Scheme and Its Applications for Large Multiprocessor Systems," *Proc. of the 1984 International Conference on Distributed Computing Systems*, pp. 486–493, May 1984.

INDEX